NEW YORK UNIVERSITY PRESS
New York and London

Library of Congress Cataloging-in-Publication Data
Mindich, David T. Z., 1963–
Just the facts : how "objectivity" came to define American journalism / David T. Z. Mindich.
p. cm.
Includes bibliographical references (p.) and index.
ISBN 0-8147-5613-1 (acid-free paper)
1. Journalism–United States–Objectivity. I. Title.
PV4888.O25 M56 1998
071'.3–ddc21 98-9090
CIP

New York University Press books are printed on acid-free paper, and their binding materials are chosen for strength and durability.

Manufactured in the United States of America

10 9 8 7 6 5 4 3 2 1

To Barbara, Talia, and Isaiah, with love

Contents

Reed, Kit Rushing, David Sachsman, Enid Stubin, Benjamin Zucker, Barbara Zucker, and Rachel Zucker.

I presented drafts of the introduction and all five chapters at conventions of the Association for Education in Journalism and Mass Communication, the Symposia on Ante-bellum and Civil War Press, and the American Journalism Historians Association. I thank the many members of these organizations who shared their expertise. A version of chapter 3 was published as a *Journalism Monograph*, whose former editor, James Tankard, helped me improve it.

My colleagues and friends from CNN (where I worked in the late eighties), including Don Ennis, Jon Orlin, Leo Sacks, and Kate Skatterbol, taught me valuable lessons.

I am also grateful for the institutional support of Saint Michael's College, and for the advice and friendship of my colleagues Dianne Lynch, Mary Jane Alexander, Jon Hyde, and Mike Donoghue.

To Niko Pfund, Despina Gimbel, and the staff of New York University Press, and to their anonymous reviewers, I owe a great debt of gratitude for their expert editing, advice, and faith in my work.

My best thoughts often came not while sitting in front of the computer but during the interruptions, and for that, my daughter, Talia, and my son, Isaiah, deserve special thanks. Had my parents, Leonard Mindich and Margot Zucker Mindich, my mother-in-law, Jeanne Richmond, and my brothers, Daniel and Jeremy, simply lured me away from the work, I would have had reason to thank them for their friendship and love. But I also thank them for their help at every stage of the writing process. Last, my wife, Barbara Richmond, was my best friend and first editor throughout the project, and I thank her for everything.

Introduction
Objectivity

You shall no longer take things at second or third hand. . . .
You shall not look through my eyes either, nor take things from me,
You shall listen to all sides and filter them from yourself.
—Walt Whitman (editor, *Brooklyn Eagle*), "Song of Myself"

If American journalism were a religion, as it has been called from time to time, its supreme deity would be "objectivity." The high priests of journalism worship "objectivity"; one leading editor called it the "highest original moral concept ever developed in America and given to the world."[1] The iconoclasts—purveying advocacy journalism, "new" journalism, and the new, new journalism of the Internet and other media outlets—see "objectivity" as a golden calf. In late 1996 one media critic, Jon Katz, encouraged journalists to "abandon the false god of objectivity" to make way for newer forms of communication, including the kind found in Katz's online magazine, *HotWired*.[2]

But what is "objectivity" anyway? That depends on whom you ask. For some it is a vague point to strive for, like the North Star. For others it involves specific practices. Still others define it in the breech, citing journalists who break its rules. And lately "objectivity" has come under fire, a casualty of a bitter battle over the future of journalism. But even as some journalists celebrate it and others call for its end, no one seems to be able to define it.

Even though it was the central tenet of American journalism for much of this century,[3] "objectivity" has had no biographer, no historian, no soothsayer. What is "objectivity" and how did it come to be? This study journeys back to the 1830s and then forward through the nineteenth century in an attempt to answer this question. Each chapter looks at a particular component of "objectivity"—detachment, nonpartisanship, a style of writing called the "inverted pyramid," facticity, and balance—and places them in a historical context. In each chapter is an examination of "objectivity's" history, structure, promise, and limits. Along the way, the book addresses what "objectivity" means today and what it might mean in the future. In the face of intense competition, from the tabloids, cable television, a plethora of new constituencies, and most especially the Internet, journalists need to ask, what is "objectivity"? Should we abandon it? And if so, what would replace it? Before we move forward, we would be wise to understand the history and structure of journalism's most celebrated and least understood practice. That is the goal of this book.

The need to understand "objectivity," important in any age, has lately taken on an added urgency. One of the great truths of journalism history is that when older news media are threatened by newer ones, an intense debate over the nature of news ensues, followed by an era of retrenchment and change. The nineteenth century, as we will see, saw constant debates over the nature of news and the veracity of journalists. Our own century has seen a series of media transformations—in terms of new technology and competition—on a scale unequaled in history. The introduction of radio in the 1920s triggered a full-scale war between the press, which collectively represented a news monopoly, and the upstart radio broadcasters.[4] After it made its first appearance in the late 1940s, television news became increasingly popular, eventually surpassing newspapers; again a struggle emerged between the dominant media (newspapers and radio) and an upstart (television). Echoing past attacks on upstarts by elites, critics still accuse television of, among other things, "stirring up emotions and shutting down minds."[5] By the 1990s the landscape of news had shifted dramatically and quickly. The new media of cable TV, syndication, faxes, computers, and the confluence of entertainment and news in the corporate sphere threatened the old guard of television journalism even as television continued to threaten print. Dan Rather, a representative of the formerly upstart television news, began to write articles fretting over encroachments from a new set of upstarts.

In the midst of these threats to his craft, Dan Rather felt compelled to end his show by affirming the tangibility of the *CBS Evening News*. Before he signed off Rather leaned forward, into our living rooms, and said, "This is real." He said this in response to the words and images just presented in a reporter's story about "reality television," the growing trend of television producers to rely on "real-life" dramas for their movies, including the movies about a young woman named Amy Fisher that ran on all three broadcast networks in 1993.[6] The "this" that is real, Rather seemed to say, is "objective" journalism.

Vladimir Nabokov once wrote that "reality" is "one of the few words which mean nothing without quotes."[7] This book is in part a discussion of why "objectivity" belongs in quotes too.[8] The terms "reality" and "objectivity" are often conflated, along with words such as detachment, fairness, accuracy, and inclusiveness. As other journalists, beyond the "objective" ones, make claims to these ideals, the established journalists are faced with new challenges to "objectivity."

The threats to "objectivity" and the old guard are manifold, a parade of new challenges to the craft. In the closing years of the twentieth century we are left with fewer and fewer daily newspapers and with network news divisions facing declining market shares and subsequent budget reductions. More Americans get their news from other sources. For example, it was reported in 1997 that one-third of all television watchers under thirty get their news primarily from late-night comedians.[9] Politicians wishing to reach the public can avoid the old guard by going through the talk shows, C-Span, the tabloids (now print *and* television), and the Internet. The line separating journalists and politicians has often blurred in history, but the line is certainly being tested now: politicians are becoming journalists, and vice versa, in alarming numbers (some recent names include George Stephanopoulos, Susan Molinari, Mary Matalin, Jesse Jackson, Patrick Buchanan, Geraldine Ferraro, and James Carville).

Finally, the line between the old guard and the tabloids is less clear than ever. The tabs are breaking stories that get picked up by the mainstream (Paula Jones, Dick Morris, Gennifer Flowers), and using "objective"-sounding leads ("Psychics have confirmed that they can communicate with the spirit of JFK").[10] The line was surely tested in early 1998 when allegations began to emerge that President Clinton and a White House intern, Monica Lewinsky, had had an affair. *Newsweek* had the story, but after much agony and soul searching, decided to withhold it. However, someone leaked all this to Matt Drudge, a self-published Internet gossip columnist. Apparently, Drudge had no overwhelming doubts about the story, and reported the rumor as a "World Exclusive." Drudge, who once said that his stories were "80 percent accurate," had no problem getting his story past his own one-man editorial board: himself. As the story came to dominate the media, journalists realized that the news cycle, already quickened by twenty-four-hour television news stations, was made even more frenzied by the Internet amateurs and by the traditional press's own online sites. By March 1998, Drudge was a celebrity, both for his story about Clinton and for publishing an account (later retracted) that a White House strategist and former journalist, Sidney Blumenthal, had a history of abusing his wife. When Drudge appeared in court to defend himself against a libel suit by Blumenthal, a journalist covering the trial shouted to Drudge, "are you a reporter?" The question suggests the need for a definition of practices, to clarify a blurred line.[11]

The success of the tabloids even compelled one local television news station to hire one of the most sensational daytime talk show hosts, Jerry Springer, as an evening commentator, a fiasco that was short-lived but full of foreboding. Most frightening of all, however, is the idea that the barbarians are at the gates of even the most elite news organizations. In 1997, when a plan was unveiled to create working partnerships between the news and business sides of the *Los Angeles Times*, journalists everywhere worried that the "wall" separating the two sides was in danger of collapse.[12]

The practice of "objectivity" has also come under scrutiny from those who point out (correctly) that it too often reflects a world dominated by white men, that it too often serves the status quo. Betsy Wade, who led a successful fight to reverse gender inequities at the *New York Times*, felt that one of the chief problems at that paper was its "white male voice . . . seldom reflecting America's diversity."[13] Jill Nelson, an African American reporter who worked for the *Washington Post*, wrote that blacks must struggle daily "with this notion of objectivity," a notion she equates with a white voice.[14]

While James Reston might have once believed that a journalist can "attain that curious quality known as objectivity," more recent journalists, particularly those with strong political views, are not so sure. "While this might work in physics, in journalism it's impossible," wrote Jay Walljasper, the editor of the *Utne Reader*. "No reporter can be truly objective."[15] In 1996 Christiane Amanpour, a reporter for CNN and CBS, called for a reevaluation of "objectivity," which means, said Amanpour, "giving all sides a fair hearing, but not treating all sides equally. . . . So 'objectivity' must go hand in hand with morality."[16]

With so many storytellers trying to tell stories (the Internet alone has millions of separate sources of news), and with so many departing from the "information model" of "objective" news, journalists once again must attempt to define their craft. Given the historical pattern, it is no surprise that the nature of news and "objectivity" should once again become an issue so important to the profession.

For more than 150 years, journalists have asserted their ability to see the world clearly, to be "objective." In his first issue of the *New York Herald*, in 1835, James Gordon Bennett announced his intention to "record facts on every public and proper subject, stripped of verbiage and coloring."[17] The implication here is that the world and its movements can be known and named authoritatively, a notion one press historian, Michael Schudson, has called "naive empiricism."[18] Walter Cronkite's nightly farewell reflected an enduring confidence in the power of empiricism: "And that's the way it is." And today the *Columbia Journalism Review* and other media journals are filled with references to "objectivity" and warnings about how it might be threatened. It is no less than remarkable that years after consciousness was complicated by Freud, observation was problematized by Einstein, perspective was challenged by Picasso, writing was deconstructed by Derrida, and "objectivity" was abandoned by practically everyone outside newsrooms, "objectivity" is still the style of journalism that our newspaper articles and broadcast reports are written in, or against.

Journalists are not naive. "Objectivity" for journalists is often a question, not an answer—a point of debate, not a dogma. Until recently, the Society of Professional Journalists' Code of Ethics highlighted "objectivity" as its central tenet; in 1996 "objectivity" was dropped from the code. And in the face of unprecedented competition from various new sources, journalists have been grappling with their mission and with the meaning of "objectivity." Journalists often reveal a skepticism that there is an "objective" "is," unfiltered by our personal lenses. A decade ago, in a seeming acknowledgment of human bias, Rather replaced Cronkite's "And that's the way it is" with his own "And that's part of our world." What you've been watching, Rather seemed to say, is not the world, or even part of the world, but part of *our* world, through *our* filters. This leads to interesting soliloquies about "objectivity": because the report on "reality" TV was the final one in the broadcast, Rather signed off, "This is real. And that's part of our world." While Rather was making claims about reality, he was in effect questioning these claims. The same can be said of the Society of Professional Journalists' Code of Ethics, the closest document that American journalists have to a professional oath. The code's changes, including the replacement of "objectivity" with words such as "truth," "accuracy," and "comprehensiveness," are creating a debate within the profession.[19]

The Slipperiness of "Objectivity": Metaphors

Defending "objectivity" is made difficult by its slippery nature; since it is often defined in negatives—a lack of bias, a lack of party affiliation, a lack of sensationalism—one is left with the impression that "objective" journalists do not do much of anything. The metaphors journalists use to describe their craft, that it is a window on the world, a mirror of life, a net, or a seesaw, reinforce this.

"You give us twenty-two minutes," suggests a local New York radio station, "and we'll give you the world."[20] The promise of this gift—the world or a reasonable facsimile of it—suggests that the listener will get a special window that somehow looks onto the world and all that is going on. The promise is not "a vision of the world through the eyes of the radio staff," but simply the world itself. But even if we see journalism as a window, we still have not proven its "objectivity." Window panes can be of various thicknesses, colors, and sizes. And in which direction is the window pointing? Window frames, just as story frames, can vary widely.[21]

The image of journalism as a mirror is pervasive too. A *New York Times* editorial offered that "the difference between news and fiction is the difference between a mirror and a painting. Let the artist boast keener vision, but don't let him palm off oil on canvas as a reflection in glass."[22] More recently, the president of the Radio-Television News Directors Association, David Bartlett, wrote that television news is a "mirror" that "reflects reality."[23] While journalism may indeed be like a mirror, sometimes journalists may hold the glass up to themselves, reflecting their own perceptions and biases. Anyway, mirrors can distort too, as a trip to any fun house will reveal.[24] This is a point made by Tom Brokaw about his coverage of campaigns: "We're not a consistent business. This is not a mathematical formula in which we're engaged. You know, journalism is a reflection of the passions of the day. It's a reflection of the change that occurs."[25] While acknowledging that journalism does reflect something, Brokaw suggested that the image may be distorted by "passions" and "change."

Journalists also see themselves as fishers. They start off with nothing but a news net, cast it out, and haul back the news of the day.[26] In 1992 I asked a CNN political producer how he decides which presidential candidates to cover. He sounded not unlike a fisherman: "Whatever candidate is most newsworthy on a given day," he said, suggesting the passivity of his job, in service to the reified notion of newsworthiness.[27] Whatever fish are in the waters, whatever is newsworthy, according to this paradigm, dictates the catch. "Our reporters do not cover stories from *their* point of view," said Richard Salant, the president of CBS News. "They are presenting them from *nobody's* point of view."[28] The net is "objective," free of human craftsmanship; the haul is dependent on what's in the waters on a given day. But as one media critic wrote, "a net has holes. Its haul is dependent upon the amount invested in intersecting fiber and the tensile strength of that fiber."[29] We must remember that nets are human-made. Understanding "objectivity" and its component parts will allow us to see the net more clearly.

A final metaphor for news making is the seesaw. "Balanced" and "fair" coverage has long been a paradigm in journalism. In 1918 Oswald Garrison Villard, the publisher of the *Nation* and the *New York Evening Post,* wrote of the need to present "both sides of every issue."[30] Seventy-five years later, an advertisement for CNN echoed this notion: "We give *both* sides."[31] The idea here is that journalists can find truth by offering two competing truth claims. But who decides who gets to sit on the seesaw? Where does one place the fulcrum? And why a seesaw? Why is there room for only two sides? Does "objectivity" really exist between two subjective sound bites?

What the window, mirror, net, and seesaw share is the idea that somehow journalism is an "objective" craft and that journalists are engaged in a basically passive endeavor. Whether sitting by a window, holding up a mirror, casting a net, or inviting participants to ride on a seesaw, journalists, the story goes, are not active constructors of a story. Even when more active verbs are used to describe reportage, as when journalists "gather" the facts or "uncover" the story, they are still basically observers, poking their noses into an area where others have not yet gone. "We don't choose the Man of the Year," read an advertisement for *Time*'s annual feature, "History does."[32] One of the reasons no one has written a history of "objectivity" is that it's difficult to discuss an ethic that is defined by its practitioners' lack of perspective, bias, and even action.

But journalists *do* do things. When Pulitzer Prizes are awarded to journalists, the honors are given less frequently to the passive than to the aggressive, such as Gene Miller of the *Miami Herald* for what the prize committee called his "persistent and courageous reporting over eight and one-half years that led to the exoneration and release" of two innocent men from death row.[33] As Jay Rosen has pointed out, "journalists are people who make things." To say that journalists *make* the news does not mean that they *fake* the news. Nor is it to say, as some sociologists have suggested, that the news *never* reflects the outside world.[34] It simply means that journalists do and must construct stories, because of their membership in the world of humanity. This book will show how "objectivity" is an active enterprise.

What "Objectivity" Means

Despite the lack of a definition from journalists, one can discern the various ethics that make up "objectivity." In journalism textbooks, for example, "objectivity" is alive and well. Of the five most widely used modern textbooks, four specifically tell students to be "objective."[35] The textbooks that discuss "objectivity" each explain it in similar terms, citing the same five components of "objective" reporting. The first of these components is *detachment*, "to make sure the facts are doing the talking, not the reporter's own preconceived notions."[36] The ethic of *nonpartisanship* is the second; reporters must offer "both sides" of each story.[37] The third is a style of writing called the *inverted pyramid,* which gives readers the most important facts in the lead paragraph.[38] *Naive empiricism*, or reliance on "facts" to "report accurately the truth or reality of the event," is the fourth quality.[39] The fifth and final component is *balance*, the impossible yet all-important goal that leads to "undistorted reporting."[40] Even the one textbook that does not discuss "objectivity" by name, a book with a pointed title, *Beyond the Inverted Pyramid*, replaces "objectivity" with similar words: "truth," "fairness," and "balance."[41] As the ethic of "objectivity" is questioned, it endures.

The *Columbia Journalism Review*, the media's periodical of conscience, and other reviews frequently cite "objectivity" as a measure of good journalism.[42] The elements of "objectivity" often match those of the textbooks. After it was disclosed that a New York City television anchor, Chuck Scarborough, had contributed to Republican candidates in 1996, he was criticized in the *Columbia Journalism Review* for departing from "objective" practices. These practices included "detachment," "nonpartisanship," fact gathering while trying to expunge biases, and "balance," roughly the equivalent of the textbooks' elements of "objectivity." While nailing down "objectivity," the writer admitted, "is like nailing Jell-O," he argued that these practices, collectively known as "objectivity," are needed to win his trust.[43]

Jon Katz, the media critic who writes for *Wired* and its online cousin, *HotWired*, frequently cites the "false god of objectivity" as the bane of journalism.[44] Defining it in similar terms as the textbooks and the article on Scarborough, Katz hates "objectivity" for some of the same reasons others favor it: detachment ("New media let people speak far more freely"), the inverted pyramid ("the knee-jerk dogma of the spokesperson culture"), and balance ("Objectivity and the *Crossfire* mentality that afflicts journalism shrink this discussion into one side or the other, both of them rigid and strident").[45]

"Objectivity" as a news strategy has dominated the mainstream press for the better part of this century. It still does. For a confirmation of this, one can peruse almost any mainstream daily newspaper from the last hundred or so years. On August 9, 1974, to cite a dramatic example, the *New York Times* ran the following lead: "Richard Milhous Nixon, the 37th President of the United States, announced tonight that he had given up his long and arduous fight to remain in office and would resign, effective at noon tomorrow." The story would satisfy the writers of the journalism textbooks. It met the goal of detachment, as the reporter's voice was merely that of a narrator; it was nonpartisan, at least insofar as the reporter's partisan preferences (if he had any) were hidden; it was written as a classic inverted pyramid, with the most important facts right at the top; it was "factual," filled with verifiable facts, including the fact that "Gerald Rudolph Ford . . . will be sworn in . . . to serve out the 895 days remaining in Nixon's second term"; and it was balanced, avoiding the partisan voice that pervaded the editorial pages of the mainstream press.[46] The resignation of a president is a powerful test of "objectivity": most people would have a strong personal or partisan reaction to such a significant event. That it was reported in an "objective" way is a testament to the enduring strength of the form.

The lead story on the front page of a more recent *New York Times* begins, "The Republican leaders of Congress today abruptly called off budget talks that had been set to take place at the White House and said they would not resume them until President Clinton produced another proposal that moved in their direction."[47] Like the report on Nixon's resignation, this story met all the criteria of "objectivity." The reporter was detached and nonpartisan, at least insofar as her actions, voice, and partisan preferences (if she had any) were not included in the story. The article was written in an inverted pyramid and factual style, and was balanced between the Democratic and Republican representatives.

Although many journalists reject the idea of pure "objectivity," they still strive for it, define themselves by it, and practice what one media critic has called the "ritual of objectivity," a series of professional routines designed to shield journalists from blame and legal action.[48] In other words, "objectivity" is, for many journalists, a goal. Journalists often say that they cannot be completely "objective," but that they try nonetheless. "Pure objectivity might not exist," said Sydney Gruson of the *New York Times*, "but you have to strive for it anyway."[49] One journalist told me that "objectivity" was not attainable, but like the North Star, was a fixed mark to help journalists stay on the right course. The problem, however, in reaching for this "objectivity" star is that it is not clearly defined and its history and development are not well explored. If we have no clear understanding of "objectivity," the practice cannot easily be defended or updated.

This study looks at the components of "objectivity" as represented in the textbooks and recent criticism and places them in certain historical moments: detachment and nonpartisanship in the 1830s and 1840s, the inverted pyramid in the 1860s, naive empiricism in the middle of the century, and balance in the 1890s. My research suggests that "objectivity" as an ethic evolved over a broad period of the nineteenth century, from its nascent years in the 1830s to the time of its greatest success in the 1890s. An examination of the evolution of these components could help to promote a better understanding of and a more precise language about journalistic "objectivity" in particular and the history and future of American journalism in general.

The work does not pretend to be an "objective" window, or any other "objective" construction. It is a history. Its author hopes that the reader will consider his interpretation and find it compelling. But the author also hopes that the reader will remember that the author's history is also *his story,* a construction.

When?

Why does this study begin in the 1830s? Why does it end in the 1890s? Michael Schudson, in *Discovering the News*, asserted that "before the 1830s, objectivity was not an issue."[50] The term "objectivity" may not have been applied to journalism before this century,[51] but a quick look back to the

Jacksonian age and before suggests that characteristics associated with "objectivity"—fairness, detachment, nonpartisanship, and balance—were venerable claims even before the 1830s. In his 1776 pamphlet *Common Sense,* Thomas Paine (writing anonymously) declared that he was "not induced by motives of . . . party."[52] James Rivington, a Tory newspaper editor in the American Revolutionary War, routinely published the pro- and anti-British perspectives. And going back all the way to 1690, Benjamin Harris declared in *Publick Occurrences,* North America's first newspaper, his intention to provide "a Faithful Relation" of "considerable things as have arrived unto our Notice."[53]

"Objectivity" was certainly an issue at least since 1690, and people appealed to various aspects of it, but no one really accepted these assertions before the 1830s. Paine's work was effective precisely because of its passionate, partisan tone. Rivington's "balance" was hated by the revolutionaries, who organized mobs that sacked his press and chased him out of the country. As Mitchell Stephens has written, the Revolution was not won by "newspapers that struggled to find a balancing quote from George III."[54] And the first issue of Harris's *Publick Occurrences,* an early attempt at news not supported by party or faction, was also his last. It took until 1833, with the birth of the penny press, for American papers to unhinge from their partisan roots. In 1833 papers started to become nonpartisan, not only in their claims, but in fact.

By the 1890s, especially with the rise of the *New York Times* and other papers that shared the "objective" paradigm, what we recognize as the traits of "objectivity" were, as I will show, all in place. It is here that our journey ends. Although this study will occasionally apply lessons from the past to the twentieth century, its main focus is the period from the sloughing of formal party ties in the 1830s to the application of the ethic of "objectivity" in the 1890s.

Where? Who?

Critics and careful readers will notice that most of my examples of American journalism (although certainly not all) come from one city, New York. From the 1830s to the 1890s, New York newspapers led the nation's press in nearly every conceivable category. In 1835, 1865, and 1895, the top U.S. newspapers in terms of circulation, size, staff size, and budget were New York papers.[55] The Associated Press was cooked up in a New York City office.[56] And in the 1990s, when press critics bemoan the celebrity status of the modern television journalist, we might remind ourselves that two New York–based nineteenth-century publishers (Horace Greeley and William R. Hearst) ran for president, and that they and other New York journalists served as congressmen and senators and in other government posts, often while running their newspapers. The story of "objectivity," at least the one I am telling, is tied to the stories of Dan Rather, other modern "objective" journalists, and their journalistic ancestors of the last century, based in New York City.

What? The Project

In order to better understand "objectivity," I looked at its traits as reflected in the textbooks and recent criticism and have examined these traits in their historical settings: the growing *detachment* and *nonpartisanship* of the 1830s and 1840s; the "objective" style of writing called the *inverted pyramid* and how it was used during the American Civil War; the idea of *naive empiricism* in the middle of the century; and claims of *balance* in the 1890s. This study places journalistic "objectivity" in its broad cultural context, but it also struggles to find definitions for the term. Each chapter corresponds to a different era and provides a different perspective on the meaning of journalistic "objectivity."

Chapter 1 looks at the first years of the "penny" press in the Jacksonian era (1828–36), the primordial soup of journalistic "objectivity." The pennies were the first newspapers to formally break from political parties, and this break caused the first step toward journalistic "objectivity": detachment. I use the beating of one New York editor, James Gordon Bennett, by another, James Watson Webb, to illustrate this issue. Because it is more detached and less partisan than the journalism of Webb, Bennett's writing represents a step in the direction of "objectivity." Along the way, the chapter rips Bennett and Webb out of the rosy and now dated narratives constructed by journalism historians and places them instead in a fractious Jacksonian America marked by change and violence. In doing so, I develop a new theory about the birth of the penny press: that it was primarily influenced not by the era's successes, but by its failures. Detachment was born in battle.

Chapter 2 is about another component of journalistic "objectivity," nonpartisanship. In the years before the American Civil War, three journalists, James Gordon Bennett, William L. Garrison, and Frederick Douglass, were displaying novel ways of looking at politics. Each showed a different shade of nonpartisanship. Bennett, the editor of the successful *Herald*, attempted to remove "color" from the news and placed himself firmly in the center of partisan politics. Garrison, the editor of the *Liberator*, refused to be "the political partisan of any man," standing outside partisan politics altogether.[57] Garrison had little use for a form that attempted to "balance" issues in partisan terms: there was generally no place in the public discourse for the enfranchisement of women, African Americans, and others. Douglass offers a third version of nonpartisanship in his acceptance of the Free Soil Party in the 1850s. The writings of the three editors reveal how much of Jacksonian discourse existed outside political party boundaries and how the antebellum press offered alternatives to partisan politics. They also offer an understanding of how complex nonpartisanship once was, and could be in the future.

Historians of journalism have long sought the first practitioners of the inverted pyramid style of news writing, a style that conveys the most important information in the first paragraphs of a story, and one mentioned by textbooks and critics as part of "objective" news writing. Conventional wisdom dates the shift from the chronological to inverted pyramid style sometime in the late nineteenth century. In chapter 3, I present evidence that it was not journalists, but the War Department that was using the form during the Civil War. Indeed, I discovered that one of the first writers of inverted pyramids was Edwin M. Stanton, Lincoln's secretary of war. Stanton has found his way into many histories of American journalism, but always because of his notoriety as a press censor. I reconcile Stanton's role as a writer of inverted pyramids with his tight rein on discourse, journalistic and otherwise, and see Stanton's "objective" news writing style and his censorship as related aspects of his repressive social control. It seems ironic, of course, to suggest that Stanton the censor may have also been a progenitor of modern journalism. But given recent criticism of "objectivity" that suggests journalists' overreliance on figures of authority,[58] a governmental source for the inverted pyramid may be less surprising and, indeed, fitting.

Naive empiricism and fact collecting are central to the "objective" ideal. In trying to understand the historical roots of naive empiricism, chapter 4 takes a sweeping look at changes in mid-nineteenth-century thought, particularly in medicine and the sciences, and compares these changes with advances in journalism. Medicine, science, art, literature, and the social sciences were shifting from a paradigm of religion and philosophy to one of science. It turns out that journalism was changing too, moving toward a more empirical and "fact-based" paradigm. During this period editors promised their readers, in the words of Charles Dana, a "daily photograph of the world's events," and the wire services began to market news "devoid of opinion."[59] I looked at the New York City cholera epidemics of 1832, 1849, and 1866 and compared the response of the medical and journalistic communities. The medical response to the epidemic evolved from the horrific "cures" of 1832, including mercury poisoning and tobacco smoke enemas, to an efficient and scientific response in the 1866 epidemic. The rise of statistical analysis and data gathering in the sciences paralleled journalism's growing reverence for "facts" and scientific method.

In chapter 5, the inquiry turns to the realization of the "objective" ideal in the 1880s and 1890s. By the last years of the nineteenth century, professional journalists' societies arose across America, textbooks told journalism students to "chronicle, don't comment," and newspapers and wire services had embraced "objectivity" and the idea that reality lies between competing truth claims. But the idea that the world can be seen without human filters is, of course, problematic. For example, the *New York Times* and other papers attempted to "balance" their coverage of lynching: on the one hand lynching is evil, on the other hand "Negroes are prone" to rape.[60] Ida B. Wells, the antilynching crusader, and others critiqued this equation and demonstrated that the underpinnings of the "objective" philosophy could be flawed. Wells's critique showed that "balance," one of the components of "objectivity" mentioned in modern textbooks, often serves the status quo, and in the case of lynching, is a skewed and dangerous construction. In return, the otherwise staid *Times* wrote an editorial calling Wells unpatriotic and a "slanderous and nasty-minded mulattress" in an attempt to discredit her criticisms.[61] This final chapter examines the mainstream notions of "objectivity" by entering into these battles.

Finally, we come back to Dan Rather, "objective" journalists, and their criticism of non-"objective" reporters and editors. The criticism by "objective" journalists of sensational and subjective journalism can tell as much about the critic as it does about the subject. In other words, the concluding section shows how "objectivity" defines itself by defining others. Finally, it explores how the modern information explosion alters the battle over "reality" and "objectivity" and challenges the mission of the modern journalist. By the end of this book I will argue that we desperately need quality journalism, but objectivity, as it is practiced and defended, must change in significant ways.

1

Detachment

The Caning of James Gordon Bennett, the Penny Press, and Objectivity's Primordial Soup

On a sunny spring day in 1836, James Gordon Bennett left his newspaper office to begin his morning perambulations around Wall Street, seeking information for the financial column of his new one-cent paper, the *New York Herald*. That morning, as he roamed the narrow, tortuous streets of the financial district, Bennett might very well have been counting his blessings. He was a man on the rise. In part because of his coverage of one of the most sensational crimes of the century—the ax-murder of a beautiful prostitute—his paper, which he had started a year before with a five-hundred dollar investment, was quickly becoming one of the most successful newspapers in New York.[1] Bennett even boasted that his paper had the highest circulation in the world. Indeed, the Scottish-born Bennett, who had single-handedly sold the ad copy, reported events, wrote the columns, and edited the newspaper, was now in a position to advertise for help: "A smart active boy wanted, who can write a good hand." Bennett also called for "a new *corps* of Carriers" to augment the growing army of those who hawked his paper. Bennett was a rare example of the total fulfillment of the American Dream, a man who could hardly keep up with his own success. It was on this brilliant spring morning that a rival editor, James Watson Webb, caught up with Bennett on Wall Street, shoved him down a flight of stairs, and beat him severely with his cane.[2]

Why Webb beat Bennett has never been explained beyond the former's penchant for violence and the latter's obnoxious character. It is true that in the weeks before the beating, Bennett's columns had included numerous jabs at Webb, the editor of New York's best selling newspaper, the staid and elitist *Morning Courier and New-York Enquirer*.[3] "We are rapidly taking the wind out of the *big bellied* sails of the Courier & Enquirer," wrote Bennett, poking fun at his rival's rotundity and the dimensions of the *Courier*'s large news sheet. Bennett promised that the *Herald* would ultimately best the "*bloated* Courier" (italics mine). In the weeks before the assault, Bennett also called Webb a "defaulter" who was guilty of "disgraceful conduct," and offered to send him a piece of the dead prostitute's bed as a "*momento mori*."[4] But Webb was not the only editor Bennett addictively insulted; one of Bennett's biographers pointed out that he "managed to attack in a single issue seven newspapers and their editors."[5] While other editors returned Bennett's verbal abuse or simply ignored it, Webb beat Bennett—three times, in fact, in 1836. So why did Webb resort to violence while others abstained? This chapter examines the rise of the first "independent," nonpartisan press through the prism of Webb's conflicts with Bennett. In doing so, this chapter grapples with the birth of "objectivity's" first element: detachment.

It is fitting that we begin our look at "objectivity" with an examination of the early "independent" press, the first American newspapers to *detach* themselves from political parties. How and why the popular, nonpartisan press arose in the 1830s is the focus of this chapter.[6] I also explain how Bennett represents a departure from Webb's brand of journalism, a departure that reflected an increasing detachment on the part of journalists. This is a step toward what journalists call "objectivity."

In order to discuss detachment, however, we must first consider the conditions that brought about its birth. How did this new kind of journalism evolve? As I will discuss, journalism historians have long maintained that the popular press of the 1830s came out of "Jacksonian democracy" in much the same way as Athena was born from Zeus's head: springing out fully formed. But while journalism historians see the birth of modern journalism as a natural outgrowth of a benign and democratic period, other scholarship would suggest that modern journalism grew out of a violent and inegalitarian era. Why is this important? Because detachment was never as clear as when the first commercial press of the 1830s detached from the violent era in which it was born.

The Penny Press

In the beginning, that is, before the founding of the first penny paper, the *New York Sun* in 1833, most daily newspapers were expensive (generally six cents each, or nearly 10 percent of the average daily wage),[7] partisan, and sedate. Many included the words "advertiser," "commercial," or "mercantile" in their titles, reflecting their business orientation. The readership of these papers, which are variously—and often interchangeably—called the "party" or "mercantile" press, may have been high, but they had few subscribers by the standards of even a few years later.[8] Before the penny era, papers were shared or read aloud to groups in the partisan clubs and inns, and sent through a partisan postal service.[9]

From 1830 to 1840, while the population grew less than 40 percent, the average total circulation for all U.S. dailies nearly quadrupled.[10] Records for urban areas show an even more marked shift. The top-selling newspaper in 1828, Webb's *Courier and Enquirer*, circulated fewer than five thousand copies a day. By 1836, fueled by his coverage of the ax-murder of the prostitute and aided by advances in printing technology, urbanization, and literacy, Bennett boasted a daily distribution of ten to fifteen thousand for his upstart paper.[11] Unlike Webb's paper, which sold for six cents a copy, the *Sun*, the *Transcript*, and Bennett's *Herald* sold for a penny, hence the term "penny press." The six-centers were sold mainly by annual subscription; the pennies were sold generally by newsboys who urgently hawked their papers in the streets and door-to-door.

The six-cent papers were connected to a tradition of party affiliation that had begun before the American Revolution; it was encouraged by the Federalists from 1789 to 1801, then by Jeffersonian and Jacksonian Democrats. The post offices, printing presses, inns, and newspapers in a city or town were often connected through party affiliation and were often run by the same person. Many postmasters were also newspaper editors; through the privilege of franking, they would have "free and certain" delivery of their papers; the government, through the granting of federal printing contracts, would enjoy the expensive, yet certain, support of their editors. The Federalists increased federal postmasterships from one hundred at the start of the period to more than eight hundred by the end, helping to create what one Democrat called a "court press." This strategy was pursued by the Democrats too; during Jackson's 1832 reelection campaign the official Jacksonian newspaper, Francis Blair's *Globe*, was franked by postmasters and congressmen to people throughout the country.[12]

The pennies resemble today's newspapers more closely than the six-centers do. For one, unlike the party or mercantile press, the pennies were not supported by political parties, and the articles were more likely to cover news outside the narrow political and mercantile interests of the six-centers. Crime news, for example, was more prevalent in the pennies, as was other news, often sensationalistic, that fell beyond the six-centers' purview. A final characteristic that separated the pennies from what came before was that they actively asserted their own nonpartisanship. The inaugural issue of the *New York Transcript* announced its political slant simply: "*we have none.*"[13]

Dates of Principal Events Discussed in This Chapter

November 1832	**Andrew Jackson is reelected president**
1833–37	**The most violent part of the antebellum period**
September 1833	**Day founds the *New York Sun***
May 1835	**Bennett founds the *New York Herald***
January 1836	**Webb beats Bennett for the first time**
April 1836	**Ellen Jewett is murdered, probably by Richard Robinson, a customer** **Bennett claims that the *Herald*'s circulation has surpassed that of the *Courier and Enquirer***
May 1836	**Webb beats Bennett for the second time**
1837	**Financial panic** **Decline of street violence and the labor press; continuing rise of the pennies**
March 1838	**Cilley-Graves duel; national outrage against dueling**

The Press "Revolution," "Jacksonian Democracy," and Historians of Journalism

Journalism historians generally place the birth of modern American journalism and the rise of "objectivity" in the Jacksonian era and tie it to the "democratic spirit" of the age. What came before, they argue, was biased and primitive, the "dark ages" of American journalism. The pennies, these historians argue, brought about a democratic revolution.[14] In *Discovering the News*, Michael Schudson advanced this view, citing the birth of universal white manhood suffrage, the "rise" of the "middle class," and an "egalitarian market economy" as reasons. Schudson also asserted that the era saw the birth of "objectivity" claims.[15] "Before the 1830s," he wrote, "objectivity was not an issue." He also asserted that "the idea of 'news' itself was invented in the Jacksonian era." Although these claims are clearly overstated, a kernel of truth remains: many newspapers formally severed their party ties and an ethic of nonpartisanship emerged, although it was practiced unevenly.[16] Unlike their six-cent ancestors, the pennies were supported by circulation and advertising, not party patronage.

That the pennies asserted their own nonpartisanship still leaves open the question of whether the papers were born out of the "democracy" of the Jacksonian age. Schudson, in *Discovering the News*, claimed that the modern press emerged during the 1830s, an era he titles the "Age of Egalitarianism."[17] Citing older studies of "progressive historians," so-called because of their whiggish faith in antebellum democracy, Schudson noted that most recent histories still confirm the earlier beliefs. The revisionist view, wrote Schudson, "far from being an attack on the idea that the 1830s were an egalitarian age, confirms just that hypothesis."[18]

But from the 1970s on, historians of the Jacksonian age have produced a body of work that thoroughly discredits the "progressive" view of Jacksonian democracy.[19] And to suggest that revisionists, led by Edward Pessen (whom Schudson cited), confirm Jacksonian "democracy" is to misrepresent them. Pessen, for one, is unequivocal in the force of his revision: "The age may have been named after the common man but it did not belong to him." At the end of his *Jacksonian America: Society, Personality, and Politics*, Pessen even suggests a new name for the period: "Not the 'age of Jackson' but the 'age of materialism and opportunism, reckless speculation and erratic growth, unabashed vulgarity, surprising inequality, whether of condition, opportunity, or status, and a politic, *seeming* deference to the common man by the uncommon men who actually ran things.' "[20]

Another forceful repudiation of Schudson's "progressive"-based view of the Jacksonian era comes from Daniel Schiller in his 1981 book, *Objectivity and the News*. Finding "a pattern of objectivity" emerging in a weekly newspaper that focused on crime news, Schiller devoted many pages to a discussion of the penny era and relied on post-"progressive" social historians for his analysis. He believed that the pennies arose out of labor's unrest in the late 1820s and early 1830s and saw a problem in Schudson's theory about the "middle class," which Schiller believed was divided into "disparate and frequently hostile" camps of merchants and artisans. The merchants' and artisans' work and welfare were being shaken by the rise of a national market system, Schiller suggested, but their interests were often contrabalanced. "That the penny press found a way to speak to both groups at once was its most ingenious and fundamental contribution," wrote Schiller.[21] Statements like the *Sun*'s "It Shines for All" reflected an appeal to the many different economic and social groups.

A New Approach to the Birth of the Commercial Press and Detachment

While historians of the Jacksonian period have become skeptical of the "democratic" promise of the age, journalism historians, with the notable exception of Schiller, have not reconciled the revisionists' new understanding. Where Schudson sees a rising middle class, Schiller sees a group, angry and divided, but united in its opposition to the elite forces. But Schiller's perceptive theory that the pennies appropriated labor's class-based anger does not go far enough in understanding the turbulent storms of the age of Jackson, the race and gender wars, and the violence, both in the streets and in the newspapers, between the elite and labor, and between men of the same class. The frantic desire to make change, to move, to build, to kill, and most of all to make money is writ large in the newspaper columns of the day as well, but journalism historians have yet to capture it beyond arguing for or against Jacksonian democracy. Understanding the era is crucial to understanding what it is the pennies detached *from*. Webb's violence against Bennett is a good place to start.

Bennett had worked for Webb in the pre-penny days, made a name for himself as a brash, entertaining Washington columnist, and left Webb's charge after the *Courier and Enquirer* switched parties to become a Whig organ.[22] Bennett, a Democrat, then tried unsuccessfully to start a Democratic paper in Philadelphia before coming to New York to found the independent *Herald* in May 1835. Within the year, Webb publicly beat his former employee twice on the streets of New York.

The first time Webb beat Bennett was on January 20, 1836. In his lead column on January 19, Bennett announced that it was "with heartfelt grief that we are compelled to publish the following awful disclosure of the defalcations of our former associate, Col. Webb. . . . But as we control an independent paper, we could not refuse it." What follows are accounts by a broker of Webb's failures in the stock market; as a result, he owed the broker more than $87,000. It was with "pain, regret, and almost with tears

HARPER'S WEEKLY
A JOURNAL OF CIVILIZATION

Vol. II.—No. 88.] NEW YORK, SATURDAY, SEPTEMBER 4, 1858. [Price Five Cents.

CONTENTS.

GENERAL JAMES WATSON WEBB.

GENERAL JAMES WATSON WEBB.—[Photographed by Fredericks.]

Figure 1. James Watson Webb. *Harper's Weekly*, 4 September 1858 (Library of Congress).

in our eyes" that Bennett published the exposé. The crocodile tears did not stop Webb from chasing down his former employee, punching him in the face, and then striking him in the head with a large club.[23]

One theme emerges in Bennett's coverage of this first fight: Webb's violence could do nothing against the inexorable success of the *Herald*, which threatened to overtake the *Courier and Enquirer*. Webb's violence is depicted by Bennett as a desperate attempt by a privileged, dishonest man to keep money and power for himself. Bennett described the blow to his head as if it were a Mexican piñata ceremony, with Webb trying to gain the contents of Bennett's skull as the prize: "[Webb] wanted to let out [of my skull] the never-ending supply of good humor and wit which has created such a reputation for the Herald, and, perhaps, appropriate the contents to supply the emptiness of his own thick skull. . . . Webb will make nothing by availing himself of his brute force against me. He cannot stop the success of the Herald."[24]

Bennett's success may very well have been on Webb's mind as he stalked the penny editor. Two days after the assault, Bennett claimed a circulation of nine thousand, which, he reminded readers, was "about three times" that of Webb's paper.[25]

By detaching from an already unpopular figure, Bennett used Webb to define his own paper. Webb's paper, too expensive for anyone but the rich, was seen by wage workers as a monopoly of knowledge at a time when knowledge was increasingly viewed as a necessary capitalist tool.[26] Employees resented that the *Courier and Enquirer* was a possession to be borrowed from the boss, after he had finished it himself. The first biographer of Bennett, Isaac Clark Pray, likened the innovation of a cheap press to that of the matchbox; no longer would people have to borrow newspapers or burning coals from their rich neighbors. This effected an economic detachment from the upper class.[27] Furthermore, Webb was connected to the most hated man of his day, the head of the U.S. Bank and enemy of Andrew Jackson, Nicholas Biddle, who bought Webb's support with a large "loan" (Webb and an associate were condemned by a House subcommittee for taking bribes from Biddle).[28] Finally, a nativist with antiIrish sentiments, Webb was an enemy to the largely immigrant, working-class New York Democrats. It would be difficult to overstate labor's hatred of the *Courier and Enquirer*'s editor, a hatred so intense that long before Bennett's public wrangling with Webb, laborers sang songs about him:

Who is't edits the blanket sheet,
And garbles statements very neat,
At No. 56 Wall street?
James Double W. . . .
Who sold himself to one Nick Biddle,
And said the Democrats he'd diddle,
Were he allowed to play first fiddle?
James Double W. . . .
Who said aristocratic rights
Should supersede the poorer wights,
And calls mechanics "troglodytes"?
James Double W.
Who, when some emigrants contrived
To reach these shores, where Freedom thrived,
Announced them "*live stock*" just arrived?
James Double W.
Whose plighted faith and consequences,
His boasted knowledge—all pretense—
Was lately valued at *six pence?*
James Double W.[29]

It is clear from Bennett's rhetoric and the working-class anger he appropriated that Webb stood for much more than merely Webb himself. It is clear that Bennett, his readers, and some modern journalism historians (including Schiller) saw Webb as a stand-in for a declining elite. Similarly, the rising Bennett was seen as a paradigm for the rising (or in Schiller's view, angry) masses.[30] But contrary to these views, Webb and Bennett are in two key ways *not* representative of the struggles of the Jacksonian era.

First, while it is true that the two men lived in an age of haves and have-nots, and while the fortunes of Webb and Bennett declined and rose, the people they have come to represent in theory did not follow their models in practice. After studying tax records, Pessen concluded that contrary to earlier beliefs, the gap between rich and poor actually *widened* during the Jackson era. Unlike Webb, the vast majority of the rich became richer. In Northeastern cities, the top 1 percent of wealth holders owned a quarter of all wealth just before Jackson came to Washington, and owned half by midcentury. Conversely, the majority of all Americans in 1850 were assessed for no property whatsoever.[31] Artisans during the years of Jackson were quickly being converted into pieceworkers. The "ten-hour" workday movement, which began in the thirties, "implicitly recognized that older, more episodic work rhythms were disappearing."[32] The decline of Webb and the rise of Bennett contravened the fortunes of members of their respective classes.

The second reason Webb and Bennett do not confirm the classic interpretations of the Jacksonian age is that these tensions are often more complicated than they seem. For example, one would expect that Bennett, representing the working classes, would have supported a guilty verdict against the upper-class suitor of the murdered prostitute, Ellen Jewett.[33] But Bennett defended the accused killer, Richard Robinson, perhaps doing so after bribes from the defense.[34] Finally, while many poorer folks may have supported the prostitutes, a number of violent working-class gangs routinely confronted and beat them, and terrorized others as well. A week after the prostitute was killed, for example, a gang known for its anti-brothel violence threw hot coals in the face of an elderly woman and savagely beat a man who came to her aid.[35] Moreover, much of the day's violence was provoked by mobs of the higher classes—merchants and the like—who feared the loss of stability that the emerging market economy had brought.[36] As I will outline, Webb was often associated with mobs. But even here, Webb's position does not exactly represent a clear elite-masses dichotomy. The elite mobs often targeted other elites: they assaulted abolitionists and their sympathizers in churches, meetings, and places of business.[37]

Webb and Bennett: Not Democracy, but Change and Mobility

Webb and Bennett are not stand-ins for a fictional declining elite and a rising middle class. What these men more plausibly represent is more complicated: the idea and fact of change and mobility, with Bennett representing a detachment from the old order. Again, this needs to be discussed in parts.

First, they represent a change in the way business was conducted in America, a change that started after the Ghent peace treaty with Britain following the War of 1812[38] and the subsequent commercial boom. The rhythms of living and business were changing, from a tight, communal, and informal market to a town- and city-based market of strangers. This is captured wonderfully in Washington Irving's "Rip Van Winkle" when Rip comes back after his long sleep and sees his own town, now livelier and "disputatious," and comes upon a "lean bilious looking fellow with his pockets full of handbills."[39] The two editors reflect this shift in lifestyles. Webb, living a life of patronage, supported by parties, special interests, and the elite who used his paper, worked short days, took time off, traveled, and engaged in politics. Bennett, in contrast, was surrounded by strangers and was supported by no one, the ultimate "independent" journalist; he worked up his paper with the intensity of a driven man, and did so by turning a basement office into a one-man, eighteen-hours-a-day, seven-days-a-week sweatshop.[40]

Second, the Webb-Bennett relationship represents the loss of deference and the rise of a working class irreverence; Webb represents an earlier era, concerned with rules of society, while Bennett's modus operandi was iconoclasm and irreverence, detaching from the rules of Webb. Alexis de Tocqueville, visiting the United States in the early 1830s, described how democracy "renders the habitual intercourse of the Americans simple and easy,"[41] a characteristic not of Webb but of Bennett. The pride and aristocratic airs of Webb, who fought duels to protect his name, are reflected in his newspaper's careful discussions about honor and social rights. In the days before Webb's second drubbing of Bennett, the *Courier and Enquirer* concerned itself with a fight, or "fracas," between two New York City men. One of the men, a Mr. Tompkins, according to accounts in the *Courier and Enquirer* and in the *Herald*, objected to being slapped on the back and treated with familiarity by a Mr. Neal. The whole thing escalated to a duel. When Tompkins failed to find a second, the duel was canceled. The friends of Neal caught up with Tompkins and his friends at a New York City hotel and a "fracas" ensued, with guns and knives drawn. Tompkins was seriously wounded. The "fracas" earned column after column in the *Courier and Enquirer*; Webb meticulously analyzed the men's "honor" and lack thereof. Webb ended one article by calling the "fracas," but not the abortive duel, "disgraceful."[42] The next day Bennett quoted Webb at length and laughed at his hypocrisy. Bennett wrote, "This homily comes with an exquisite grace from a man who has kicked up more disgraceful brawls than any other of the same dimensions ever did." Bennett then criticized Webb for not taking a stand against dueling. "Who has the courage" to oppose dueling, Bennett asked. "If no other will, we shall." Finally Bennett insinuated that Webb was a coward.[43] Bennett's attacks on Webb's coverage were less a careful critique than a public demonstration that Bennett could take a measure of his former boss's "dimensions" and hold him up to ridicule.

One of the *Herald*'s chief innovations was its detachment from the six-centers' concern with propriety and honor. The articles in the *Herald* about the beatings contain no suggestion that Bennett was offended or indignant over Webb's violence. The emotion that comes through is feigned pity over Webb's declining condition, and an irreverence calculated to further affront Webb's honor and to entertain the *Herald*'s readers. Bennett's ability to mock the airs of the aristocracy can be seen in the days immediately following his beating. Claiming that the *Herald* has produced a "new era" in the city, Bennett wondered why the other papers did not support him after the beating and even compared himself to Socrates and the other papers to the ancient sophists who tried to destroy him. "The days of Webb and his impotent paper are numbered," promised Bennett—empty bombast indeed, but fiery and irreverent too.[44]

Even a glimpse at the daily fare in both papers would reveal the sea change from a mannered to irreverent journalism. On one day in April 1836, the *Courier and Enquirer*'s dry political reports included one of a Rhode Island election ("The Providence Journal brings us full returns of the recent election in that State, from every town but New Shoreham") and a vapid account of a failed congressional bill. On the same day, the *Herald* mentioned Congress too, but the topics, tone, and terseness of the two papers contrast markedly. Here are two snippets from the *Herald*:

> Nothing done in Congress—equally idle at the Five Points.
>
> How lovely the ladies looked yesterday on Broadway![45]

Bennett employed the "simple and easy" lack of deference that de Tocqueville noticed and Webb deplored.

Mobility and Change

The directions of Webb's and Bennett's mobility ran opposite to that of the elite and working classes. But the very fact of their change in fortunes is important, because if there is one characteristic that marks the early penny era it is mobility—the promise of mobility and the fear of it as well. Bennett's detachment from the mannered society of Webb is reflected in this shift. And Bennett's optimism and exuberance are too.

In the 1830s people moved. More canals, steamboats, railroads, roads, turnpikes, and bridges were built under Jackson, who was often skeptical of public works, than under any previous president.[46] The changing market

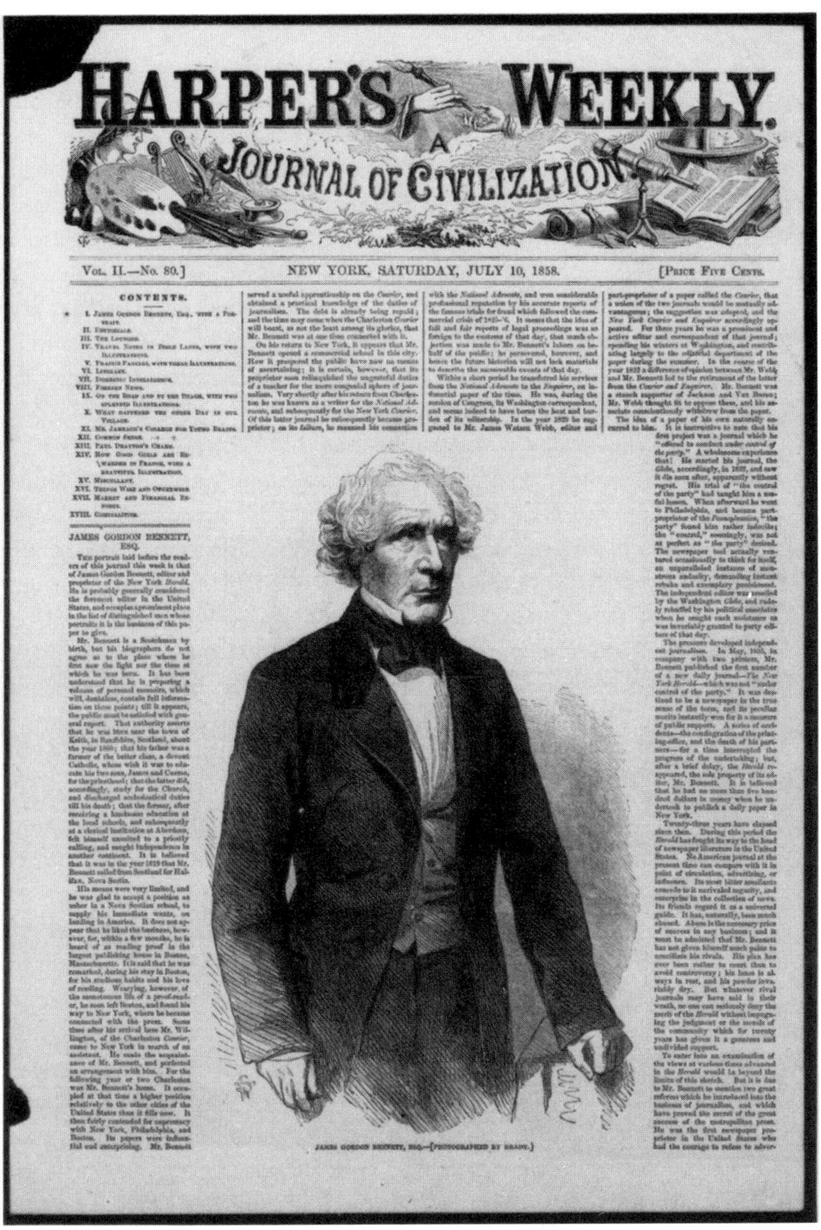

HARPER'S WEEKLY.

A JOURNAL OF CIVILIZATION

Vol. II.—No. 80.] NEW YORK, SATURDAY, JULY 10, 1858. [Price Five Cents.

CONTENTS.

JAMES GORDON BENNETT, ESQ.

JAMES GORDON BENNETT, ESQ.—[PHOTOGRAPHED BY BRADY.]

Figure 2. James Gordon Bennett. *Harper's Weekly,* 10 July 1858 (Library of Congress). After Bennett interviewed the madam of Ellen Jewett, other editors suggested that the "visit to the scene" was not his first. To this he replied that he had visited a brothel only once before, and was turned away for being "too ugly." Stephens, *A History of News,* 352.

economy uprooted families and individuals; increasingly, people began to move away from rural homes and to the cities to find work. The fiction of the Jacksonian era and beyond, until the Civil War, reflects this traveling age: Irving's Rip Van Winkle travels through time, while Ichabod Crane flits from town to town; James F. Cooper's Natty Bumpo is forever foraging in the woods; some of Nathaniel Hawthorne's characters wander the woods too, while others seek kinsmen in other cities; on a grander scale, ships carried people across the country and the world, as reflected in Herman Melville's great narratives of the sea, written about his younger days in the nascent years of the pennies.[47]

Politically and socially it was an exciting and heady age for those who were fortunate enough to be born white, male, and Protestant. It is difficult to imagine a definition of democracy that would include the Jacksonian kind (Southern blacks, of course, were generally slaves, and Northern ones were badly abused and politically disenfranchised; American Indians generally fared no better than free blacks; Irish and other non–native-born Americans were often deprived of their civil rights; women, too, politically powerless, did not gain suffrage until the twentieth century, and some even compared their plight to that of the slaves).[48] But the era was deeply concerned with the *idea* of democracy. Although Jackson did not introduce universal white manhood suffrage (it preceded him, in fact), for the first time the votes of all white men did matter. And while Jackson's laissez-faire policies may have hurt the poor, Jackson and his Democratic confreres appealed to the poor for their votes, in what one historian called an era of "lowest common denominator" politics.[49] While the upward economic mobility of the working classes was greatly exaggerated, the increasing currency of the *myth* of mobility is evident from the press and political rhetoric of the day. The myth of politicians rising from humble origins was employed by both major political parties. Jackson himself was a beneficiary of this myth: he had never been poor, and at the time of his first presidential campaign he held great wealth and owned more than one hundred slaves.[50]

People began to feel empowered by new religious beliefs. By the coming of the Jacksonian age, a revivalist faith began to supplant the old Calvinist doctrine of predestination. The revivalists brought with them a belief in eternal mobility. Charles Finney, the leading revivalist of his time, was a lawyer turned preacher who believed that salvation was possible for all. Gaining national attention for the revivals he staged, Finney encouraged his followers—many of whom were recently empowered by suffrage—to "vote" for salvation. Come up to the bench, he would beckon them, and elect yourself to heaven.[51] Finney's beliefs influenced and echoed those of reformers everywhere: revivalism, abolitionism, temperance, anti-tobaccoism, vegetarianism, and other isms were seen as necessary tools with which to build a perfect life fit for salvation. "All great reforms go together," said the abolitionist Frederick Douglass, reflecting a belief of the reformers, or what some called the "anti-everythingarians" of the day.[52] The antebellum reformers held the common belief that admission to heaven (or, for the doubters, to a utopia), would be gained only through a total separation from evil. Thus abolitionists called for Northern secession, temperance advocates called for anti-drinking laws, and others, like Thoreau in his journey to Walden, simply dropped out completely. This activist approach to heaven was embraced by many, including the wealthy Tappan family, which secured a New York City church for Finney; it was also feared by many, including Webb, who organized a mob that sacked Finney's church.[53]

While Bennett hated the abolitionists, calling them "crazy-headed blockheads," he did share their faith in change and perfectibility.[54] All of the above dimensions of mobility can be seen in the following passage from Bennett's editorial page. Notice how the promise of the age is played out in the passage, and how mobility, in its variegated forms, and detachment from the old order are demonstrated:

> We mean to elevate the daily press to the same rank in literature and influence that Shakespeare did the low-sunk Drama in the days of Elizabeth, or Milton the Epic during the Commonwealth, or Scott the Novel in our own time. Do not smile, gentle reader, at our ambition—at our enthusiasm. Hitherto, the daily newspaper press has . . . possessed no soul—it was enlivened with no genius—it was actuated with no breathing spirit of fire,—it was dull as the lake of Asphaltides—or as the Courier and Journal—brimstone and saltpetre combined. The daily newspaper press is one of the most important elements of modern civilization. Its power—its brilliancy—its secret charms—its hidden mysteries,—have never yet been revealed—never yet been dug out from the dullness of montebanks, ninnies, or miserable twaddlers. We mean to call forth these hidden treasures so far as our strength and talent and energy can. To do so requires perseverance—which we have, experience—which we have, fearlessness—which we have, a private character untainted—which we have, a moral and physical courage that nothing can intimidate—which also we have, and a circulation and advertising patronage unequaled in the world—part of which we already have, and the rest will soon follow. See if it don't.[55]

Figure 3. "The Herald Establishment." *New York Herald*, 27 August 1845 (Library of Congress). In August 1845, Bennett ran a series of sketches of his premises. The sturdy five-story building reflects the success of the *Herald*, which by this time had passed Webb's *Morning Courier and New-York Enquirer* to become New York's top-selling newspaper.

From the hyperbolic beginning of the passage, where he promised to reach immortal heights, to the final sentence, where he used slang to underline his working-class irreverence, Bennett brought his American dream to the people and invited them, however vicariously, to share in it.

Public and "Personal Outrages": A Press Born out of a Violent Era

The penny press did not emerge from a period of democracy or from the growth of the middle class; instead, it detached from an era of change and complex, occasionally violent conflict. But the nature of the violence is important too, and here we will turn to an examination of Webb's violence and what it says about the conflicts of the era as a whole.

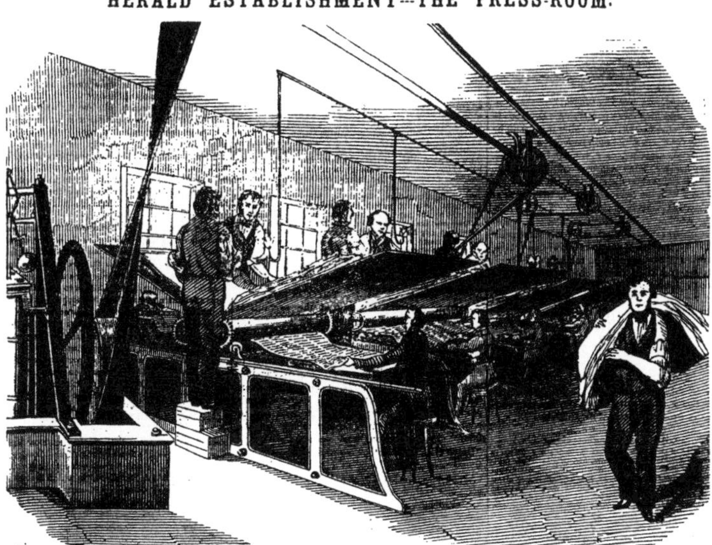

Figure 4. "The Herald Establishment—The Press Room." *New York Herald*, 28 August 1945 (Library of Congress). The double-cylinder steam presses at the *Herald*'s office are starting their daily run. The two modern presses, according to Bennett, "are capable of throwing off 5,000 copies per hour each." By four in the morning, the news carriers, about twenty in number, gathered to deliver the paper by subscription. By six o'clock "several hundred" newsboys gathered to hawk the *Herald* on the streets of New York.

The day after his second beating, the headline in Bennett's *Herald* screamed out from the first page: "OPENING OF THE SUMMER CAMPAIGN—JAMES WATSON WEBB'S SECOND FRACAS—WALL STREET IN COMMOTION—RETREAT OF THE BELLIGERENT—RETURN OF THE KILLED AND WOUNDED." Bennett was exuberantly reporting on his favorite topic—himself—and was using his misfortune to sell papers. But while he often wrote about his life with hyperbole, comparing himself to Socrates and even Moses at times, this time he had a narrower goal: to detach from Webb and paint him as a dangerous outsider. "The violent and disgraceful personal outrages which have so frequently disgraced the city, were yesterday repeated by James Watson Webb, the editor and proprietor of the Courier and Enquirer," wrote Bennett, who offered to convince the head of "Bellevue Asylum" to have the "insane" Webb committed.[56]

Although Bennett was merely having some public fun at his rival's expense and boosting the *Herald*'s circulation, Webb may very well have made it to Bellevue in later times. A violent man in any age, Webb was nevertheless representative of the era's violence and the instigator of physical attacks on individuals and groups. According to one chronicler of Jacksonian violence, the years from 1833 to 1837 were the most violent of antebellum America.[57] This time also corresponds with the birth and rise of the pennies *and* the height of Webb's violence. In 1833, after the abolitionist newspaper the *Liberator* denounced the reactionary American Colonization Society, the society called a meeting, held in Webb's office, and staged a massive riot, which included seizing and tormenting an elderly African American man.[58] In 1834 Webb led a mob in the bloody election riots in New York City. In 1836 he beat Bennett (on three occasions), and in 1837 he almost fought a duel with Congressman Samuel H. Gholson of Mississippi. Webb's feud with Congressman Jonathan Cilley of Maine in 1838 led to a duel between the latter and Webb's friend, W. J. Graves, a congressman from Kentucky. Graves killed Cilley, the only example in American history of one congressman killing another. In 1842 Webb himself fought a duel with a congressman, Thomas Marshall of Kentucky; Webb was injured, and then briefly jailed for breaking New York's anti-dueling laws.[59]

A Violent Era

The years from 1833 to 1837 were violent in a number of ways. The violence of the Old West reaches us through the filters of B-movies and other mass media, but a more complete and general picture emerges through the work of the post-"progressive" revisionist historians. While shootouts may have been less common in the nineteenth century than they are in twentieth-century Hollywood, antebellum life was, like Webb, extremely violent, even by our standards. The violence, from mob riots to the quaint antebellum custom of "eye-gouging," was most certainly affected by the enormous quantities of hard liquor consumed by Americans—an annual consumption of four gallons *per capita* by one estimate—and was a daily fact for many city-dwellers.[60] One historian counted nearly fifty reported riots nationwide in the years 1834 and 1835 alone.[61]

Setting the tone for the violent era were the U.S. and state governments. Jackson's own bellicosity rivaled and probably surpassed Webb's; as he acknowledged himself, his violence was part of his nature: "I was born for a storm and calm does not suit me."[62] A hero of the 1812 war, Jackson was also representative of the various forms of violence in the era, especially with regard to Native Americans, slaves, political rhetoric, and personal confrontations. In 1818 then General Jackson led an expedition through Spanish-owned Florida to attack Seminole Native Americans. Without permission from superiors he killed countless Indians, took a Spanish fort, and executed two British citizens.[63] Indian "removal" was at a peak in the Jacksonian era; removal was often a euphemism for genocide.

A wealthy man by the time of his election, Jackson lived well off the backs of his slaves at his farm, the Hermitage. Obviously the very fact of slavery was another great form of violence in antebellum America, to say nothing of the routine beatings, rapes, and other abuses by white masters and their surrogates. Jackson himself kept runaway slaves in chains and once placed an advertisement to recover a runaway that offered fifty dollars, plus "ten dollars extra, for every hundred lashes any person will give him, to the amount of three hundred."[64]

Jackson's presidential tenure was also marked by political bellicosity and violence. While the United States was at peace for most of the era, two internal conflicts, the nullification crisis of the early thirties and the battle over the second Bank of the United States, which took up Jackson's attention for much of his tenure, were marked by brinksmanship and violent rhetoric. The nullification crisis was sparked when South Carolina tried to nullify a federal treaty. After South Carolinians threatened to call up a militia over a fight with the president about states' rights, Jackson vowed to hang leading nullifiers as traitors "on the first tree I can find." During the bank conflict Jackson said, "The bank . . . is trying to kill me, *but I will kill it.*"[65] In 1835 Jackson was also the victim of the first assassination attempt on an American president, during the height of the era's violence. It was a "sign of the times," remarked New York's *Evening Post*.[66] Jackson, like many in the era, fought duels, including the one over a horse race that left Jackson injured for life. Perhaps the bullet won in this duel, which was lodged in Jackson's side near his heart, caused internal bleeding, and gave him a funereal air, best represented the violence and pain of the man and the era that took his name.[67]

In the North, street violence peaked from 1832 to 1837; mob violence probably troubled people the most, especially the blacks, abolitionists, and

Irish immigrants who were the most likely targets. But even members of the elite were alarmed, including Philip Hone, who called 1834 the "riot year."[68] Northern anti-abolitionist violence peaked in 1837 with the killing of an abolitionist editor, Elijah Lovejoy, in Alton, Illinois. After this incident the violence abated somewhat, and public opinion in the North became increasingly tolerant of abolitionism, so much so that even officials who fought against the rights of blacks began to regret their actions.[69]

Why were the mid-1830s so violent? Two historians, Richard Hofstadter and Carl Prince, saw the inegalitarianism of the era as an important factor. Hofstadter called the violence a "symptom" of the "pathology of a nation growing at a speed that defied control, governed by an ineffective leadership . . . , bedeviled by its internal heterogeneity, and . . . cursed by a . . . wrong [slavery] that many of its people had even come to cherish as a right." Prince argued that the violence may have been "encouraged by an ideology that espoused political democracy without paying much attention to its social and economic substance." The year 1834, Prince argued, was the first year in the nineteenth century that people in urban centers believed that their interests were suddenly and radically different from their neighbors'.[70]

Dueling and Drubbing

Two forms of violence, duels and beatings, were widely practiced in antebellum America and were also favored by Webb. A look at the social function of these forms can give us a deeper understanding of the relationship of Webb and Bennett, and of Bennett's detachment from the culture of dueling and violence. Dueling was a particularly Southern ritual, but it was practiced in the North and by Northerners too. In 1804 Aaron Burr killed Alexander Hamilton in a duel in New Jersey. And Webb himself displayed a lifelong interest in duels, both through his coverage of the "fracas" and other duels, and as a participant. The ritual of the duel is a way of both resolving conflicts and reaffirming ideals of society and honor through the *code duello*. Just as modern litigants reaffirm their faith in the validity of the courts by participating in legal structures, men embarked on the "social drama" of the duel with its intricate rules to renew their membership in the antebellum gentry. The duel would often start with an exchange of notes and escalate to the choosing of weapons and seconds and the drawing up of rules. The vast majority of cases were resolved peacefully in the hours or minutes before the scheduled fight, and even bellicose men like Jackson and Webb settled many duels for every one they fought.[71]

Why did Webb beat Bennett instead of challenging him to a duel? Even by its proponents and participants, dueling was not considered the appropriate method of conflict resolution for all parties. Specifically, dueling was not practiced by two men of different "classes." Masters did not duel slaves, for example; they beat them. Occasionally the choice to beat rather than to duel was in itself a comment on the character of the victim. After Charles Sumner of Massachusetts stood up on the Senate floor in 1856 to criticize Andrew P. Butler from South Carolina, Preston Brooks, a congressman from South Carolina and Butler's cousin, beat the Massachusetts senator with his cane. Brooks was demonstrating that Sumner was no gentleman, unworthy of a duel, and fit to be beaten like a dog, or more to the point, like a slave. The *Richmond Enquirer* wrote after the caning, "The Vulgar Abolitionists in the Senate are getting above themselves. . . . They have grown saucy and dare to be impudent to gentlemen!. . . . They must be lashed into submission."[72] This passage reveals the social or "class" aspects of the choice to beat rather than to duel. It also shows how the *Enquirer* felt that the remedy to Sumner was to keep him down, both in terms of political power and by the use of actual force.

It is no coincidence that there are parallels between the Sumner-Brooks conflict and Bennett's accounts of Webb's beatings, with Webb trying to beat down Bennett, and Bennett always getting up and forever climbing. Webb's violence is part and parcel of the violence of the day and the social/political framework in which it operated. Because they represented different classes, Webb could not duel Bennett. And despite Bennett's increasing wealth (or perhaps because of it), Webb thought that his only option was to beat him.

Bennett's coverage of the beatings carefully subverts the gentry-servant relationship that Webb's cane had sought to establish. Bennett and, vicariously, the nonelite readers of the *Herald* would not be kept down by anyone. In the classic master-slave narrative, the master beats the slave and breaks his will, but Bennett had rewritten the gentry-servant relationship so that the servant uses the pen to fight back, detach from the master's rules, and ultimately conquer. Bennett had tapped into the myth of mobility, based on the evangelical spirit of the age, the feeling that people can change their situation (even though only white men could participate in the adventure and even this group saw their fortunes decline), and a rare embodiment of the American Dream, Bennett himself.

Bennett's heroic self-portrait was in keeping with the heroic if nonviolent image of the press as a check on monied interests, including the elite newspapers. The following is from a labor paper, the *Working Man's Advocate*:

> No weapons we'll use, nor for aught do we care
> But knowledge and union to bring on the field
> For those are the keenest and those will we bear
> Whilst the *press* will inspire us and be our safe shield.[73]

The lesson is unmistakable: not actual weapons but the press would help to win the battles for the working men. While Bennett did not naturally align himself with "working men's" or union causes, he did use his pen to attack. And attack he did. With his indiscriminate attacks on Catholics (of which he was one), Protestants, Jews, natives, immigrants, blacks, men, women, drunkards, temperance advocates, abolitionists, slave owners, six-penny papers, penny papers, and everyone else, Bennett was the scribbler's equivalent of a one-man mob. But Bennett's violent rhetoric, unlike Webb's, generally did not lead to actual violence.

What Bennett's attacks did lead to was a sort of proto-"objective" style of writing. Bennett's attacks followed the textbooks' edict to be "detached" in that they seemed totally random and without provocation. Many years later, Joseph Pulitzer said of his own paper, "the *World* has no friends."[74] This can be said of Bennett's paper too: the *Herald* had only enemies. In its major break from the partisan papers (which always had at least one friend—their own party), the penny press detached itself from alliances.

Within months of Jackson's departure from office and the arrival of his handpicked successor, Martin Van Buren, the economy collapsed, due in part to eight years of laissez-faire economics and inflated paper money. The Panic of 1837 also marked two major turning points: the decline of street violence and the supremacy of the pennies. To illustrate the pennies' detachment from the culture of violence, one of the most important contributions of the pennies, we turn to one final example, the Cilley-Graves duel.

After a *Courier* reporter had accused him of corruption, Jonathan Cilley, a Democratic congressman from Maine, attacked Webb on the floor of the House, noting the infamous bank "loan." Webb's friend, W. J. Graves, a congressman from Kentucky, then delivered a letter from Webb to Cilley, which the latter refused to read. Cilley told Graves that he could not be held responsible for "language used in debate," meant no discourtesy toward the Kentucky congressman, but could not say that Webb was a gentleman. According to the *code duello,* Cilley, by impugning Webb's reputation, had also cast doubt on the honor of Graves. Notes were exchanged and finally the two met on a Maryland field, each holding rifles at one hundred yards. Webb claimed that he searched for the dueling parties so that he might substitute himself for the Kentucky congressman. He arrived after Graves shot Cilley dead on the third round of shooting.[75]

Bennett's response to the duel was predictable. He called Webb a "murderer" and reported that "upwards of a hundred subscribers of the *Courier* yesterday withdrew their patronage from the wicked and blood-crimsoned sheet." But the *Herald*'s coverage also suggested how Webb symbolized the violence of the era, how that violence was coming to an end, and finally, how the penny press would replace it. Calling the duel an "atrocious plot against the tranquillity and well being of society," Bennett placed the violence of the era on Webb's doorstep:

> For five or six years past there has been an organized conspiracy to set aside all order, and to make passion the interpreter, in fact, the substitute for law. Open incitements to rioting, public denouncings of persons opposed to their desires, and violent assaults upon quiet and unoffending citizens, have been the claims this Wall street gang, and its ruffian leaders, have preferred to the respect and confidence of us all.[76]

In this passage Bennett creates a dichotomy between "tranquillity," "order," "law," and "us all" on one side and the violent, privileged cabal of Wall Streeters on the other. While Bennett had used rhetoric like this before, now it had begun to resonate. Now other newspapers joined Bennett in denouncing Webb. And they all suggested that Webb was a threat to civilized discourse. The *Transcript*, another penny paper, asked whether Webb will "be allowed to take his editorial chair and will the public take his paper from his bloody hands?" The *Sun* pointed out that Webb's "turbulent spirit" had "more than once carried him to Washington on similar errands." Does Webb, asked the *Sun*, "stand ready to defend his paragraphs with his pistol case?"[77] Newspapers of all stripes denounced the duel and Webb; but the above passages show more than a general censure: they all show horror that violence and newspapering would be coupled together. Will laws be abandoned? Will the public buy from bloody hands? Will the editor defend himself not with words, but with bullets? The editors had found a better method than violence, the newspaper business, and were now detaching from the ideological and violent Webb.

It is impossible to evaluate the veracity of Bennett's report of the following week that "over one hundred and fifty young men have enrolled themselves, for the purpose of inflicting a marked personal indignity on James W. Webb, or any of his associates, the first time they are seen in the streets." But Bennett used this report to condemn these "young men" *and* Webb. By "detaching" himself from the conflict and getting between two bellicose sides, Bennett had cast himself in the role of a person in the middle—a familiar role in modern journalism—while at the same time plotting the demise of his rival's paper. "No, no, no," Bennett cried in his column at the prospect of more violence. "Let the moral, legal, and respectable inhabitants of New York, only indicate their horror at the late doings, by calmly, but firmly withdrawing all patronage, all subscriptions, all advertisements, from the blood-stained sheet."[78]

The pennies had taken the measure of the ideological and violent Webb and had seen something in him that represented the age as a whole. Other representations of ideology, such as the labor press, and violence, such as the violent street struggles and the anti-abolitionist mobs, all abated by the late thirties. Schiller points out that the labor press did not survive the panic and ensuing depression of 1837, and that the pennies did survive.[79] Similarly, a historian of Jacksonian violence wrote that violence declined after the panic (Webb himself became more respectful of the law after he was tried, convicted, and briefly jailed for dueling), in part due to lagging funds for both abolitionist and anti-abolitionist groups.[80] And while some mainstream partisan and commercial newspapers would survive in one form or another until the Civil War, after the Panic of 1837 none would keep up with the success of the pennies.[81] But why did the pennies survive the panic? Only one explanation seems plausible: the public accepted the pennies' rejection of divisiveness, partisanship, and violence.

The textbooks tell young journalists to be detached. Because of this, Webb can be seen as anti-"objective": violence and uncontrolled rage are the opposites of the "objective" mind. The word "detachment," with all the implications of pulling oneself out of one's life, is still problematic, but we can concede that Webb's violence, including his mob actions, duelings, and beatings, show that the editor could separate his mind from his body less successfully than Bennett could. Bennett, with his humorous looks at his own misfortune, had matched Webb's passion (he is not what we would recognize as a dispassionate modern journalist) but had transformed it. Although Bennett used aggressive rhetoric, it was contained in the columns of his paper. Bennett and his penny confreres detached themselves from Webb's brand of ideology and violence. In this way the pennies took a big step toward "objectivity."

The birth of the penny press and detachment came not from democratization and a rising middle class, and not only from factors already acknowledged—sensationalism, urbanization, the rise of literacy, and technological advances—but also as a response to a difficult and violent era. For if we accept Prince's notion that the mid-1830s were violent because for the first time in the nineteenth century neighbors felt that their interests were incompatible, we are struck by the pennies' creation of an opposite paradigm: that neighbors could transcend party and share interests, specifically the interest in buying a detached and nonpartisan paper. The pennies, in replacing divisive ideology and violence with a detached nonpartisanship, had discovered a sound business practice.

2

Nonpartisanship

Three Shades of Political Journalism

Well, people on the right say we're too liberal and people on the left say we're in league with the status quo, which probably means we're right where we should be, right in the middle.

—Sam Donaldson, *ABC News*

Most reporters are members of the extreme center—I am.

—John Chancellor, *NBC News*

In 1836 James Gordon Bennett supported Martin Van Buren, a Democrat, for president. In 1840 he endorsed Van Buren's opponent, William Henry Harrison. Bennett then supported a Democrat, James K. Polk, in 1844, a Whig, Zachary Taylor, in 1848, a Democrat, Franklin Pierce, in 1852, and a Republican, John C. Fremont, in 1856. Three things distinguish Bennett's record of presidential endorsement. First, aside from Fremont, Bennett always picked the winner. Second, aside from Fremont and possibly Taylor, his endorsements always favored the position of most slaveholders. Third and most important to this study, Bennett's eclectic endorsements were rare, if not unique, in an era of strong party affinity. In a time when the two major parties each had newspapers that broadcast the party line (the Democratic *U.S. Telegraph* and *Globe*, and the Whig *National Intelligencer*), a newspaper not supported by party was a newfangled notion. Even Bennett's competitors, the *Sun*, the *Tribune*, and the *Times*, had strong party affiliations. The *Sun* was strongly Democratic and the *Tribune* and *Times* were Whig/Republican until Greeley's famous break with the Republicans in 1872 to support his own ill-fated presidential campaign. But even Greeley's switch, dramatic as it was, represented a onetime shift. Bennett, on the other hand, moved across party lines every few weeks. He was one of America's first nonpartisan newspaper editors.[1]

Nonpartisanship is the second of the five components of "objectivity" mentioned by modern textbooks, journalists, and critics. When journalists promise to give "both sides" in political debates, when they avoid a formal affiliation with political parties, they are said to be nonpartisan. Nonpartisanship is easier to discuss than "objectivity" as a whole because we can be reasonably certain of a number of its historical features. We know, as we discussed in the first chapter, that true nonpartisanship was not possible before the newspapers' formal sloughing of party ties in the 1830s; by definition, editors cannot be nonpartisan if their main source of income is a single political party. We also know that as journalists had less and less access to party patronage, they wrote more and more nonpartisan news stories.[2] This chapter is an examination of nonpartisanship from the 1830s to the start of the Civil War.

The chapter has two goals. First, it aims to demonstrate how nonpartisanship functioned, in various forms, in the years after the partisan press domination in the 1820s and early 1830s. Second, it seeks to explore different kinds of nonpartisan participation. To this end I have analyzed the political journalism of three editors—James Gordon Bennett, William Lloyd Garrison, and Frederick Douglass—in an attempt to understand the structure of early American nonpartisanship. What emerges is not one, but three paradigms of nonpartisanship, exemplified by the journalism of Bennett, Garrison, and Douglass. Because they were interested in the government yet not supported by or beholden to a political party, each was nonpartisan. However, the three editors represent three distinct nonpartisan stances. Bennett could be called a *centrist nonpartisan*, Garrison an *antipartisan*, and Douglass an *activist nonpartisan*.

"Objectivity" and nonpartisanship are so closely linked that they are often confused. But they are different. For the reasons outlined in the introduction—reasons that some journalists would be the first to acknowledge—true objectivity as a goal is not attainable, but nonpartisanship, insofar as it is defined as keeping personal political preferences (if a reporter has any) out of news stories, is quite possible. During the Vietnam War, for example, a study showed that most respondents who considered themselves "hawks" thought that the leading TV newsmen of the day, Walter Cronkite, Chet Huntley, and David Brinkley, shared their views. But the three anchors were considered to be against the war by a majority of "doves." Masking one's preferences for a political party is possible, according to studies, especially in our two-party system.[3] For the most part we do not know with certainty how mainstream journalists have voted, a point made recently by George Stephanopoulos, Clinton's ex-advisor: "I don't think there's one reporter now—I'm not talking about columnists—who acts out of an ideological bias that can be detected,"[4] a remarkable claim for a presidential advisor, and one that could not have been made 150 years ago. This is a point of pride for many journalists. "If people knew how I felt on an issue," wrote Cronkite in his memoirs, "I had failed in my mission." Study after study has shown that contrary to the press critics of the left and right, American journalists occupy the middle of the political spectrum. Journalists take pride in the fact that they are both praised and criticized by people of all political persuasions, and Cronkite, citing criticism from both the right and the left, announced that he must be doing something right. I don't like "group conformity," Cronkite wrote, and I don't like "conspicuous nonconformity" either.[5] You can't get more center than that.

If John Chancellor seeks the extreme center, as the epigraph at the start of this chapter suggests, he is not alone. Journalists are frequently both disparaged and praised for "not taking sides," for voicing opinions only after others have already done so. Eric Sevareid, a *CBS News* commentator, was dubbed Eric "Severalsides" for his moderate views.[6] But nonpartisanship serves an important function in democracies: it provides a voice distinct from those of the partisans. Nonpartisanship, at its best, can allow for a national dialogue between politicians and the public unpolluted by partisan interpretation.

Of course, as the media critic Robert A. Hackett pointed out, "an electorally oriented notion of bias and fairness is a very limited one."[7] Nonpartisanship in American journalism means in essence favoring both of the two major parties because it implicitly accepts the two-party system. "We give *both* sides," stated an advertisement for CNN.[8] Equal time for minor parties is not given by any mainstream media outlets; the FCC's so-called Fairness Doctrine, for example, announced that it is not intended "to make time available to Communists or the Communist viewpoints." So when we discuss "nonpartisanship" in this chapter, we mean not "objectivity" or even "balance," only that a news organization is not openly tied to a single political party. This, as we discussed, is a *component* of the modern notion of "objectivity."[9]

If you are seeking an understanding of nonpartisanship, don't look in the history books. Historians have not yet developed a clear understanding of the structure of early nonpartisanship, especially how it fit into the political world of antebellum American politics. Historians of journalism and historians of the Jacksonian period have yet to develop a synthesis of the disparate theories that they hold about party and nonpartisanship. Jacksonian historians have concentrated on political history, while journalism historians have written about nonpartisanship, but no one has tried to place early nonpartisans in their political milieu. Doing so would reveal at least three distinct strands of antebellum nonpartisanship, three strands that broadly define the practice.

Schlesinger and His Critics

The last fifty years of historical scholarship on Jacksonian politics can be seen in part as a referendum on Arthur M. Schlesinger, Jr.'s book *Age of Jackson* (1945).[10] First came Schlesinger's vision of the Democratic Party, the party of "the people," that swept in democracy and egalitarianism over the protests of the elite Whigs, a battle fought primarily in the northeastern United States. Schlesinger saw the Jacksonian age primarily in terms of conflict between Democrats and Whigs, ideological battles between a few prominent white men of distinct political parties. The battle over the Second Bank of the United States (B.U.S.), according to Schlesinger, was the defining conflict of the era, with the "people" opposing the bank and the elites supporting it.[11]

Since Schlesinger, a number of historians have responded to his vision of class-based party, pointing out that the Whig supporters of the B.U.S. were not always elite, and that the Democrats' opposition was based not on principle but on a greedy desire to speculate; they argued that the electorate were not divided as much by class as by other factors—ethnicity, religion, national background, section, and types of wealth. And they showed that major slave owners were generally Democrats.[12] Others viewed Jacksonian politics in the frame of an emerging partisan system, coming out of a formation based on section and faction and influenced by market forces.[13]

Included in the struggle to define the two major parties is a fifty-year attempt to discern the position of African Americans. Much is left out of Schlesinger's view of Jacksonian political life, as the author himself admitted in hindsight: "When I wrote *The Age of Jackson*, the predicament of women, of blacks, of Indians was shamefully out of mind."[14] Leading abolitionists, such as Garrison, and leading African Americans, such as Frederick Douglass, are notably absent from Schlesinger's vision of the populace during the Jacksonian era. Schlesinger did not go beyond Jackson's plantation for evidence of black views of Jackson.[15] The verisimilitude of Schlesinger's brief sketch of the plantation, with docile and loving slaves, is not as important to understanding antebellum racial views as the findings of Pessen and others that voting was often split along racial and ethnic lines; unlike the Democrats of the 1930s and 1940s, the 1830s Democrats were hated by blacks, and Whigs received "almost all Negroes' votes."[16] Jackson as a major slaveholder and supporter of slavery convinced at least the free blacks—the only black voters—that their cause was better served by the Whigs.

In their attempts to define the two major parties, revisionist historians have analyzed these parties, their message and membership, and discussed alternative parties. But much of antebellum political life existed *outside* the parties. The position of the nonpartisans is largely ignored by historians. The role of newspaper editors was, according to the historical narratives, to support parties and causes. Thus party-supported editors and the partisan editors, like Greeley, are given more attention than the nonpartisan Bennett. Indeed, the editor of the *Herald* is ignored in three of the five synthesis studies read for this chapter and mentioned only in passing in the other two.[17]

Journalism Historians

As we have seen, historians of journalism, including Frank L. Mott, Michael Schudson, Daniel Schiller, Mitchell Stephens, and Michael Emery and Ewin Emery, have written extensively about Bennett. But with the exception of Schiller, their notion of antebellum party is colored by dated historical information, a whiggish view of nonpartisanship, and, with the exception of Schiller and Stephens, a general distaste for Bennett's sensationalism. Furthermore, while Bennett is discussed in all of the above journalism histories, the non- (or anti-) partisan political positions of two other leading journalists, Garrison and Douglass, are completely ignored.[18] With only slight oversimplification, one can say that the mainstream histories have ignored nonpartisanship and journalism histories have misunderstood antebellum parties. I have not yet found a study that combines a modern understanding of party with a discussion of nonpartisanship.[19]

Dates of Principal Events Discussed in This Chapter

January 1831	**Garrison founds the *Liberator***
May 1835	**Bennett founds the *New York Herald***
November 1835	**Garrison is mobbed in Boston**
November 1837	**Lovejoy is killed in Alton, Illinois**
September 1838	**Douglass escapes to the North**
December 1847	**Douglass founds the *North Star*, renamed *Frederick Douglass' Paper* in 1851**
July 1848	**Douglass supports the Free Soil Party**
May 1850	**Garrison and Douglass speak in New York at the sixteenth anniversary of the Anti-Slavery Society**
September 1850	**Compromise reached by Southern and Northern interests**
July 1852	**Douglass announces, "This fourth of July is *yours,* not *mine.*"**
July 1854	**Garrison burns a copy of the U.S. Constitution**
November 1864	**Garrison, Bennett, and Douglass all endorse Lincoln**

Bennett: Centrist Nonpartisan

Within months of starting the *New York Herald*, James Gordon Bennett took a stand on the bank battle. He placed himself firmly between Nicholas Biddle, the head of the Bank of the United States, and Jackson's anti-bank advisors, called the Kitchen Cabinet. As usual, his stance was at once self-serving, critical of his rivals, and boastful of his paper's independence:

> The Times makes a great outcry on one side against Mr. Biddle—The Courier, on the other, is equally vociferous about the kitchen [both for reasons of stock speculation]. All these large papers are in the hands of stock-jobbers. None are "free as the mountain wind" but the small dailies. We are the fellows that tell the truth.[20]

Bennett's stance is ignored by Schlesinger and only hinted at by Pessen and others; it is centrist and skeptical of partisan ties. Schlesinger does give countless examples of politicians who switch political affiliation, and Pessen suggested that "on most social and political issues—including [the parties'] willingness to gerrymander 'under the guise of reform'—there was little to choose between the major parties."[21] But neither book concerns itself with people, like Bennett, who stand publicly and firmly apart from either party. This is why I choose to call Bennett a *centrist nonpartisan.*

Bennett's penchant for switching sides fits right into the political milieu of his time. During the 1830s and 1840s, according to Richard McCormick in *The Presidential Game*, national politics in the United States moved from the "game of faction" to the "party game." That is, the medium of political ascendancy shifted from sectional coalitions to a national push for a unified message. The new reality of American politics was that a president could no longer get elected without a strong national party behind him. The first national political conventions were held in 1831 and 1832. Because of universal white manhood suffrage, the emergence of the "party game" meant that vast political engines sought power not from fellow politicians, but from the people, at least the men who voted. "People . . . were now to be acknowledged, courted, appealed to, and heard as never before," wrote McCormick.[22] Parties would now shift as much as needed to capture the majority of voters and electoral votes. As the content of the parties' message became secondary and the goal of winning elections became dominant, a parallel rise in the journalism of the day occurred: the political content became secondary to selling papers and advertising. The purveyor of this type of journalism is described by James Carey as a "professional communicator": "The distinguishing characteristic of the professional communicator—as opposed to the writer, novelist, scholar and others who produce messages—is that the message he produces has no *necessary* relation to his own thoughts and perceptions."[23] Although Carey lists purer forms of professional communicators, such as translators who merely stand as "brokers or links" between two linguistic groups, Bennett too can be seen as an example.

Bennett can be seen as a "professional communicator" because his editorial policy often seems motivated less by his "thoughts and perceptions" than by his profit motive. For example, as I have already mentioned, Bennett's support for Richard Robinson, the accused ax-murderer of the lovely prostitute Ellen Jewett, may very well have been motivated by bribes from the defense.[24] Similarly, despite Bennett's long-standing feud with the promoter P. T. Barnum, he shamelessly plugged Barnum's promotions in paid news stories. "Arrival of Jenny Lind—Tremendous Enthusiasm—Immense Turn-Out of the People," screamed Bennett, in a two-column editorial about the "heroism, goodness, and genius" of a singer who had just arrived in New York for a series of concerts sponsored by Barnum.[25] Finally, Bennett, more than the other New York penny editors, accepted all advertisements from those who could pay his price, including illegal abortionists and purveyors of quack medicines. His reply to critics who blamed him for accepting unsavory ads was simple: pay me more and I will drop the ads.[26]

Bennett's view of party was similarly detached from a known political philosophy. In fact only three characteristics seemed to remain consistent during Bennett's three decades as publisher of the *Herald*—his proslavery position, his immoderate stance on everything, including moderation, and his patriotism—and these characteristics can be traced to the sign of the dollar.

Bennett's proslavery was consistent. "For twenty odd years," Bennett wrote in 1858, "the New York Herald has been the only Northern journal that has unfailingly vindicated the constitutional rights of the South."[27] In Bennett's galaxy of shifting positions, why did proslavery remain true? An answer can be gleaned from one of Bennett's critics, writing to the Springfield *Republican* from Washington, DC:

> It is amusing to see the greed with which the *Herald* is snatched up and devoured on its earliest arrival here in the evening; and what is worse, to see the simplicity of these Southern fellows who seem to pin their whole faith upon it. Where Northern men look at it only for amusement, as they look at *Punch* or *Frank Leslie,* Southern men swallow it gravely with a sigh and a knowing shake of the head.[28]

Quite simply, Bennett's proslavery stance sold newspapers. In fact, Bennett sold more newspapers in the South than any other Northern publisher.

A second constant in Bennett's writing was his stridency. As one of Bennett's biographers wrote, "His editorials were notorious for their rhetorical extremism—strident, vituperative, and emotional—in behalf of politics that were basically moderate and balanced."[29] Politicians were often "blockheads," and as with the bank battle and slavery, Bennett often stood between two groups of "blockheads," making sense of the conflict through his own "independence" for his independent readers.

The third way Bennett can be seen as a professional communicator is his patriotism and its effect on the public. "Nothing is more embarrassing," wrote Alexis de Tocqueville after he visited the United States during the age of Jackson, "than the irritable patriotism of the Americans."[30] For those who find patriotism irritable, a perusal of editorials on any given week of Bennett's long tenure at the *Herald* would be maddening. This patriotism, which might be better described as jingoism or xenophobia, colored nearly every subject that Bennett addressed. When discussing the Catholic Church, for example, Bennett screamed, "If we must have a Pope, let us have a Pope of our own,—an American Pope, an intellectual, intelligent, and moral Pope,—not such a decrepit, licentious, stupid Italian blockhead as . . . Rome condescends to give the Christian world."[31] If Bennett's views on America were enough to irritate genteel aristocratic Frenchmen like Alexis de Tocqueville, they certainly did not prevent the wild success of the *Herald*. In fact, as I will show later in this chapter, Bennett's irritable patriotism was applauded by many, and it may have even contributed to his success.

Bennett's political position can be understood through a model of "objective" journalism set up by Daniel Hallin in his book about the press and the Vietnam War, *The Uncensored War*. Hallin constructed a diagram (see figure 5) of three spheres: the spheres of Consensus, Legitimate Controversy, and Deviance. The Sphere of Consensus, Hallin's inner circle, is the place in which most people are supposed to agree. Most modern journalists and news consumers would agree on the legitimacy of the government as embodied in the Constitution, the Bill of Rights, and the other amendments. Legitimate Controversy includes the debates over laws: Should the deficit be eliminated? If so, how so? The Sphere of Deviance includes issues beyond the pale: Should the United States be violently overthrown? Should we ignore the Constitution? Often, as in the above example, the first and last spheres operate as opposites: everyone agreeing with the Sphere of Consensus would uphold the Constitution; the deviants might overturn it. These spheres also shift from time to time, as politicians, journalists, and the public shift their views. The support of women's suffrage, for example, moved over time from Deviance to Legitimate Controversy to its present position: deeply embedded in the Sphere of Consensus. These adjustments are a necessary feature of a working democracy.

In the context of Bennett's position, the Sphere of Consensus might include the assumptions that an "independent" press is superior to all other forms, that America is a great country with unlimited potential, and that blacks are inferior to whites. Bennett placed his *Herald* in the very center

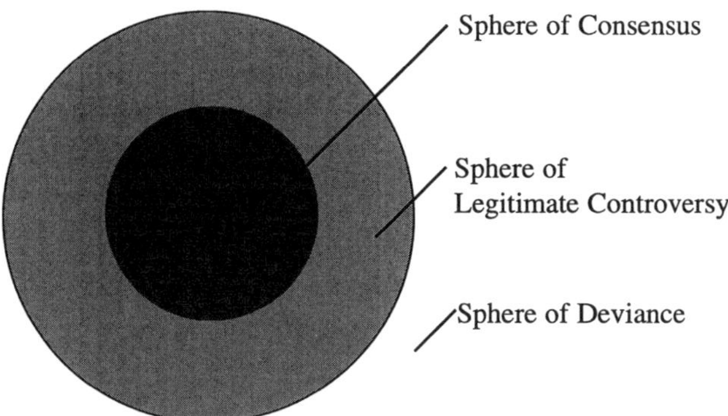

Figure 5. Hallin's spheres. Daniel Hallin, *The Uncensored War: The Media and Vietnam*, 117. Reprinted by permission.

of his inner Sphere of Consensus, with its appeal to North and South, its fierce independence, and its love of country. Legitimate Controversy, the place in which "mainstream" topics are debated, included, for Bennett, battles over the bank and debates over which party served the interests of the Sphere of Consensus. For Bennett, the Sphere of Deviance included everything not debated, including many of the matters raised by Garrison and Douglass, who were truly seen as deviants by Bennett and much of the white press.

"Not the Partisan of Any Man": Garrison the Antipartisan

William Lloyd Garrison, like Bennett, can be used to illustrate nonpartisanship. However, Garrison's nonpartisanship was a rejection of all politics, an *antipartisanship*, if you will. Garrison's career as a newspaperman began in 1818, when he was thirteen. It was then that he began a seven-year apprenticeship with the *Newburyport* (Massachusetts) *Herald*, which he later bought and renamed the *Free Press*. Upon selling the *Free Press* in 1827, Garrison became editor of a temperance journal, the *National Philanthropist*, through which he also expressed his antislavery views. "We have warmed in our bosom a serpent," Garrison wrote of slavery, "the poison of whose sting is felt through every vein of the republic."[32] Garrison's writings caught the eye of the leading abolitionist editor of the time, Benjamin Lundy, who walked from Baltimore to Bennington, Vermont, ostensibly to convince Garrison to become the editor of his newspaper, the *Genius of Universal Emancipation*. Garrison accepted the position in 1829. Like Bennett, Garrison was a vituperative editor; after blasting a Northern slave trader, Garrison was convicted of criminal libel and jailed for several weeks.[33]

On January 1, 1831, Garrison founded the *Liberator*, which, from its beginning to the end of the Civil War, would be the most radical, strident, and influential abolitionist periodical in the nation. Although the *Liberator*'s circulation was small by Bennett's standards, Garrison used a network of newspaper exchanges to gain a vast readership; although the paper was banned across much of the South, its words were widely read and dutifully cut and pasted into even the most radical proslavery sheets, where they were held up as examples of Northern fanaticism.[34] When the proslavery faction accused Garrison of inciting Nat Turner and his followers to kill fifty-five white men, women, and children in 1831, they probably did not imagine that slaves were actually reading the *Liberator*, but that Garrison's views, so widely quoted in the Southern press, were on everyone's mind.[35]

Garrison, like Bennett, stood apart from the parties. But unlike the *Herald*, which sought a middle ground between parties in the bank battle, the *Liberator* avoided politics in favor of a direct appeal to people who put principles above party, and to blacks whose ties to the abolition cause would transcend partisan affiliation. While refusing to be "the political partisan of any man," Garrison appealed to the "religious," the "patriotic," and "our free colored brethren" for aid.[36]

Unlike the *Herald*, which sought balance *inside* the political spectrum, Garrison clung to the outside. He railed against moderation:

> Tell a man whose house is on fire, to give a moderate alarm; tell him to moderately rescue his wife from the hands of a ravisher; the mother to gradually extricate her babe from the fire into which it has fallen;—but urge me not to use moderation in a cause like the present. I am in earnest—I will not equivocate—I will not retreat a single inch—AND I WILL BE HEARD.[37]

That there was "little to choose between" the two major parties was especially true for slavery, the big issue of the era and the one that eventually consumed all others. Garrison's extra-party stance was a necessary part of his movement; neither Whigs nor Democrats had immediate abolition on their agendas. It is precisely Garrison's exclusion from the parties that allows him to be intransigent and to demand to "be heard."

Figure 6. William Lloyd Garrison (Library of Congress).

Because it positioned itself outside politics, the *Liberator* needed to find a nonpolitical justification for its stance. To this end, Garrison appropriated images and icons that transcended party politics. Ironically, this often meant looking to the Revolutionary period, an era no more successful in ending slavery's evils than Garrison's. The *Liberator*, Garrison wrote, would lift the standard of emancipation "within sight of Bunker Hill and in the birth place of Liberty." The Capitol, "American People," and "Liberty" are all mentioned by Garrison on the *Liberator*'s first page. Garrison cites the " 'self-evident truth' maintained in the American Declaration of Independence, 'that all men are created equal and endowed by their Creator with certain inalienable rights.' "[38] The position of the *Liberator*, therefore, is outside rather than in the middle of party conflicts. Garrison's appeal to a past America is an attempt not to enter politics, but to force what he sees as American values onto an unwilling government. In this way Garrison can be called an "antipartisan." Perhaps even more than Bennett does, Garrison clings to the image of America's great potential; while this "potential" lay in economic laissez-faire for Bennett, for Garrison it was deeply rooted in the American dream of equality, his Sphere of Consensus, outside politics altogether.[39]

The Principles of Profits and the Prophet of Principles: Bennett and Garrison Compared

The *Herald* took a stance similar to the *Liberator*'s in that it was not partisan. But there the similarity ends. Bennett called the abolitionists "crazy-headed blockheads" outside mainstream thought. He balanced the abolitionists against the anti-abolitionist mobs, disapproved of them both, and then went on to blame their actions on demagogic newspapers that try "merely to acquire a hold upon the public passions." Bennett was meticulous in his criticism of the two extremes, announcing gratuitously, "We dont [*sic*] like the abolitionists" and calling an anti-abolitionist meeting "one of the greatest blunders of the day." Then Bennett wrote something interesting in his editorial column about the anti-abolitionist meeting:

> *The people were not there.* Yet the people here are not abolitionists. . . . On this question the South wants no sympathy, no protection, no public meetings at the North. *They only want to be let alone.*[40]

The "people were not there"? People were, of course, at the meeting, so what was Bennett saying? He was, it seems to me, defining the Sphere of Consensus, positioning himself in the middle of his imagined centrist majority. Ever suspicious of ulterior motives, Bennett suspected the participants of being merchants with Southern ties and "young idle lawyers, who want to marry young southern heiresses, and conciliate southern mothers . . . who hold the title deeds."[41]

Ironically, Bennett called for an absence of ulterior motives at the same time that he cast his appeal for moderation in economic terms: "Almost every one is full of beef and business—is growing fatter and wiser every day . . . and yet both North and South, east and west, are lashing themselves into a fury."[42] Whereas Garrison likens the status quo to a burning building, Bennett sees it as a great smorgasbord. Bennett fears the forces that would disturb white men's access to the trough.

By understanding the remunerative value of nonpartisanship, Bennett was able to make a fortune,[43] as he sensed he would, with prescience, in one of his first issues:

> We are again in the field[44] . . . and more independent than ever. . . . Avoiding the dirt of party politics, we shall yet freely and candidly express our opinion on every public question and public man . . . and [merchants] are beginning to find out that a brief advertisement in our sheet is seen and read by six times as many as it would be in the dull prairies of the Courier & Enquirer.[45]

The connection between being "independent" and being successful is the converse of the connection between the "dirt of party politics" and the dull readership of the rival partisan papers; both connections suggest that advertisers and subscribers would flock to an extra-party newspaper. Partisan papers sought only part of a region's readership; readers of other political persuasions would read other papers. But Bennett's nonpartisan stance allowed him to seek a much more inclusive readership.

An examination of the first issues of the *Herald* reveals that Bennett's centrist and skeptical stance supported an eclectic advertising community. Despite Bennett's views on abolition, or perhaps because of them, the Anti-Slavery Society ran an advertisement defending its right to send material (recently confiscated) to Charleston. "We address not the slave but his master," protests the advertisement. The United States Bank, in the swirls of controversy, also advertised, as did dozens of "doctors" with their outrageous claims of miraculous panaceas promising to cure "Spasmodic Cholera," "Cholera Morbus," "urinal diseases," and a "well known disorder," which may have been well known but was too delicate to name.[46]

Bennett's public suspicion of motives and his claims to be "independent" and "free from the dirt of party politics" all privilege the partisan and occasionally outrageous claims of advertisers. Bennett's ballooning circulation and advertising revenues show that a place apart from partisan politics, a "centrist nonpartisan" stance, could be profitable. Garrison's stance, similarly outside party debates until Lincoln and the nation came around to *his* views, showed that his position, an "antipartisan" one, could also be effective, not financially, but in terms of its ability to challenge American public opinion.

Wanting In: Frederick Douglass and His "Activist Nonpartisanship"

Frederick Douglass's nonpartisanship combined Garrison's activist zeal with Bennett's acceptance of the U.S. political system. I therefore call him an *activist nonpartisan.* Douglass is almost completely ignored by journalism historians, and when he is remembered, it is merely in a passing compliment to a "great" journalist.[47] An examination of the journalism of Douglass and the other abolitionists must account for *why* they felt compelled to write. The *why* here is crucial in understanding Douglass's brand of nonpartisanship and his ideas about party.

Born in 1818 to a slave mother and a white father—probably his master—Douglass would rise to become one of the leading African American advocates of the nineteenth century. In 1838 Douglass escaped from Baltimore to the North. Walking down Broadway in Manhattan, he felt exhilaration. Bennett, of course, had tapped into the exhilaration of the street ("How lovely the ladies looked yesterday on Broadway!")[48] but probably never approached the thrill of the runaway slave with the Maryland dust still on his boots:

> In less than a week after leaving Baltimore, I was walking amid the hurrying throng, and gazing upon the dazzling wonders of Broadway. The dreams of my childhood and the purposes of my manhood were now fulfilled. A free state around me, and a free earth under my feet! What a moment this was to me! A whole year was pressed into a single day. . . . I felt as one might be supposed to feel, on escaping from a den of hungry lions.[49]

From New York, Douglass went to New Bedford, laid low, and worked odd jobs. A few months after he reached New Bedford, he was approached by a newsboy who asked him to subscribe to the *Liberator.* When Douglass said that, having escaped only recently from slavery, he was too poor to subscribe, the boy signed him up anyway, and Douglass started receiving his weekly issues on credit. The *Liberator*, Douglass wrote later, "took its place with me next to the bible."[50] Soon after this, Garrison spoke in New

Figure 7. Frederick Douglass (Library of Congress).

Bedford and the ex-slave stood up and spoke; his words were covered in the *Liberator*.[51] From then on, until Emancipation and beyond, Douglass would tell about the horrors of slavery to anyone who would listen. He spoke so eloquently that people doubted that he was born a slave.

As early as 1827, with the publication of *Freedom's Journal*, the first paper published and edited by African Americans, there were tensions over who got to discuss black issues. "We wish to plead our own cause," announced the first *Freedom's Journal*. "Too long have others spoken for us."[52] The need to "plead" was made much more pressing because most of the white papers, even the more progressive ones, were generally against black labor and black rights, at least until the late 1850s. In 1846, for example, when blacks tried to change the New York Constitution's racist exclusion of many black voters, even the *Sun*, with its famously progressive slogan, "It shines for *all*," was against the change. When a black man sent a letter to the editor, the *Sun* published it as an advertisement and charged the man fifteen dollars. The editor explained, "The *Sun* shines for all white men, and not for colored men."[53] It was this exchange that launched Douglass on his long career as a newspaperman, first as editor of the *Ram's Horn* in 1847, and then as editor/publisher of his own paper, the *North Star*, which later became *Frederick Douglass' Paper*. Like Garrison's "I WILL BE HEARD" and *Freedom's Journal*'s "We wish to plead," Douglass's opening editorials asserted his desire to enter the Sphere of Legitimate Controversy: "the truth must be told. . . . I will not be silent."[54]

At first glance, one wonders why Douglass published a paper when the *Liberator* was so closely identified with the radical abolitionist movement, so willing to print Douglass's words, and so influential. Indeed, Garrison wondered this as well! But Douglass no longer agreed with Garrison's antipartisan stance. Douglass, quite simply, began to support a political party (the antislavery Free Soil Party). By including a political party in his Sphere of Legitimate Controversy, Douglass firmly broke from Garrison. Although Bennett and Douglass might have shared no political beliefs, Douglass's shift meant that they at least shared a faith in the possibility of political solutions. Garrison felt betrayed by Douglass, and did not understand his newfound respect for the political system.[55]

Douglass, in his support of Free Soil, found himself among friend and foe alike. Included with the serious abolitionists were many, like the racist James Watson Webb, who were attracted to the party because of its position that the territories were to be free of slavery, perhaps even of free blacks, and thus a good place for poor whites to work without fear of competition from free and enslaved blacks.[56] Douglass's endorsement represented a compromise that Garrison, the antipartisan, was unwilling to make.

Douglass's most recent biographer, William McFeely, points out that Douglass's life journey can be compared to the fictional journey/escape of Thoreau's *Walden*.[57] But if both stories contain an escape, or self-emancipation, from a corrupt society, there the similarity ends. After Douglass's initial escape from slavery, it was Garrison, not Douglass, whose life could be best described as a Walden-like escape. The central difference between Garrison and Douglass can be reduced, with little exaggeration, to the following: Garrison spent much of the antebellum era trying to drop out of America; Douglass spent these same years trying to enter it. Much like Thoreau's trip to his little shack, Garrison's journey away from American politics left him isolated. We must remember, however, how much easier dropping out of society must have been for Thoreau and Garrison than it was for Douglass. When Thoreau went to Walden he took many meals at Emerson's house; when he refused to pay taxes, his aunt paid the fine.[58] When Thoreau and Garrison left society they knew that, as white men, they were welcome back. With popular politicians advocating sending blacks back to Africa, and with the 1857 *Dred Scott* decision questioning whether blacks could even be citizens, blacks were always on the verge of total exclusion. Douglass's position was marginal at best.

Thoreau's fictional journey toward independence begins, significantly, on July 4.[59] On this date, so much at the middle of the Sphere of Consensus, Garrison made a declaration against America, Douglass tried to join it, and Bennett tried to preserve the lack of difference between the two parties.

Variations of Nonpartisanship and the Three Editors' Celebration of the Fourth of July

In 1854 a large crowd gathered in Framingham and bore the "extreme" heat of the summer sun to hear William Lloyd Garrison present his oration on the occasion of America's seventy-eighth birthday. Standing under an American flag, "Union down," and "draped in black," Garrison produced a copy of the Fugitive Slave Law and set fire to it. According to the *Liberator*'s report, there was a "unanimous cheer" from the crowd. Garrison then held up a copy of the United States Constitution. Saying that the Constitution was "an agreement with hell," Garrison burned it too. The

Liberator's report admitted that the shouts of approval were "mingled with a few hisses and wrathful exclamations," but attributed this to a minority who were in a "rowdyish state of mind."[60] While rowdies, mostly anti-abolitionist Democrats, did dog abolitionist groups wherever they went, we should not be too quick to attribute the boos and hisses to people outside the movement: perhaps some of the abolitionists in attendance disagreed with Garrison's assessment of the Constitution.

Douglass did not burn the Constitution, if for no other reason than the act would have moved him further away from his goal of inclusion. By burning the Constitution, Garrison was indicating that he was an antipartisan, not a part of political America, a position he held publicly as early as 1839 when he announced in front of a crowd that he equated voting with sin.[61] But for Douglass—who expended much energy in supporting female and black suffrage, and the Free Soil Party—to advocate not voting would be hypocrisy.[62] Rejecting the Constitution would have meant a rejection of the possibility of a political solution to America's problems. As a biographer of Douglass wrote, "there was not a great deal of point in having the vote if it was not to be used."[63]

In his "Fifth of July" speech in 1852, subsequently printed in the *North Star*, Douglass uttered the now-famous lines,

> I am not included within the pale of this glorious anniversary! Your high independence only reveals the immeasurable distance between us. The blessings in which you, this day, rejoice, are not enjoyed in common. . . . This fourth of July is *yours,* not *mine. You* may rejoice, *I* must mourn.[64]

On the face of it, Douglass's words seem more radical and less accommodating than Garrison's. But while Douglass here was telling his listeners and readers that he could not celebrate the Fourth of July, later in the speech he left open the possibility of doing so in the future. Unlike Garrison, who accepted the promise of the Revolution but not the Constitution, Douglass, in this speech and others, mourned the loss of the Revolution's *and* the Constitution's idealism. Soon after Douglass's Fifth of July speech, he underscored his faith in the political world with his endorsement of a political party. After years of following Garrison's policy of not supporting parties, Douglass through his *North Star* endorsed, albeit uneasily, the Free Soil Party. Douglass's activist nonpartisanship and his endorsement of the Free Soilers and later the Republicans represented a political stance that would vex him through old age, as generations of party men would em-

Rochester to throw Douglass's "printing-press into Lake Ontario and to banish [Douglass] to Canada,"[70] was now trying to counter the force of the impending convention. He did this by casting the abolitionists as enemies of everything normal. "There will be arrayed all the men fit for petticoats," wrote Bennett just before the abolitionists came to town, "And all the women ready for breeches." According to a *Herald* editorial, Garrison's aim was nothing less than "utter overthrow of the churches, and the Bible."[71] Bennett was clearly placing the abolitionists in the Sphere of Deviance.

The abolitionists, according to Bennett, would destroy one of the centerpieces of American Consensus, the pursuit of wealth. These "mad people" and "religious lunatics," according to Bennett, would wreck the nation's business:

> The merchants, men of business, and men of property, in this city should frown down the meetings . . . if they would save themselves. What right have [the abolitionists] to gather in this commercial city for purposes which, if carried into effect, would ruin and destroy its prosperity?[72]

When the abolitionists arrived on May 7, 1850, a group of proslavery Democrats, a temporary but loyal army in the service of Bennett, had already gathered at the convention site, the Broadway Tabernacle Church, to intimidate Garrison and Douglass. Headed by a "Captain" Isaiah Rynders, the leader of a local Democratic club with a long history of breaking up Whig and abolitionist meetings, the group heckled each of the antislavery speakers. The group's mission was, of course, to keep the abolitionists out of the Sphere of Legitimate Controversy. Garrison, in turn, tried to widen that sphere, and, as always, tried to challenge the Constitution and other Consensus icons. The times when Rynders stood up and challenged Garrison were when Garrison denied that Jesus supported slavery and when he criticized President Taylor as an owner of slaves and a "dealer in human blood." It was at this point that the hecklers went wild and Rynders ran onto the stage and announced, "I will allow no man to insult the President of the United States."[73] The Consensus had been attacked and defended.

In an attempt to end the heckling and to start a debate, Garrison offered Rynders the platform to debate antislavery. Garrison wanted antislavery included in the debate, not for it necessarily to be the only view. Bennett, on the other hand, resisted debate, as reflected in his editorial column: "When free discussion does not promote the public good, it has no more right to exist than a bad government, that is dangerous and oppressive to the common weal."[74] But Rynders accepted Garrison's offer and ceded the platform to a "Dr." Grant, who gave a pseudoscientific speech about how blacks descended from apes. At the end of Grant's speech, Garrison suggested that no white man reply.

Douglass then stood up and gave an articulate rebuttal to Grant, which included the argument that Douglass himself was a man. Even Rynders must have been persuaded by the force of his argument, because he blurted out, "*You* are not a black man; you are only half a nigger." Douglass's response brought down the house and left Rynders speechless: "He is correct; I am, indeed, only half a negro, a half-brother to Mr. Rynders."[75]

Douglass's retort did two things to Rynders's argument. First, it pointed out a weakness in the proslavery argument, that freedom would mean "amalgamation," or black-white sexual relations. As Douglass implied by his retort and elsewhere in his speech, it was the Southern master who has contributed most to "amalgamation." "From my own experience," Douglass announced, "I can safely say that the portion of this country given up to wholesale amalgamation lies South of Mason and Dixon's line." Second, the retort established a familial relationship, one of Douglass's central goals. If blacks can be related to whites, then slavery and even exile are more difficult to defend.[76]

The battle between Bennett's representatives and Garrison and Douglass reveals that the editors, each nonpartisan, saw their place in political America in radically different ways. Bennett, the moderate, used his editorials to push politics to protect business interests, the status quo of laissez-faire capitalism, and a system that perpetuated slavery. Bennett understood that the two-party system, which succeeded because of its denial of slavery, was put at risk by the abolitionists, and he tried to hold back the slavery debate by intimidating the abolitionists. Garrison, like Bennett, avoided any political affiliation but was fundamentally different in that he rejected politics entirely. Douglass, too, remained nonpartisan for the antebellum period, and would neither reject a discussion of slavery, as did Bennett, nor reject politics generally, as did Garrison.

Bennett, Garrison, and Douglass positioned themselves in a political place hitherto missing from historical scholarship, a location apart from political parties. The political (or antipolitical) positions of the three editors also represented a departure from what came before; nonpartisanship is a big step away from the days of partisan journalism, with its attachment to political parties. This chapter illustrates that three journalists, each nonpartisan, can arrive at radically different destinations. Still, it is difficult to argue that nonpartisanship yields an "objective" truth, free of human filters. If it did, Bennett, Garrison, and Douglass would have arrived at the same conclusions. When they finally did come to share certain beliefs, during the Civil War, it was because the political arena had changed, not their ideals of journalism.

By the eve of Lincoln's reelection in 1864, the first reelection of a president since Andrew Jackson in 1832, three things had forever changed American politics. The first was that it was now clear that the North would win the war, finally bringing antislavery into the Sphere of Consensus. Second, slavery as a political issue was dead, partly because of the North's success, but also because the Emancipation Proclamation had effectively ended the possibility that Lincoln would be able to keep the institution alive. Finally, while equal political rights for blacks would not be realized for another century, Douglass knew that the question of their existence as Americans was decided by, among other things, the U.S. emblem on the uniforms of black soldiers, and by the muskets on their shoulders.[77]

The Republican Party would continue its domination of American politics for years to come. Bennett sensed a winner in Lincoln and voted for him. Douglass, who had split with Garrison because the ex-slave could not leave the world he was trying to enter, voted for Lincoln as the slaves' best hope. Finally, Garrison, who had boycotted partisan America for thirty-four years after his first *Liberator,* saw a politician, Lincoln, finally come knocking on Garrison's moral *Walden,* his radical antislavery. Garrison's antislavery had not changed, and he had not joined society: society joined him. Garrison, too, voted for Lincoln.

To reconfigure an American political landscape in such a way as to include Bennett, Douglass, and Garrison required the end of slavery. Otherwise, the three could never have voted the same way. But the end of slavery only set the stage for another necessary step, the ability to communicate to a new national audience. Lincoln was the first president to do so, with the help of his war secretary, Edwin M. Stanton. Lincoln and Stanton were able to accomplish this aim only because of the existence of nonpartisanship, the telegraph, and the continuing evolution of "objectivity."

3

The Inverted Pyramid

Edwin M. Stanton and Information Control

> [The telegraph] will have a prodigious, cohesive, and conservative influence on the republic. No better bond of union for a great confederacy of states could have been devised. . . . The whole nation is impressed with the same idea at the same moment. One feeling and one impulse are thus created and maintained from the centre of the land to its uttermost extremities. —James Gordon Bennett

> Let a man only tell you his story every morning and evening and at the end of a twelvemonth he will have become your master.
> —Edmund Burke

Until the end of the nineteenth century the telling of news nearly always took the form used in classical storytelling: first, an announcement of the utility or importance of the story, as in the start of the *Iliad,* "Sing, goddess, the anger of Peleus' son Achilleus and its devastation, which puts pains thousandfold upon the Achaians"[1] or the penny papers' "By Telegraph!" or the familiar "You'd never believe what I saw at the office." The storyteller, having given a promise of astonishment, narrated in chronological order, leaving the surprise, or what Aristotle called "Reversal of the Situation," for last.[2] The *Morning Courier and New-York Enquirer*'s 1832 story, promising astonishment with the heading "Melancholy Loss of Life," fits this pattern. It begins at the beginning and narrates in a chronological fashion:

> A most distressing occurrence took place at Alstead, East Providence on the 18th of last month.
>
> On the Saturday evening preceding between the hours of 10 and 11, a family consisting of Capt. Kidder and wife, one son, one daughter, a nephew . . . and a boy . . . retired in health, and under circumstances of comfort.

> About one o'clock in the morning Mrs. K. was suddenly awaked [*sic*] from a sound sleep, and found the house was on fire.

The reporter withholds what would be the modern "lead" until the final paragraph: the fire consumed the house and claimed two lives.[3]

When Theodore Dreiser entered the world of journalism and the office of the *Chicago Globe* in 1892, his editor told him that the first paragraph of a news story must reveal "Who or what? How? When? Where?" giving away the punch line, or lead, in the first paragraph.[4] Between 1832 and 1892 someone, or someones, somehow, at some time, somewhere, did something to change the way newspapers tell stories. What happened in the interim?

On or about April 15, 1865, the character of news writing changed. At least that is the date most cited by historians as the first example of a new journalistic style, the "inverted pyramid," a system of ordering facts in descending order of importance. An 1894 textbook mentioned the inverted pyramid form by name and explained that a "well constructed story begins with its most important fact and ends with the least important."[5] Or, as a modern textbook explained,

> The inverted pyramid form demands that the most important elements of a story be placed at the beginning of the article (or at the wide end of the inverted pyramid) and that the least important information be placed at the end of the article (or at the lower point of the inverted pyramid).[6]

The importance of the inverted pyramid, which supplanted the chronological style of antebellum news writing, is difficult to overstate. It is a system that appears to strip a story of everything but the "facts," and changes the way we process news. The new style, as Mitchell Stephens wrote, reflects a new age concerned with facts. It is an age with no time to hear a good story: "The essay—perfected by eighteenth-century journalists . . . placed too much emphasis on point of view; there was to be no point of view in the new world of unambiguous fact."[7] Often called "objective" or "straight" news writing, the inverted pyramid system is also one of the five components of "objectivity" cited in this book. The inverted pyramid style dominated news writing for the past hundred years and is still widely used today.[8] A recent story in the *New York Times* begins, "A 19-month-old girl was killed and her baby sitter seriously injured on the Upper West Side yesterday when an out-of-control car turned a leisurely stroll into a journey of horror, dragging them across the sidewalk and slamming them into the plate-glass window of a health food store."[9] In a chronological

by their nature, assert their own factuality (what Daniel Schiller has called a "pattern of objectivity") and include a few of the Ws, often the "what" and "when."[17] But it seems that the careful, "objective" ordering of facts into an inverted pyramid style did not appear in the *Herald* until 1865.[18] One researcher, Harlan Stensaas, conducted a content analysis of six U.S. dailies and found that the inverted pyramid form was not common until the 1880s and not standard until the turn of the century.[19]

Donald L. Shaw and others have suggested that the rise of the wire services and the telegraph contributed to the development of an "objective" style of writing. In a study of news reports of the antebellum period, Shaw found that news via telegraph was practically nonexistent before 1847 (Morse unveiled his telegraph in 1844) and rose to 8 percent of all stories between 1847 and 1860. This wide dissemination of wire news led to the realization that "facts were more safely marketed than opinion."[20] Shaw's study, however, did not look for the inverted pyramid form. Stensaas's findings suggest that inverted pyramids were not widely used in wire and nonwire news until the 1880s. In a separate project, Shaw studied stories about presidential campaigns in Wisconsin dailies from 1852 to 1916 and found that the use of the telegraph had a direct correlation to the emergence of "unbiased" stories. However, Shaw's findings revealed that while "bias" declined in tandem with the rise of the telegraph in 1876, "bias" was highest in 1872, a generation after the first telegraphs were used.[21]

True inverted pyramids written by reporters were probably not, as Jones put it, "war-born." None of the above journalism historians, including Jones, cite Civil War examples of inverted pyramid articles. Gobright's account of Lincoln's assassination, which many of the historians cite, occurred a week after Lee's surrender at Appomattox, at the very end of the war. Mott and Schudson suggested that the innovations were mainly post-war, and it seems that they are correct. Four years of war reporting, prior to the assassination, were chronological and self-conscious; at the earliest, it seems, the lead was born with the coverage of Lincoln's death.

The Night of the Assassination

In his 1869 autobiography Lawrence Gobright, the Washington agent for the Associated Press, recalled the events of April 14, 1865. It was late in the evening and Gobright had just written a tidbit about General Grant missing that night's performance of "Our American Cousin" at Ford's Theatre. As

Gobright sat alone in the AP telegraph room, puffing on a cigar, he scanned the out-of-town papers for news. Washington was in a celebratory mood that night: the rebels were defeated and were suing for peace. The South had lost its largest army with Lee's surrender, and Gobright expected a slow night.[22]

Suddenly a friend burst through the door, excited and shouting. Minutes later, Gobright dispatched the following to New York:

> WASHINGTON, APRIL 14, 1865
> TO THE ASSOCIATED PRESS:
> THE PRESIDENT WAS SHOT IN A THEATRE TONIGHT AND PERHAPS
> MORTALLY WOUNDED.[23]

Although his dispatch is often cited as an early example of a lead, "lead" implies that something is led; Gobright had no other information at hand and was merely telegraphing the sum of his knowledge. He would later write a detailed, *chronological* account to the dailies.[24]

The same hour found the secretary of war, Edwin Stanton, dressing for bed when he heard a knock at the door. "Mr. Seward is murdered," was the cry. Suddenly people began pouring into the house, each with a different story. Some were saying that Lincoln, too, was murdered. Stanton found a hack and took it to the house of William Seward, where he found the secretary of state and his son wounded and unconscious. Blood was everywhere. A doctor was treating the injured men. Stanton then rushed to Ford's and went across the street to a small boardinghouse where doctors were ministering to Lincoln.[25]

Lincoln lay diagonally across a short bed, his breathing labored and erratic, his face discolored and pained. Soldiers and messengers rushed in and out of the boardinghouse, and many of the cabinet members stood around the president, not knowing what to do. Meanwhile, Stanton ordered an unofficial court, with the chief justice, the attorney general, a military shorthand clerk, and representatives from the local police, the military, and the U.S. marshall's office to gather as much evidence as they could from witnesses.[26] Stanton immediately put the city under martial law, organized squads to capture the assassins, and wired the New York chief of police to "send here immediately three or four of your best detectives."[27] Gideon Welles, the navy secretary, wandered into the room, but given the weight of the events, felt "indisposed," and "oppressed . . . physically" by the crowds.[28]

Charles A. Dana, an assistant secretary of war, remembered being summoned to the boardinghouse by Stanton, who

> dictated orders, one after another, which I wrote out and sent swiftly to the telegraph. All these orders were designed to keep the business of the Government in full motion until the crisis should be over. It seemed as if Mr. Stanton thought of everything, and there was a great deal to be thought of that night. . . . The coolness and clearheadedness of Mr. Stanton under these circumstances were most remarkable.[29]

It was Stanton's ability to manage men and information that allowed him to control events that night. And control he did: "in the next eight hours [following Lincoln's death] the country was run by a dictator. . . . Edwin McMasters Stanton," said one chronicler.[30]

Gathering and interpreting a daunting amount of data under adverse conditions, Stanton tried to piece together what had happened. At first he thought that the assassination was part of a massive Southern plot to overthrow the government. But by 1 A.M., less than three hours after Lincoln was shot, Stanton had the names of Booth, Atzerodt, and Herold, three of the four conspirators, and was beginning to understand the relatively limited scope of the scheme. Stanton wrote a number of dispatches to be released to the New York dailies, some by his own hand and some by Dana's. Stanton himself wrote the letter that would inform Vice President Andrew Johnson of Lincoln's death.[31] Although Dana was an excellent writer (he had been an editor of the *New York Tribune* and would become the editor and part owner of the *New York Sun* after the war), on this night he merely took dictation from his boss, Stanton. Dana wrote,

> I remember that one of his first telegrams was to General Dix, the military commander of New York, notifying him of what had happened. No clearer brief account of the tragedy exists to-day than this, written scarcely three hours after the scene in Ford's Theater, on a little stand in the room where, a few feet away, Mr. Lincoln lay dying.[32]

The first dispatch, sent to the New York papers through General Dix, may very well be one of the first inverted pyramids in history.

Stanton's dispatch appeared as the *New York Herald*'s lead story the following morning. The editors divided the paragraphs into shorter units, but the contents were unchanged. Below is how the story appeared in the *Herald* (for its placement on the page, see figure 9):

THE OFFICIAL DESPATCH.

WAR DEPARTMENT,
WASHINGTON, April 15—1:30 A. M.

Major General Dix, New York:—

This evening at about 9:30 P. M., at Ford's Theatre, the President, while sitting in his private box with Mrs. Lincoln, Mrs. Harris and Major Rathburn, was shot by an assassin, who suddenly entered the box and approached behind the President.

The assassin then leaped upon the stage, brandishing a large dagger or knife, and made his escape in the rear of the theatre.

The pistol ball entered the back of the President's head and penetrated nearly through the head. The wound is mortal.

The President has been insensible ever since it was inflicted, and is now dying.

About the same hour an assassin, whether the same or not, entered Mr. Seward's apartments, and under pretence of having a prescription was shown to the Secretary's sick chamber. The assassin immediately rushed to the bed and inflicted two or three stabs on the throat and two on the face.

It is hoped the wounds may no the mortal. My apprehension is that they will prove fatal.

The nurse alarmed Mr. Frederick Seward, who was in an adjoining room, and he hastened to the door of his father's room, when he met the assassin, who inflicted upon him one or more dangerous wounds. The recovery of Frederick Seward is doubtful.

It is not probable that the President will live through the night.

General Grant and wife were advertised to be at the theatre this evening, but he started to Burlington at six o'clock this evening.

At a Cabinet meeting, at which General Grant was present, the subject of the state of the country and the prospect of a speedy peace were discussed. The President was very cheerful and hopeful, and spoke very kindly of General Lee and others of the confederacy, and of the establishment of government in Virginia.

All the members of the Cabinet except Mr. Seward, are now in attendance upon the President.

I have seen Mr. Seward, but he and Frederick were both unconscious.

EDWIN M. STANTON,

Secretary of War.

Figure 8. Stanton's dispatch of 15 April 1865 as it appeared in the *New York Herald* (Library of Congress).

War Department,
Washington, April 15—1:30 A.M.

Major General Dix, New York:—
This evening at about 9:30 P.M., at Ford's Theatre, the President, while sitting in his private box with Mrs. Lincoln, Mrs. Harris and Major Rathburn, was shot by an assassin, who suddenly entered the box and approached behind the president.

The assassin then leaped upon the stage, brandishing a large dagger or knife, and made his escape in the rear of the theatre.

The pistol ball entered the back of the President's head and penetrated nearly through the head. The wound is mortal.

The President has been insensible ever since it was inflicted, and is now dying.

About the same hour an assassin, whether the same or not, entered Mr. Seward's apartments, and under pretense of having a prescription was shown to the Secretary's sick chamber. The assassin immediately rushed to the bed and inflicted two or three stabs on the throat and two on the face.

It is hoped the wounds may not be mortal. My apprehension is that they will prove fatal.

The nurse alarmed Mr. Frederick Seward, who was in an adjoining room, and he hastened to the door of his father's room, when he met the assassin, who inflicted upon him one or more dangerous wounds. The recovery of Frederick Seward is doubtful.

It is not probable that the President will live through the night.

General Grant and his wife were advertised to be at the theatre this evening, but he started to Burlington at six o'clock this evening.

At a Cabinet meeting, at which General Grant was present, the subject of the state of the country was discussed. The President was very cheerful and hopeful, and spoke very kindly of General Lee and others of the confederacy, and of the establishment of government in Virginia.

All the members of the Cabinet except Mr. Seward, are now in attendance upon the President.

I have seen Mr. Seward, but he and Frederick were both unconscious.

Edwin M. Stanton,
Secretary of War.[33]

Stanton's most thorough biographer, Benjamin S. Thomas, praised Stanton for assembling "a logical narrative of the attacks on Lincoln and Seward from the incoherent accounts he had heard."[34] However, while Stanton deserves praise, the above dispatch is no narrative in the classic, storytelling sense. It doesn't reserve or withhold attention-getting information, nor does it provide a chronological account of events. Rather it is a striking example of an inverted pyramid. Stanton opens with a sentence that conveys the central fact—that the president had been shot. He briefly discusses the particulars and then moves to the assassination attempt on Secretary Seward. Stanton ends with relatively minor points: General Grant's whereabouts, a cabinet meeting, and the condition of the Sewards.

Stanton's dispatch, while not perfect as a modern news story, is still much closer to the inverted pyramid style than Gobright's longer narrative that followed his initial one-sentence "lead." Gobright begins, "President Lincoln and wife, with other friends, this evening visited Ford's Theatre, for the purpose of witnessing the performance of the 'American Cousin.' "[35] The first eleven paragraphs are written in straight chronological order, and it takes the reader four paragraphs of narrative to get to Lincoln's injury. Unlike Stanton, whose aim was to present important facts quickly, Gobright reported events nearly in the order that they occurred. Gobright's chronological report, while perceptive and well wrought, has neither a paradigmatic nor prototypal relation to later inverted pyramids.

Ironically, some of the articles hailed as a new beginning in the history of journalism were written not by reporters but by Stanton. In trying to place an early example of a lead, Jones wrote, "the Chicago *Tribune's* noteworthy story began . . ." and then quotes a dispatch written by Stanton![36] Jones's argument may be that the papers, in their choice and placement of dispatches, were in effect creating a de facto inverted pyramid. However, the papers' choices better support Mott's contention that the press was still operating in chronological structures; dispatches were usually laid out in the order they came in. On April 15, 1865, it was the War Department, not the press, that adhered most closely to the new style.

The "objective" news report is, at best, an honest attempt to assemble facts as fairly and accurately as possible; but it can also be a deliberate ordering of "facts" to manipulate public perceptions. Stanton's conveyance of the facts in the above dispatch includes Lincoln's "kindly" stance toward General Lee and "others in the confederacy, and of the establishment of government in Virginia." This information, not centrally important to the assassination itself, may well have been used to enrage Northerners (by

THE NEW YORK HERALD.

WHOLE NO. 10,456. NEW YORK, SATURDAY, APRIL 15, 1865. PRICE FOUR CENTS.

IMPORTANT.

ASSASSINATION OF PRESIDENT LINCOLN.

The President Shot at the Theatre Last Evening.

SECRETARY SEWARD DAGGERED IN HIS BED, BUT NOT MORTALLY WOUNDED.

Clarence and Frederick Seward Badly Hurt.

ESCAPE OF THE ASSASSINS.

Intense Excitement in Washington.

Scene at the Deathbed of Mr. Lincoln.

[illegible]

J. [illegible] Booth, the Actor, the Alleged [illegible]

THE OFFICIAL DESPATCH.

War Department, Washington, April 15—1:30 A. M.

Major General Dix, New York:—

This evening, at about 9:30 P. M., at Ford's Theatre, the President, while sitting in his private box with Mrs. Lincoln, Mrs. Harris and Major Rathburn, was shot by an assassin, who suddenly entered the box and approached behind the President.

The assassin then leaped upon the stage, brandishing a large dagger or knife, and made his escape in the rear of the theatre.

The pistol ball entered the back of the President's head and penetrated nearly through the head. The wound is mortal.

The President has been insensible ever since it was inflicted, and is now dying.

About the same hour an assassin, whether the same or not, entered Mr. Seward's apartments, and under pretence of having a prescription was shown to the Secretary's sick chamber. The assassin immediately rushed to the bed and inflicted two or three stabs on the throat and two on the face.

It is hoped the wounds may not be mortal. My apprehension is that they will prove fatal.

The noise alarmed Mr. Frederick Seward, who was in an adjoining room, and he hastened to the door of his father's room, when he met the assassin, who inflicted upon him one or more dangerous wounds. The recovery of Frederick Seward is doubtful.

It is not probable that the President will live through the night.

General Grant and wife were advertised to be at the theatre this evening, but he started to Burlington at six o'clock this evening.

At a Cabinet meeting, at which General Grant was present, the subject of the state of the country and the prospect of a speedy peace were discussed. The President was very cheerful and hopeful, and spoke very kindly of General Lee and others of the confederacy, and of the establishment of government in Virginia.

All the members of the Cabinet except Mr. Seward, are now in attendance upon the President.

I have seen Mr. Seward, but he and Frederick were both unconscious.

EDWIN M. STANTON,
Secretary of War.

THE HERALD DESPATCHES.

Washington, April 14, 1865.

Assassination has been inaugurated in Washington. The bowie knife and pistol have been applied to President Lincoln and Secretary Seward. The former was shot in the throat, while at Ford's theatre to-night. Mr. Seward was badly cut about the neck, while in his bed at his residence.

SECOND DESPATCH.

Washington, April 14, 1865.

An attempt was made about ten o'clock this evening to assassinate the President and Secretary Seward. The President was shot at Ford's Theatre. Result not yet known. Mr. Seward's throat was cut, and his son badly wounded.

There is intense excitement here.

Details of the Assassination.

Washington, April 14, 1865.

Washington was thrown into an intense excitement a few minutes before eleven o'clock this evening, by the announcement that the President and Secretary Seward had been assassinated and were dead.

The wildest excitement prevailed in all parts of the city. Men, women and children, old and young, rushed to and fro, and the rumors were magnified until we had nearly every member of the Cabinet killed. Some time elapsed before authentic data could be ascertained in regard to the affair.

The President and Mrs. Lincoln were at Ford's theatre, listening to the performance of the American Cousin, occupying a box in the second tier. At the close of the third act a person entered the box occupied by the President, and shot Mr. Lincoln in the head. The shot entered the back of his head, and came out above the temple.

The assassin then jumped from the box upon the stage and ran across to the other side, exhibiting a dagger in his hand, flourishing it in a tragical manner, shouting the same words repeated by the desperado at Mr. Seward's house, adding to it, "The South is avenged," and then escaped from the back entrance to the stage, but in his passage dropped his pistol and his hat.

Mr. Lincoln fell forward from his seat, and Mrs. Lincoln fainted.

The moment the astonished audience could realize what had happened, the President was taken and carried to Mr. Petersen's house, in Tenth street, opposite to the theatre. Medical aid was immediately sent for, and the wound was at first supposed to be fatal, and it was announced that he could not live; but at half-past twelve he is still alive, though in a precarious condition.

As the assassin ran across the stage, Colonel J. B. Stewart, of this city, who was occupying one of the front seats in the orchestra, on the same side of the house as the box occupied by Mr. Lincoln, sprang to the stage and followed him; but he was obstructed in his passage across the stage by the fright of the actors, and reached the back door about three seconds after the assassin had passed out. Colonel Stewart got to the street just in time to see him mount his horse and ride away.

This operation shows that the whole thing was a preconcerted plan. The person who fired the pistol was a man about thirty years of age, about five feet nine, spare built, fair skin, dark hair, apparently bushy, with a large moustache. Laura Keene and the leader of the orchestra declare that they recognized him as J. Wilkes Booth the actor, and a rabid secessionist. Whoever he was, it is plainly evident that he thoroughly understood the theatre and all the approaches and modes of escape to the stage. A person not familiar with the theatre could not have possibly made his escape so well and quickly.

The alarm was sounded in every quarter. Mr. Stanton was notified, and immediately left his house.

All the other members of the Cabinet escaped attack.

Cavalrymen were sent out in all directions, and despatches sent to all the fortifications, and it is thought they will be captured.

About half-past ten o'clock this evening a tall, well dressed man made his appearance at Secretary Seward's residence, and applied for admission. He was refused admission by the servant, when the desperado stated that he had a prescription from the Surgeon General, and that he was ordered to deliver it in person. He was still refused, except upon the written order of the physician. This he pretended to show, and pushed by the servant and rushed up stairs to Mr. Seward's room. He was met at the door by Mr. Fred Seward, who notified him that he was master of the house, and would take charge of the medicine. After a few words had passed between them he dodged by [illegible] and rushed to the Secretary's bed, and struck him in the neck with a dagger, and also in the breast.

It was supposed at first that Mr. Seward was killed instantly, but it was found afterwards that the wound was not mortal.

Major Wm. H. Seward, Jr., paymaster, was in the room, and rushed to the defence of his father, and was badly cut in the melee with the assassin, but not fatally.

The desperado managed to escape from the house, and was prepared for escape by having a horse at the door. He immediately mounted his horse, and sung out the motto of the State of Virginia, "*Sic Semper Tyrannis!*" and rode off.

Surgeon General Barnes was immediately sent for, and he examined *Mr. Seward and pronounced him safe.* His wounds were not fatal. The jugular vein was not cut, nor the wound in the breast deep enough to be fatal.

Washington, April 15—1 A. M.

The streets in the vicinity of Ford's Theatre are densely crowded by an anxious and excited crowd. A guard has been placed across Tenth street and F and E streets, and only official persons and particular friends of the President are allowed to pass.

The popular heart is deeply stirred, and the deepest indignation against leading rebels is freely expressed.

The scene at the house where the President lies *in extremis* is very affecting. Even Secretary Stanton is affected to tears.

When the news spread through the city that the President had been shot, the people, with pale faces and compressed lips, crowded every place where there was the slightest chance of obtaining information in regard to the affair.

After the President was shot, Lieutenant Rathbun, caught the assassin by the arm, who immediately struck him with a knife, and jumped from the box, as before stated.

The popular affection for Mr. Lincoln has been shown by this diabolical assassination, which will bring eternal infamy, not only upon its authors, but upon the hellish cause which they desire to avenge.

Vice President Johnson arrived at the White House, where the President lies, about one o'clock, and will remain with him to the last.

The President's family are in attendance upon him also.

As soon as intelligence could be got to the War Department, the electric telegraph and the Signal corps were put in requisition to endeavor to prevent the escape of the assassins, and all the troops around Washington are under arms.

Popular report points to a somewhat celebrated actor of known secession proclivities as the assassin; but it would be unjust to name him until some further evidence of his guilt is obtained. It is rumored that the person alluded to is in custody.

The latest advices from Secretary Seward reveals more desperate work there than at first supposed. Seward's wounds are not in themselves fatal; but, in connection with his recent injuries, and the great loss of blood he has sustained, his recovery is questionable.

It was Clarence A. Seward, instead of Wm. H. Seward, Jr., who was wounded. Fred. Seward was also badly cut, as were also three nurses, who were in attendance upon the Secretary, showing that a desperate struggle took place there. The wounds of the whole party were dressed.

One o'Clock A. M.

The President is perfectly senseless, and there is not the slightest hope of his surviving. Physicians believe that he will die before morning. All of his Cabinet, except Secretary Seward, are with him. Speaker Colfax, Senator Farwell, of Maine, and many other gentlemen, are also at the house awaiting the termination.

The scene at the President's bedside is described by one who witnessed it as most affecting. It was surrounded by his Cabinet ministers, all of whom were bathed in tears, not even excepting Mr. Stanton, who, when informed by Surgeon General Barnes, that the President could not live until morning, exclaimed, "Oh, no, General; no—no;" and with an impulse, natural as it was unaffected, immediately sat down on a chair near his bedside and wept like a child.

Senator Sumner was seated on the right of the President's couch, near the head, holding the right hand of the President in his own. He was sobbing like a woman, with his head bowed down almost on the pillow of the bed on which the President was lying.

Two o'Clock A. M.

The President is still alive, but there is no improvement in his condition.

THE PRESS DESPATCHES.

Washington, April 14—12:30 A. M.

The President was shot in a theatre to-night, and is perhaps mortally wounded.

SECOND DESPATCH.

Washington, April 15—1 A. M.

The President is not expected to live through the night. He was shot at a theatre.

Secretary Seward was also assassinated. No arteries were cut.

Additional Details of the Assassination.

Washington, April 15—1:30 A. M.

President Lincoln and wife, with other friends, this evening visited Ford's theatre, for the purpose of witnessing the performance of the American Cousin.

It was announced in the papers that General Grant would also be present; but that gentleman took the late train of cars for New Jersey.

The theatre was densely crowded, and all seemed delighted with the scene before them. During the third act, and while there was a temporary pause for one of the actors to enter, a sharp report of a pistol was heard, which merely attracted attention, but suggested nothing serious, until a man rushed to the front of the President's box, waving a long dagger in his right hand, and exclaiming "*Sic semper tyrannis*" and immediately leaped from the box, which was in the second tier, to the stage beneath, and ran across to the opposite side, making his escape, amid the bewilderment of the audience, from the rear of the theatre, and, mounting a horse, fled.

The screams of Mrs. Lincoln first disclosed the fact to the audience that the President had been shot, when all present rose to their feet, rushing towards the stage, many exclaiming "Hang him! Hang him!"

The excitement was of the wildest possible description, and of course there was an abrupt termination of the theatrical performance.

There was a rush toward the President's box, when cries were heard:—"Stand back and give him air." "Has any one stimulants?"

On a hasty examination it was found that the President had been shot through the head, above and back of the temporal bone, and that some of the brain was oozing out.

He was removed to a private house [illegible] surgeons sent for to attend to his condition.

On an examination of the private box blood was discovered on the back of the cushioned rocking chair on which the President had been sitting, also on the partition and on the floor. A common single barreled pocket pistol was found on the carpet.

A military guard was placed in front of the private residence to which the President had been conveyed. An immense crowd was in front of it, all deeply anxious to learn the condition of the President. It had been previously announced that the wound was mortal, but all hoped otherwise. The shock to the community was terrible.

At midnight the Cabinet, with Messrs. Sumner, Colfax and Farnsworth, Judge Curtis, Governor Oglesby, General Meigs, Colonel Hay, and a few personal friends, with Surgeon General Barnes and his immediate assistants, were around his bedside.

The President was in a state of syncope, totally insensible, and breathing slowly. The blood oozed from the wound at the back of his head.

The surgeons exhausted every possible effort of medical skill; but all hope was gone.

The parting of his family with the dying President is too sad for description.

The President and Mrs. Lincoln did not start for the theatre until fifteen minutes after eight o'clock. Speaker Colfax was at the White House at the time, and the President stated to him that he was going. Mrs. Lincoln had not been well, because the papers had announced that General Grant and they were to be present, and, as General Grant had gone North, he did not wish the audience to be disappointed.

He went with apparent reluctance, and urged Mr. Colfax to go with him; but that gentleman had made other engagements, and, with Mr. Ashmun, of Massachusetts, bid him goodby.

When the excitement at the theatre was at its wildest height reports were circulated that Secretary Seward had also been assassinated.

On reaching this gentleman's residence a crowd and a military guard were found at the door, and on entering it was ascertained that the reports were based on truth.

Everybody there was so excited that scarcely an intelligible word could be gathered. But the facts are substantially as follows:—

About ten o'clock a man rang the bell, and the call having been answered by a colored servant, he said he had come from Dr. Verdi, Secretary Seward's family physician, with a prescription, at the same time holding in his hand a small piece of folded paper, and saying, in answer to a refusal, that he must see the Secretary, as he was entrusted with particular directions concerning the medicine.

He still insisted on going up, although repeatedly informed that no one could enter the chamber. The man pushed the servant aside, and walked hastily towards the Secretary's room, and was then met by Mr. Frederick Seward, of whom he demanded to see the Secretary, making the same representation which he did to the servant.

What further passed in the way of colloquy is not known; but the man struck him on the head with a billy, severely injuring the skull and felling him almost senseless.

The assassin then rushed into the chamber and attacked Major Seward, Paymaster United States Army, and Mr. Hansell, a messenger of the State Department, and two male nurses, disabling them all.

He then rushed upon the Secretary, who was lying in bed in the same room, and inflicted three stabs in the neck, but severing, it is thought and hoped, no arteries, though he bled profusely.

The assassin then rushed down stairs, mounted his horse at the door, and rode off before an alarm could be sounded, and in the same manner as the assassin of the President.

It is believed that the injuries of the Secretary are not fatal, nor those of either of the others, although both the Secretary and the Assistant Secretary are very seriously injured.

Secretaries Stanton and Welles, and other prominent officers of the Government, called at Secretary Seward's house to inquire into his condition, and there heard of the assassination of the President.

They then proceeded to the house where he was lying, exhibiting of course intense anxiety and solicitude.

An immense crowd was gathered in front of the President's house, and a strong guard was also stationed there, many persons evidently supposing he would be brought to his home.

The entire city to-night presents a scene of wild excitement, accompanied by violent expressions of indignation and the profoundest sorrow; many shed tears.

The military authorities have despatched mounted patrols in every direction, in order, if possible, to arrest the assassins. The whole metropolitan police are likewise vigilant for the same purpose.

The attacks, both at the theatre and at Secretary Seward's house, took place at about the same hour—ten o'clock—thus showing a preconcerted plan to assassinate those gentlemen. Some evidences of the guilt of the party who attacked the President are in the possession of the police.

Vice President Johnson is in the city, and his headquarters are guarded by troops.

THE STATE CAPITAL.

Rejection of the New York Fire Commissioners—Passage of the Central Railroad Fare Bill—Great Excitement Over the Health Bill, &c.

Albany, April 14—11:30 P. M.

Legislation each day is now so rapid here that a detail or analysis of its progress is out of the question. To-day the long pending Central Railroad bill passed the Senate, and is virtually a law if the Governor does not veto it. But the result may be foreshadowed in the vote sent in to-day of the Dry Dock and Battery Railroad.

The Health bill, which two days since was bound by caucus rules to have a sure passage, was to-night defeated by republican votes. The Collector of the port of New York, who has had an elaborate organization up for his retention in the office of Commissioner of Charities, was thrown overboard and the power of all his patronage disregarded in the strife to secure this position, which has been his pet desire and speciality for many years. All these occurrences have a political significancy which it would take too much time and space to develop. The excitement of the day has been the Health bill, and that excitement has been so incoherent as to be indescribable. The attempt made last night to kill off the bill was renewed to-day at an early hour. It has been lost for want of a sufficient vote, and laid on the table for reconsideration. A motion was made to call it up for a final vote, a short time after the reading of the Journal, by its opponents. The tactics against the measure were led by Wood, of Clinton, in whose fresh abilities the democrats have gained their ablest accession in this Legislature. He moved to take from the table, and upon that the previous question. The vote of fifty-three to sixty-one disclosed the fact that the friends of the bill were in the minority, and a panic at once was created among them. An adroit suggestion was sent to the Speaker understood to be from Henry J. Raymond, who was on the floor [illegible] Wood and others insisting that such action was out of order.

While the vote was being taken a few more republicans were drummed up, and the motion carried by one or two votes. Hereupon the wildest scenes of confusion took place, all the members gathered in a crowd before the Speaker's desk in the most excited condition, shouting, disputing and threatening each other and the Speaker. One member from New York got upon a desk, and in the midst of a clamor for bets, offered at a thousand dollars, shouted and taunted the republicans, daring any man to bet. He shook his two fists with handsfull of greenbacks. Others clamored in like manner, and the scene resembled the most exciting days at the gold room in New York. In the midst of all this were heard the clapping of hands and the triumphant imitations of the mock chanticleer of the republicans, while the democrats uttered the most violent denunciations of the Speaker to his face for his rulings.

This scene was disposed of only to be reproduced for the evening session. Mr. Wood renewed his assaults upon the bill to bring it to a final vote, while its dismissed friends sought to postpone this action. Messrs. Van Buren, Stuart, Reed, Brandreth, Wood and Parker sought alternately to postpone or to kill time by filibustering, after prolonged, excited and most disorderly proceedings.

A final vote was forced upon the friends of the bill at a late hour. Sixty-one voted for the bill and fifty-one against it. Sixty-five votes being necessary to its passage, it was lost. Mr. Salmon, of New York, who had made himself obscure by the vehemency of his opposition to the bill, was sought to be involved in proceedings before the bar of the House; but the Speaker was evidently discouraged from any such attempts. The management for the bill on the floor of the House was understood to be in the hands of the radicals, under the lead of Fields. Boole was in the lobby in person. Mayor Gunther, Carr and others of his opponents were here yesterday to urge on the passage of the bill. It is alleged that the republican interest was sold out by the radicals.

The Fire Commissioners encountered a decided capsize in executive session. The defeat of the Health bill was pending on their consideration, and the Assembly had adjourned in the extraordinary manner of the morning. The names were at first confirmed, Senator Laimbier, who had made the chief opposition, moving the confirmation. This action was, however, reconsidered on motion of Senator Andrews, on the ground of the promises made in the Assembly to the democrats, who passed it, that the board would comprise two democrats. The names were accordingly sent back to the Governor.

The continuation of Boole in office by the defeat of the Health bill is accompanied by the passage of a resolution continuing the Senate investigating committee, to sit during the summer and examine the other departments. The feeling here is that Boole was treated as an invidious exception, and the thing will be made even all round.

The action determined on in caucus yesterday in regard to Draper and the Board of Charities, was decked by resolution to-day, and is coupled with the defeat of Rufus F. Andrews as candidate for United States District Attorney at New York, as a satisfactory manifestation of Thurlow Weed's power.

The passage of the Central Railroad Fare bill was conducted through the form of third reading with no excitement, and with the limit of seven per cent dividends. The increase of half a cent per mile for three years is thought only reasonable.

IMPORTANT FROM SOUTH AMERICA.

Surrender of Montevideo to Gen. Flores—Brazil in Possession of the City, &c.

The Brazilian mail arrived at Lisbon April 2, bringing the following advices:—

Montevideo has surrendered to General Flores.

The Brazilians now (March 11) occupy the city.

Rio Janeiro, March 11, 1865.

Exchange 25¼ a 25½.

Coffee—Sales of good firsts at 65.00. Shipments, 100,000 bags. Stock, 100,000 bags. Freights, 50.[illegible]

Bahia, March 11, 1865.

Exchange 26¼. Cotton nominal.

Pernambuco, March 11, 1865.

Exchange 26½ a 27.

News from San Francisco.

San Francisco, April 13, 1865.

The exports of treasure for the quarter just ended show a falling off of about six and a half millions as compared with the same period last year.

San Francisco, April 14, 1865.

The Pacific mail steamship Sacramento sailed to-day, with a large number of passengers, for New York, and $1,130,000 in treasure, of which nearly $700,000 go to New York.

The steamship Moses Taylor sailed for San Juan del Sur, with numerous passengers.

The market continues variable and unsettled, and traders pursue a hand-to-mouth policy. Prices of Eastern goods are steady falling.

Sailed, ship *Flying Eagle*, for Boston.

New Orleans Markets.

New Orleans, April 8, Via Cairo, April 14, 1865.

The New Orleans markets are at a stand still. Low middling cotton is quoted at 45c per pound, and good superfine flour at $8 per barrel.

THE REBELS.

JEFF. DAVIS AT DANVILLE.

His Latest Appeal to His Deluded Followers.

He Thinks the Fall of Richmond a Blessing in Disguise, as it Leaves the Rebel Armies Free to Move from Point to Point.

He Vainly Promises to Hold Virginia at All Hazards.

Lee and His Army Supposed to be Safe.

Breckinridge and the Rest of Davis' Cabinet Reach Danville Safely.

The Organ of Governor Vance, of North Carolina, Advises the Submission of the Rebels to President Lincoln's Terms, &c., &c., &c.

Jeff. Davis' Last Proclamation.

VIRGINIA TO BE HELD BY THE REBELS AT ALL HAZARDS.

Danville, Va., April 5, 1865.

The General-in-Chief found it necessary to make such movements of his troops as to uncover the capital. It would be unwise to conceal the *moral and material injury to our cause resulting from the occupation of our capital* by the enemy. It is equally unwise and unworthy of us to allow our own energies to falter and our efforts to become relaxed under adverses, however calamitous they may be. *For many months the largest and finest army of* the confederacy, under command of a leader whose presence inspires equal confidence in the troops and the people, has been greatly trammelled by the necessity of keeping constant watch over the approaches to the capital, and has thus been forced to forego more than one opportunity for promising enterprise. It is for us, my countrymen, to show by our bearing under reverses how wretched has been the self-deception of those who have believed us less able to endure misfortune with fortitude than to encounter dangers with courage.

We have now entered upon a new phase of the struggle. Relieved from the necessity of guarding particular points, *our army will be free to move from point to point* to strike the enemy in detail far from his base. *Let us but will it and we are free.*

Animated by that confidence in spirit and fortitude which never yet failed me, I announce to you, fellow countrymen, that it is my purpose to maintain your cause with my whole heart and soul; that I will never consent to abandon to the enemy one foot of the soil of any one of the States of the confederacy. That Virginia—noble State—whose ancient renown has been eclipsed by her still more glorious recent history; whose bosom has been bared to receive the main shock of this war; whose sons and daughters have exhibited heroism so sublime as to render her illustrious in all time to come—that Virginia, with the help of the people and by the blessing of Providence, *shall be held and defended*, and no peace ever be made with the infamous invaders of her territory.

If by the stress of numbers we should ever be compelled to a temporary withdrawal from her limits, or those of any other border State, again and again will we return, until the baffled and exhausted enemy shall abandon in despair his endless and impossible task of making slaves of a people resolved to be free.

Let us, then, not despond, my countrymen; but, relying on God, meet the foe with fresh defiance and with unconquered and unconquerable hearts.

JEFFERSON DAVIS.

The Evacuation of the Rebel Capital.

THE FIRST REBEL ACCOUNT OF HOW THE CITY WAS ABANDONED.

[From the Danville (Va.) Register, April 5.]

Persons who left the capital Sunday night and Monday morning represent that the scene which followed the evacuation of the city by our troops beggars description. To preserve order and protect the property of the citizens who unavoidably remained there, as far as could be done, the Nineteenth Virginia militia, under Colonel Evans, was placed on police duty in the city, to await the coming of the enemy; but accounts state that they failed to render any aid or protection to the people whatever. On Sunday night a mob of the lower classes of the city, composed, it is said, mostly of the foreign element, visited a number of the largest storehouses of the city and robbed them of their contents. It is affirmed that Main street was pillaged, and then burned, and that some of the milling establishments were also committed to the flames. We have no doubt that a considerable portion of that brave city has been laid in ashes, and a number of its people insulted, outraged, robbed and massacred. How painful the thought that the place should be given over to rapine and plunder, even before the public enemy entered its limits. But the fact only proves that the people of Richmond have had secret enemies in their own midst scarcely less savage and even more treacherous and vindictive than the open foe.

We are told that the people banded together during the violent proceeding of the mob and resisted them with force, a street fight ensuing, in which several persons were killed.

No intelligence has reached us of the enemy's troops occupying the city. The last trains on the Danville railroad which came out of the place left Monday morning, and passengers upon them had heard nothing from the enemy. The greater portion of Grant's army was transferred to the south side of James river some days ago, only the command of General Ord, which is composed mostly, if not entirely, of negro troops, being left on the north side. This command will enter and occupy the city. Some of our people who are acquainted with the character of General Ord think they have reason to hope that his treatment of the unfortunate people of Richmond will not be so hard, and cruel and inhuman as that which has fallen upon the heads of our fellow citizens in some other captured cities.

The newspapers of Richmond, we suppose, all fall into the hands of the enemy. The evacuation of the city was so sudden and unexpected—scarcely any one being prepared for it—that no time was left for the removal of so cumbrous an establishment as a city newspaper office. In a few days we may expect to hear that the *Enquirer* or the *Whig* or the *Examiner* is issued as a Yankee paper.

All the rolling stock of the Richmond and Danville Railroad in running order was saved on the retreat from Richmond. A few old ones, not in a movable condition, were left at Manchester. No train was captured by the enemy near the junction, as was at one time reported; and, indeed, we do not believe that any body of Yankees had struck the road at any point up to yesterday evening.

The Secretary of War, the Quartermaster General, Commissary General and a number of other officers of the government, left Richmond on horseback, and will probably arrive at this place to-morrow.

Should General Lee establish his lines east of the junction, we suppose the State Legislature will be convened at Lynchburg.

All the specie and other valuables belonging to the banks in Richmond were removed from the city on Sunday, and have been carried to places of safety.

A considerable amount of goods purchased by the State for distribution to the people, we regret to learn, had to be left behind. Also the State archives remained in the city; but we perceive no motive the enemy can have in destroying them, as they will, no doubt, endeavor to occupy the city permanently, and establish a State government at Richmond under the federal Union.

Lee's Army Supposed to be in a Safe Position.

[From the Raleigh Confederate, April 7.]

This is the time for rumor manufacturers who are engaged in a wholesale business. Sometimes they kill [illegible] that whole brigades deserted in the last [illegible] among others, Cook's brigade is [illegible] We are assured [illegible] foundation whatever; that no hostility induced the disaster at Petersburg; that our forces fought splendidly, and the enemy only succeeded by overwhelming numbers. We are convinced, too, from facts which we cannot mention, that Lee's army is in a safe position, and that [illegible]

[illegible] In the Southern [illegible] independence certain. It is with the people themselves whether they are to [illegible] their liberties.

Rebel Particulars of the Battle at Petersburg.

[From the Raleigh Confederate, April 7.]

An officer who left Richmond at nine o'clock on Monday morning last informs us that at the time he left the city was in flames from Cary to Canal streets. The Shockoe warehouse and other entrepots of supplies were burning. The bridges also had been fired.

No mob or violence of any kind had occurred up to the period when he left, so that the reports of a destructive mob on Sunday night are untrue. The enemy's cavalry entered the city as the train moved off that he came out in. The story of the mob, therefore, we hope, is entirely erroneous.

This officer describes the fighting on Saturday as terrific beyond description. The enemy forced column after column on our works, lapping our lines on the extreme right. They came nine columns deep. Eight lines faltered and were broken by the obstinacy of our defences; but the ninth broke over our forces like a whirlwind. He says the destruction of the enemy was immense. Our loss, we think, consisted mainly in the prisoners taken by the enemy. All the prisoners whom we captured were drunk, having been prepared according to Yankee tactics for this dreadful ordeal. Lieutenant General A. P. Hill was certainly killed. General Fitz. Lee was not killed, as reported, nor General W. H. F. Lee. No general officer from North Carolina was killed, as far as he heard. On Monday Sheridan attacked Fitz. Lee and was handsomely repulsed.

The Organ of Governor Vance, of North Carolina, Advising General Lee to Submit on Mr. Lincoln's Terms.

[From the Raleigh Confederate, April 7.]

The *Conservative* occasionally seems to fall into very mysterious hands, and to come under the control of an incomprehensible influence. On the day before yesterday that paper availed itself of a period of extreme reverse and disaster to renew the attempt to instil odium on a portion of our own citizens, which has been a favorite policy with its political leaders ever since the reverses began, and after it was no longer politic to claim that they "made the revolution." Yesterday it sends to the public a leader of still more extraordinary import. From what we comprehend of it, it seems to be a *distinct proposition to submit and surrender upon the terms proposed by Lincoln.* This has never yet, that we recollect of, been more distinctly proposed, even by journals whose loyalty has been called in question. The *Conservative* [illegible] to propose [illegible] of the conclusion that the confederacy is a government," and hence, says the *Conservative*, "if our authorities are determined to force this condition upon the North as a basis of negotiation, then the North will never negotiate." What is this but surrender? Not only surrender, but an assertion to the world that the defence of the last four years has been of a position which is one of sheer nonsense—one which the North "never could admit!" We have not seen in this controversy so bold and unconditional a justification of the Northern invasion; for, if we sought to force a claim inconsistent with reason, and to demand an "admission" which "is an absurdity in anything like government," and the North only resisted such claim and refused such admission, then we are in the wrong and the Yankee government is right, and the writer of the article to which we are replying does well when he *advises General Lee not to "block up his way, at the threshold, by presenting a basis to which he knows the enemy will not yield,"* but "to meet him on his own ground," as "the only way to open the negotiation." When we remember what "his own ground" is, upon which the *Conservative* proposes to meet the enemy, we may readily understand how much it is prepared to concede. "His own ground" measured the length of three propositions; submission to the laws and constitution of the United States, the laying down of our arms, and acquiescence in Lincoln's proclamations. This is the ground on which the author of the editorial desires General Lee to meet Lincoln and "secure a talk about peace." We have no idea that Governor Vance will support this idea; but it is very unfortunate that now, at the very moment when everything should be said to uphold the hopes and confidence of the army and people, such sentiments should obtain publication in the organ of the Governor.

High Prices in an Overstocked Market.

[From the Raleigh Confederate, April 7.]

Our market, on the arrival of the Weldon train, on yesterday, *became overstocked with shad; they went off slowly at $50 per pair.*

Exchange of the Rebel General Vance.

[From the Ashville (N. C.) News.]

The exchange of prisoners seems to go steadily on. We have seen a large number of our mountain boys, who have reached home after a protracted imprisonment. Among others we were gratified to meet Brigadier General R. B. Vance, who reached home some days since. He looks rather worsted by his long confinement, but, as usual with him, is full of life, cheerful and buoyant. The General is a great favorite of the people of this section, and everybody was glad to see him.

City Intelligence.

Easter Sunday at St. Ann's Church.—The admirers of sacred music, made truly effective by a well trained choir, have an opportunity of indulging their taste by repairing to St. Ann's church on Easter Sunday evening, the doors opening at seven, the concert beginning at eight. Three of the pieces are from Gordigiani, three from Rossini and one from each of the composers Verdi, Donizetti, Verrimst, Dachauer and Gounod. We need only mention the names of Signor Rossi and Messrs. Schmitz, Schubert and Dachauer to insure confidence in the vocal results. The ladies are quite distinguished for contralto and soprano execution, and no exertion will be spared to make the musical feast worthy of the day.

A New Church.—An advertisement among our religious notices announces the opening of the new Church of the Holy Trinity, Madison avenue, corner of Forty-second street, on Sunday. Sermons will be preached at the three services by Rev. Dr. Tyng, of St. George's; Rev. Dr. Dyer, and the Rev. Stephen H. Tyng, Jr., the pastor of the church. It promises to be an occasion of great interest to residents on Murray Hill.

Croton Aqueduct Contracts.—The following contracts have been issued by this department:—Laying crosswalks from southeast corner of Fifty-ninth street and Broadway to the junction of Broadway and Eighth avenue, Matthew Murray, $480. Cobble stone pavement in [illegible] street, west of Thirteenth avenue, Christy [illegible] $1,380 [illegible]. Sewer in Forty-third street, from Lexington avenue to Fourth avenue, John Duffy, Jr., $1,[illegible]. Sewer in Forty-sixth street, from Eleventh avenue to seventy-five feet west of Tenth avenue, John Rogers, $4,[illegible]. Fifty-second street [illegible] Sewer in [illegible] street, from Fifth avenue through [illegible] street to Tenth avenue, James Cunningham, $[illegible].

Miss Emma Hardinge delivers her able lecture on "Politics in the Pulpit" this evening, at Dodworth Hall. To test the lady's ability, any question the audience desire to ask will be answered.

Man Drowned.—On the morning of the 13th instant a journeyman hatter [illegible], whose name is believed to be Bernard Burns, was accidentally drowned at Gravesend [illegible], Long Island. His body has not yet been claimed by his friends. Mr. J. B. Acker, of No. 9 [illegible] street, will give facilities to any one who can identify the corpse.

emphasizing Lincoln's benevolence even to traitors) and instruct Southerners of their mistake. In fact, at the final cabinet meeting Lincoln was not especially conciliatory toward the South, and apparently accepted much of Stanton's harsh reconstruction plan.[37] Stanton's "objective" facts are used to mask his personal agenda.

During his tenure as war secretary, Stanton was fanatical about controlling the dissemination of information. In this attempt to establish a connection between Stanton's controlling and repressive acts and his writing style, we need to examine the nature and structure of his attempts to control discourse and attain power through his manipulation of information.

Stanton's Background

By the end of 1861 the U.S. War Department had become corrupt and inefficient, and the House set up a special committee to investigate it. The committee found that the War Department had purchased "rotten blankets, tainted pork, knapsacks that came unglued in the rain, uniforms that fell apart . . . hundreds of diseased and dying horses—all at exorbitant prices." The committee found "colossal graft" and a "prostitution of public confidence to purposes of individual aggrandizement" under war secretary Simon Cameron. Lincoln needed a change and picked an unlikely candidate, Edwin McMasters Stanton.[38]

Stanton had a fitting background and temperament for a man who would be at the forefront of a new, "factual" style of news writing. An extremely ambitious man, he became a lawyer in 1835 (at age twenty-one) and earned early recognition as a skillful rhetorician and a brilliant legal strategist. He shared many of the views of abolitionism (his grandmother had manumitted her dead husband's slaves at the turn of the nineteenth century), but he carefully avoided the sensitive subject. It might have been this trait that attracted Lincoln to Stanton; the president was looking for a

Figure 9. Facing page: New York Herald, 15 April 1865 (Library of Congress). Stanton's dispatch is in the lead (left) column, below the final heading, "The Official Despatch." The "Press Despatches," including Gobright's, can be found in the third column, after Stanton's dispatches. The *Herald*'s placement of official and unofficial dispatches reflects the general reliance on "authoritative" sources during the second half of the Civil War.

war secretary who could avoid discussion of slavery until strategic issues were settled. In this, Stanton did not disappoint Lincoln. A tight control of utterance was central to Stanton's value to his president.[39]

From his early years as a lawyer, Stanton's chief concern was with minutiae, leading him to find loopholes in the law. The case of a Lisbon, Ohio, wagoner, who was accused of damaging a road, is an example. The man had driven his cart uphill with its brakes on, creating deep ruts in the already ill-kept road. Stanton successfully argued that since the town's ordinance forbade drivers to go *down* the street with their brakes on, his client, going uphill, was innocent.[40] Stanton's most sensational case was the murder trial of his friend Daniel Sickles, a New York congressman who killed Philip Barton Key (son of the author of "The Star Spangled Banner"). Stanton and his associates successfully defended Sickles and were the first in U.S. history to use the defense of "temporary insanity."[41] By 1859 Stanton had become one of the nation's leading lawyers. It was then that James Buchanan, in the final year of his presidency, named Stanton his attorney general.[42]

Stanton thought Buchanan was becoming too conciliatory to the South, and while he maintained Buchanan's trust, he was also apprising Republican leaders of threats to the Union. Stanton, a Democrat, was able to keep the trust of the president and conservatives back home while secretly planning strategy with radical Republicans in Congress. He was able to accomplish this difficult task only by a careful management of information: during Stanton's tenure as attorney general, he met with Republican Senator Charles Sumner a few times in complete secrecy; Stanton always understood how quickly a subordinate would take information to a newspaper.[43]

In 1855, when Stanton was working as an attorney on an important patent case, a young lawyer from Illinois was retained to assist him. Stanton and his associates were rude to the man, did not include him in their stratagems, and generally ignored him. The young man sat quietly through the trial and tried to learn as much as he could. The snub would never be forgotten by the man, and when this gangling young attorney from Illinois was elected president in 1860, the insult was still fresh in his memory. If Lincoln resented Stanton, the sentiment was mutually displayed; Stanton, through letters, disclosed his mistrust of Lincoln's administration, which he perceived as corrupted and bureaucratic.[44] If his secret dislike of Lincoln resembled his previous disapproval of Buchanan, it also foreshadowed his surreptitious machinations against General George McClellan and his public

Figure 10. Edwin M. Stanton, photographed by Matthew Brady (Library of Congress).

wrangling with President Andrew Johnson, who tried to dismiss him. Stanton's complex relationships with his superiors often displayed his conspiratorial mind.[45]

When Lincoln had to replace War Secretary Cameron, the powerful Republicans may have remembered Stanton's favors to them and recommended him to Lincoln. But Lincoln may have also considered Stanton's legal expertise, put his personal feelings aside, and picked the man because he would be a discreet and able administrator. As a lifetime civilian, Stanton could offer no military background; however, his legal expertise would allow him to quickly train himself in military matters.

More than one of Stanton's biographers and many of his contemporaries saw him as a misanthrope. L. A. Whiteley, chief of the *Herald*'s Washington office, wrote to James Gordon Bennett, "Stanton absolutely stinks in the nostrils of the people and the army. His manner has made him offensive to every one who approaches him."[46] It is consistent with Stanton's character that the telegraph was his preferred form of discourse: it was far less personal than the courier system used by many of his colleagues.

It is true that he was often rude to his generals and subordinates, but it may have been Stanton's repugnance that drew Lincoln to him. In a fascinating book, David Bates, a telegrapher during the Civil War, describes the two men closely. He wrote, "Lincoln's heart was greater than his head, while Stanton's head was greater than his heart."[47] Lincoln needed someone to end favoritism in the War Department and he may have seen Stanton's lack of ardor as an asset; during his secretaryship, Stanton was impeccable in his hiring practices, even denying an appointment (signed by Lincoln!) to his own favorite nephew. His vigilance paid off, saving the department $17 million in adjusted contracts.[48]

Stanton Takes Control of Discourse in the North

It is strangely fitting that the author of what might be the first inverted pyramid was also one of the most notorious censors of the nineteenth-century press: both sides of Stanton reflect his control of information.[49] Henry Villard, of the *Herald* and the *Tribune*, wrote in his memoirs about what Stanton did to the War Department: "This change, while of immeasurable benefit to the country, proved a decided disadvantage to my profession; for whereas Cameron was always accessible and communicative—no doubt too much so for the public good—his successor had the doors of the War Department closed to newspaper men."[50] Not only did Stanton close the doors, he rerouted the telegraphs, created a secret police force, arrested reporters, restricted press passes, and even usurped the authority of his generals.

Stanton was confirmed in January 1862, at the height of Lincoln's impatience with George McClellan. McClellan, Hamlet-like in his timidity, was constantly stalling for more time and resources. "If General McClellan does not want to use the army," the president said to his war council, "I would like to borrow it for a time."[51] McClellan's procrastinations were aided by his complete control of telegraphic dispatches. Less than two weeks after his appointment, Stanton penned a letter to Lincoln asking for total control of the telegraphs. On the reverse side of Stanton's request is a message, dated the same day, from Lincoln: "The Secretary of War has my authority to exercise his discretion in the matter within mentioned. A. Lincoln." That day, Stanton wrote to Dana, then the editor of the *Tribune*, "The champagne and oysters on the Potomac must be stopped." Two weeks later, Stanton dismantled McClellan's telegraph office and rerouted all lines into the room adjacent to his own.[52]

On the same day he received control of the telegraphs, Stanton also created a new assistant-secretaryship for his trusted friend Peter Watson. Watson was put in charge of press releases and the newly formed secret police, his dual role reflecting Stanton's concern with the dissemination of information.[53]

On February 10, a reporter for the *New York Herald*, "Dr." Malcolm Ives, told a War Department assistant that the *Herald* expected to hear of all classified and nonclassified War Department decisions in advance of the other dailies, and that the newspaper would decide whether to withhold information. He suggested that this was simply the price of the *Herald*'s support of the administration. Ives then stormed into Stanton's busy office, saying that as a *Herald* reporter, he had freedom to come and go as he pleased. When Ives went to sleep that night, he was a reporter; the next morning he was a prisoner in Fort McHenry and an accused rebel spy.[54] Certainly Ives was guilty of rudeness, but the charge of espionage was clearly an attempt by Stanton to establish power over the powerful press. Two days later, the War Department was given control over all political arrests, and one historian credits Stanton with more than a quarter of a million seizures.[55] At one point late in the war, a salesman was caught trying to smuggle $25,000 worth of military goods into the South. Ninety-seven of Baltimore's leading businessmen were implicated by the salesman's receipts; all were promptly arrested by Stanton.[56]

Although the press almost universally applauded the arrest of Ives (the *Herald*'s misfortunes were always widely applauded), they soon began to realize that news gathering would be severely curtailed under Stanton. Newspaper reporters could not send their stories directly to their papers; instead they had to pass through Stanton's office and his censors. Stanton

Figure 11. A covered wagon serving as the field headquarters of the *New York Herald*, near the front (Library of Congress).

restricted press passes to the front and arrested reporters and telegraphers.[57] At one point in the war, a dishonest investor circulated a phony letter, said to be written by Lincoln, to the New York dailies. The sham letter had Lincoln calling for many more troops and practically admitting surrender. Of the papers that had received the letter, only two, the *World* and the *Journal of Commerce*, printed it. Stanton quickly ordered the arrest of their editors. The other dailies considered the imprisonment a violation of First Amendment rights. Indeed, Stanton did keep the editors in jail after their innocence was determined, and it was due only to Lincoln's intervention that they were released at all.[58] In order to track the source of the hoax, Stanton ordered an investigation of the Independent Telegraph Company, and when its manager refused to surrender its records, Stanton sent agents to telegraph bureaus across the country and jailed the company's entire national staff.[59]

Stanton's control of telegraphic information extended well beyond the press dispatches. General Grant, who basically liked Stanton, wrote in his memoirs about his only wartime disagreement with the war secretary. Because he had split his field communications in two, Grant asked an army telegrapher to give his cipher to one of Grant's trusted captains. The telegrapher refused. Grant wrote,

> Mr. Stanton had taken entire control of the matter of regulating the telegraph and determining how it should be used, and of saying who, and who alone, should have the ciphers. The operators possessed of the ciphers . . . were practically independent of the commanders whom they were serving immediately under, and had to report to the War Department . . . all the dispatches which they received or forwarded. . . . The operator refused [Grant's request] point blank . . . , stating that his orders from the War Department were not to give it to anybody—the commanding general or any one else. . . . He said that if he did he would be punished. I told him if he did not he most certainly would be punished. Finally, seeing that punishment was certain if he refused longer to obey my order, and being somewhat remote . . . from the War Department, he yielded.

When Stanton found out, he promptly relieved the dispatcher, and Grant had to intercede on the man's behalf.[60]

Reactions to the Secretary's Control

The various impressions of Stanton came from two distinct groups: those who were hurt by Stanton's restrictions and those who saw their necessity. Gideon Welles, the navy secretary, complained in his diary of the difficulty of getting information from Stanton. On many occasions, Welles wrote, his ships would show up to battles long finished. Welles interpreted Stanton's control of information as greed: "He wants no general to overtop him, is jealous of others in any position who have influence."[61] William T. Sherman hated Stanton. When Sherman made a provisional peace with Joseph E. Johnston, a Confederate general, days after Lincoln was assassinated, Stanton was furious and sent down Grant to Sherman's command, "to direct operations against the enemy." Then Stanton used his office to send press releases informing the public of Sherman's error and implying that Sherman might help Jefferson Davis escape.[62] Stanton may have been injudicious in publishing the story; Sherman was a loyal soldier who, at worst, acted on his own initiative in the absence of specific orders from

Washington. But Stanton tolerated no forays into his command, and one of the results of his tenure as a strict press censor was his effective use of the press as an instrument of control. In his memoirs Sherman tells about refusing to shake Stanton's outstretched hand at a parade, although Dana wrote that it was not offered.[63]

It is a testament to Stanton's stature that he was often contrasted with Lincoln. They were usually seen as opposites. For example, Grant compares Lincoln's pleasant, yielding, but forceful personality with an odd mixture of traits in Stanton: "He cared nothing for the feelings of others. . . . Mr. Stanton never questioned his own authority. . . . The Secretary was very timid."[64] Stanton also lacked Lincoln's waggishness (some say Stanton lacked a sense of humor altogether), as reflected in a participant's observation of a cabinet meeting: "President mentioned [a funny] book. Proposed to read a chapter which he thought very funny. Read it, and seemed to enjoy it very much—the Heads also (except Stanton) of course."[65] David Bates, the telegrapher, wrote that Stanton often wrote dispatches and releases himself. Bates contrasts the slow, clean, and deliberate writing style of Lincoln with that of Stanton, "whose drafts or letters and memoranda were jotted down at a terrific pace, with many erasures and interlineations."[66] This attention to detail gave Stanton the "attitude of a man who is always trying to catch a mental train," said one writer.[67]

Stanton told Lincoln repeatedly to stay away from crowds and was always convinced that the president was in danger. When Lincoln visited the fallen Richmond, just weeks before the war's end, Stanton warned against exposing "the nation to the consequences of any disaster to yourself."[68] Stanton assigned a guard around Lincoln, who tried for a time to avoid it, only to give in: "If Stanton should learn that you had let me return alone," he joked to his guard, "he would have you court-martialed and shot." Two weeks later, on April 14, 1865, Stanton told Lincoln not to go to Ford's Theatre. Although the Lincolns invited the Stantons to accompany them that night, Stanton refused, hoping to sway the president.[69]

Stanton's control over the telegraphs made his office the North's nucleus of information, and Lincoln often spent more time in the telegraph office than his own; the president even had a special chair in which he read the daily dispatches.[70] Stanton, in turn, often came late to cabinet meetings, refused to speak if noncabinet members were present, and would occasionally bypass the meetings completely, speaking directly with Lincoln.[71]

According to James Rhodes, a nineteenth-century Lincoln biographer, and Stephen Oates, a recent one, Lincoln considered Stanton an important

aide and one of his favorites.[72] Lincoln's fortune was to have a tough secretary "who never questioned his own authority." Lincoln could stand by his secretary when force was needed, and he could stop him when necessary. At Lincoln's final cabinet meeting, on the day he died, he allowed Stanton to present a reconstruction plan more radical than his own, accepting most of it, while letting Navy Secretary Welles and others have their way on some particulars.[73] Lincoln seemed to enjoy his secretary's superciliousness. Once, upon hearing that Stanton had called him a fool, he returned, "Did Stanton call me a fool? Well, I guess I had better go over and see Stanton about this. Stanton is usually right."[74]

Stanton's "War Diary"

Until Lee's surrender in 1865, Grant's 1864 Wilderness Campaign was one of the most important maneuvers of the war. Grant and Lincoln agreed that they would not communicate for the duration of the battle, but after a week of silence Lincoln and Stanton were getting nervous. It was then that a young reporter from the *New York Tribune*, Henry Wing, sent a message to the War Department. Wing had just broken through enemy lines and wanted to send a battle report to his paper. Stanton himself answered the request, telling the reporter to send an account to the War Department and refusing Wing's request for a message to the *Tribune*. When Wing rejected these terms, Stanton made a counterproposal: Wing's immediate arrest.

Just as Stanton made his threat, Lincoln walked into the telegraph office. "Ask him if he will talk with the President," Lincoln told the dispatcher.[75] Wing stated that he wanted to send one hundred words to his newspaper before he answered the president's questions. Lincoln quickly agreed, and did not limit the length of Wing's article, under the condition that Wing report to Washington the next day.

Wing's dispatch begins in a chronological style. Reporting information occurring from a Wednesday to a Friday, Wing began at the beginning "The grand Army of the Potomac crossed the Rapidan on Wednesday." Wing took four paragraphs to describe the events of Wednesday, anoth six for Thursday's skirmishes, and in the thirteenth paragraph of a fiftee paragraph story, Wing came to the point: "heavy firing had commenc on our right when I left at 5 o'clock [this morning] . . . there has bee grand victory."[76] Unreliable telegraph lines and enemy presence did stop Wing from saving his best material for last.

A dispatch, hastily written in Stanton's hand, was immediately sent to New York:

> A dispatch of the New York Tribune reporter just received states that yesterday the Army of the Potomac came in collision with Lee's army in Chancellorsville; that Lee's whole army is there, and that a general battle would take place to-day. After he left the army on his way in, heavy cannonading was heard, showing that the engagement was going on. Burnside reached the field with his forces last night.
> Edwin M. Stanton, Secretary of War.[77]

Stanton's dispatch, as compared with the longer narrative of Wing, is much closer to the inverted pyramid style: informative, terse, factual, detached, and impersonal. Unlike Wing's dispatch, Stanton's doesn't start at the beginning of the action, and avoids all mention of Wednesday's activities. He first discusses the lead (Friday's battle), then he moves to Thursday, and finally takes a more cautious position than Wing's: Stanton did not echo Wing's announcement of a "grand victory," choosing instead to wait for an "official" word before announcing it (Stanton immediately sent down his assistant, Dana, to get official statements).

In the last year of the war, Northerners received most of the important news through Stanton's daily dispatches to General Dix, stationed in New York, who released the dispatches to the New York dailies. Stanton, after getting information from generals, Dana, reporters, deserters, and sick soldiers, would consolidate the information under the heading "War Diary." He had a journalist's love for "breaking the story," and Gideon Welles, who on rare occasions beat Stanton to the telegraphers, wrote that Stanton "craves to announce all important information."[78] In assessing Stanton's role in creating the new journalistic style, one should remember the prominence of these daily editions of the "War Diary": major battles, especially near the end of the war, were almost always announced by Stanton's dispatches on the front pages of papers across the Union. In fact, the bigger the battle, the more likely were Stanton's dispatches to appear on the front page. No other writer in the press or government could boast of such a readership.

It is important to place Stanton's dispatches in the context of the political shift in America from a loose confederation of states to a strong centralized executive branch. "Before the war," said Shelby Foote, "it was said 'the United States are . . . ' It . . . was thought of as a collection of independent states. After the war it was always 'The United States *is* . . . ' And that sums up what the war accomplished. It made us an 'is.' "[79] The scope of the

Civil War required unity, and Lincoln, in suspending habeas corpus and giving his war secretary a long leash, must have considered that unity is gained by extralegal and other maneuvers that strengthen executive power. To lead a nation into a nondefensive war, the bloodiest in its history, Lincoln himself had to appeal to *all* Americans. He did so by surrounding himself with a cabinet of Democrats and ex-rivals for the presidency. He did so by his conciliatory speeches to the South. And he did so by his special relationship with the press.

The relationship of the executive branch with the press changed markedly with Lincoln. Before the 1860s, presidents maintained a semiofficial organ among the Washington newspapers.[80] Lincoln broke with this tradition and relied on a direct appeal to the burgeoning low-priced newspapers, which, significantly, were asserting their own nonpartisan stances. With less unquestioned newspaper loyalty, Lincoln had to market himself as a president for the whole country—at least the mainly white, male voters—and this marketing included the selling of his rhetoric. The Associated Press, a young organization in the Civil War, has always prided itself on its ability to write "objectively" to different news audiences. Lincoln, too, had to take his words to the market.

The U.S. Government Printing Office was founded in 1860. Although not widely seen as a major event in the history of the United States, it did have profound implications for journalism, effectively ending partisan printing contracts and hence the party press. Combined with a telegraphic network, which allowed for rapid communication from Washington, and the emerging wire services, which delivered a single message to newspapers of all political stripes, the end of the party press forever altered the nonpartisan press as well.

As with most changes, something was gained and something lost with the end of the party press. What was gained was that politicians suddenly had greater audiences, made up of newspapers of all parties, and in turn granted access to journalists. President-elect Lincoln made his famous trip to Washington from Illinois accompanied by a *New York Herald* reporter. Journalists were granted greater access than they ever received as partisans, but in giving up their partisanship, gave up their partisan voice. Because of this the media were now free from direct political control *and* deeply connected to the actions and operations of the government.[81] When, to use a recent example, aides to President Reagan told television journalists that they could no longer ask questions of the president during meetings with foreign dignitaries, the television journalists protested and immediately began a boycott of these meetings, only to give up the boycott within hours. Michael Deaver, Reagan's deputy chief of staff, had predicted that the administration would win the confrontation with the press: competitive economic forces were so strong that journalists would not be able to resist covering the nation's most important newsmaker.[82]

This shift from the party-based press organs to a wider dissemination gave the executive branch far greater powers. Stanton's "War Diary" appeared on the front pages, usually in the lead column, often in larger type, in newspapers across the Union. Imagine the effect of these terse statements on news-hungry families of hundreds of thousands of soldiers. Stanton's dispatches were read by the North, and helped to create a shared discourse, which in turn pushed the nation toward what one historian calls an "American federal community," a community sharing a common interest in what Washington says and does.[83] "Mr. Stanton sends a cheerful bulletin touching the advance movements of General Grant," wrote a *Herald* editorialist near the end of the war, emphasizing Stanton's role as conveyor.[84] That the *Herald* and the other papers would accept freely what "Mr. Stanton sends" speaks to the North's need for authoritative news, especially in the vacuum created by Stanton's censorship, telegraph and press pass restrictions, and jailings. The "War Diary," then, is welcome, even though the dispatch's overt role, the dissemination of information, masks the intentions of suppression, distortion, propaganda, and curtailment of press freedom.

While not always written in descending order of importance, Stanton's daily dispatch was never chronological and was always terse. Stanton's biographers suggest that the pressures of the Civil War nearly killed him. For a man so busy, to write a long chronological dispatch would be impossible. Instead, Stanton wrote his "War Diary" in a hurried style. Journalism historians have suggested that the inverted pyramid style best serves people who don't have time to read a narrative. It may be that the style was started by a man with no time to write one.

Although Stanton left no memoirs behind, he did make comments on writing that reflect his stance on clarity and terseness. Dana's dispatches, clear, impersonal, and written from the perspective of an impartial spectator (if there is such a thing), were appreciated by Stanton "for their clearness of narrative and their graphic pictures of the stirring events they describe."[85] Because it was brief, Stanton loved Lincoln's Gettysburg Address. The speech was not universally hailed at the time, and was terse compared to Edward Everett's two-hour lecture of the same day. "Mr. Lincoln has made a speech of perhaps forty or fifty lines," Stanton told Dana. "Everett's is the speech of a scholar, polished to the last possibility . . . but Lincoln's speech will be read by a thousand men where one reads Everett's, and will be remembered as long as anybody's speeches are remembered." Stanton's fondness for concision was shared by Dana, who, as an editor, once admonished a particularly gushing reporter, "Hereafter, in sending your reports, please specify the number of the hymn and save telegraph expenses."[86]

Dana, the ex-*Tribune* editor, may have been the freest reporter in the Civil War. With Stanton's restrictions, other reporters had difficulty gathering information; if they learned anything the War Department did not know, they could not send it by telegraph. Dana had no such restrictions. In 1863 Stanton dispatched Dana to provide the government with "semiofficial" reports on Grant's movements. As Lincoln balanced allegations of Grant's drunken misconduct with his own realization that "I can't spare this man. He *fights*,"[87] Dana's observations may very well have swayed Lincoln's decision to keep Grant. Dana's dispatches from Vicksburg are detailed, factual, and terse, and in an impartial tone convey the competence of Grant and his men.

Dana's detached style may suggest a connection between "objective" writing and sociopolitical repression, the two sides of Stanton. Dana's autobiography seems to include an example of how he neglected to report one of General Grant's drinking binges: Grant's steamer was stopped by Union boats, who warned Dana of danger ahead. The general was "sick and asleep . . . too sick to decide" whether to turn back. Dana decided to turn back, and Grant awoke the next morning "fresh as a rose" and not remembering a thing. That Dana did not mention Grant's "sick" episode in his dispatches, which could have resulted in Grant's dismissal, shows how "objective" reporting may be less than honest while still keeping an impersonal and "factual" tone. Dana, the reporter, while asserting facts, had left out some as well.[88]

"Strategic Ritual" of Manipulation

"Objectivity" has been called by one journalism critic, Gaye Tuchman, a "strategic ritual."[89] By this she means that reporters must rely on authoritative quotes and other measures as a defensive gesture, to avoid lawsuits and professional censure. The press, Tuchman says, tends to choose the discourse of power because it is more reliable and verifiable. Stanton's rituals of manipulation also revolved around a central strategic question: how to minimize the damage from unofficial press leaks to the enemy. Stanton's solution was to assert the factuality of his own dispatches while diminishing the importance of all nonauthoritative sources.

Stanton's careful control of information was often not enough to stop the South from profiting from the Northern dailies. A *New York Tribune* article announced that "General Sherman would not be heard from about Goldsboro because his supply vessels . . . were known to be rendezvousing at Morehead City," a fact that Sherman was trying to keep quiet. The *Tribune* editor must have known he had a scoop because he announced his "satisfaction to inform his readers" of the information. Unfortunately for Sherman, Confederate general William J. Hardee was a *Tribune* reader that day and gave Sherman a fight he never forgot. Robert E. Lee was an avid reader of the Northern dailies, and often, much to the amazement of his enemies, anticipated Union moves. Once he discovered from the pages of the *New York Daily News* that General Burnside was moving alongside Grant. On another occasion, a statement in the *Philadelphia Inquirer* about McClellan's movements convinced Lee that a withdrawal from Richmond was a safe move.[90]

Stanton's terse communiqués were the "official" statements that were supposed to be believed. Given the difficulty of getting news, and given the penalties for printing false material, an emphasis on the "official" word could be seen in newspapers across the Union. Similarly, in his "War Diary," Stanton often announced that an "official report" or "official word" had been received by his department.

Another example of the way facts were used to manipulate perceptions is Stanton's dispatch (an inverted pyramid except for its personal nature) to Lincoln on January 17, 1865, and sent to the papers, about the battle for and surrender of Fort Fisher. It begins,

> The rebel flag of Fort Fisher was delivered to me on board the steamer, *Spaulding*, off that place, yesterday morning, Jan. 16, by Major-Gen Terry.

The dispatch's touching conclusion reminds readers of the cost of victory and why they must keep fighting:

> On Monday, everything was quiet as a Sabbath day. The dead were being buried and the wounded collected and placed in transports and field hospitals.[91]

That is how the newspaper account ended, but Lincoln's copy ended with a paragraph about Sherman's movements, life in Savannah, and seized rebel cotton. Of this expunged information only Sherman's movements seem classified, but the news consumers saw none of the material about Savannah and the cotton. Because it has no narrative flow, the inverted pyramid is easier to manipulate than the chronological account; it is easy to delete paragraphs and facts without disturbing the sense of the story. The Fort Fisher dispatch shows how Stanton was able to omit nonessential facts to convey a different impression of the event.[92]

The reports of major battles reflect the stark differences between Stanton's dispatches and those of the reporters. Sherman's march on Atlanta is an excellent example. Stanton's terse, unemotional communiqué to Dix, "General Sherman's official report of the capture of Atlanta has just been received by this Department . . . ," announces the news. This is followed in the *Tribune*, *Times*, and *Herald* by an Associated Press summary of the celebrations of cities throughout the North. A reporter's article then follows, written chronologically by the newspaper's "Special Correspondent":

> Before Atlanta, Ga., *Aug. 25, 1864.*
>
> *Early on the morning of the 18th* [italics mine] the 1st Brigade of this Division, Col. R. H. G. Minty, commanding, with the Second Brigade, Col. Eli Long, now Brigadier General, commanding, were ordered to march rapidly to our right flank.[93]

The story, written on the twenty-fifth, begins with events of the eighteenth. It proceeds in the classic storytelling mode, withholding the most important news until the end.

Another example of the differences between Stanton and reporters can be seen in the coverage of the fall of Richmond, ten days before Lincoln was assassinated. Stanton relied on reports from Lincoln, who was in Virginia to witness Lee's defeat firsthand. With Lincoln as a reporter and Stanton writing in his anomalous style, the battle for and surrender of Richmond was a great news event. Sometimes Stanton would send along Lincoln's dispatches to the newspapers. Occasionally he would refuse to name his august source:

> To Major General Dix,
>
> The following telegrams [from the President] announcing the victory won yesterday by Major General Sheridan over Lees army [the enemy's force at Burk's Station] has just been received by this department.
>
> Edwin M. Stanton
> Secretary of War

The above dispatch, with Stanton's deletions in brackets, displays a deliberate attempt to conceal Lincoln as the source of Stanton's information. The words "from the President" are crossed out, allowing Stanton to announce the "victory" himself.[94] After the fall of Richmond, Stanton received Lincoln's dispatches and, as usual with important information, penned the following dispatches himself:

> Secretary Stanton to General Dix:
> The following telegram from the President, announcing the EVACUATION OF PETERSBURG, and probably of Richmond, has just been received by this department.
>
> Edwin M. Stanton,
> Secretary of War

> The President's Despatch:
> Hon. Edwin M. Stanton, Secretary of War:—
> This morning Lieut.-Gen. Grant reports Petersburgh evacuated, and he is confident that Richmond also is. He is pushing forward to cut off, if possible, the retreating rebel army.
>
> A. Lincoln

> Secretary Stanton to General Dix:
> It appears from a dispatch of Gen Weitzel's, just received by this department, that our forces under his command are IN RICHMOND, having taken it at 8:15 this morning.
>
> Edwin M. Stanton,
> Secretary of War.[95]

The effect of Stanton's dispatches on reporters is evident in their articles on the surrender of Richmond. Stanton's and Lincoln's dispatches were given the lead position in April 4's *New York Tribune*, followed by a long dispatch by the paper's reporter. The reporter may well have understood that Lincoln and Stanton's short paragraphs would serve as a lead because he began his story, "As you doubtless have accounts of the operations in progress here up to yesterday, I will confine myself to a brief synopsis. The heaviest fighting has been done by the Fifth Corps and Sheridan's Cavalry."[96]

If not *infantilized* by Stanton's monopoly of information, the reporter was at least relegated to telling the non-"authoritative" elements of the story. It is quite apparent that his role in the dissemination of information was reduced to recalling his experience as a participant. But a close reading of Stanton's orchestration of the above news event shows that Lincoln's role was similarly diminished. Stanton wrote that "the following telegram from the President . . . has just been received by this department." This usurps Lincoln's role by anticipating Lincoln's news and announcing it before Lincoln does (indeed, the front pages lead with Stanton's dispatch). That Stanton has "received" the news, and that this is important to convey, suggests that it is only with Stanton's release that it becomes "official." This is all similar to the ritual of hierarchical privilege that takes place daily on today's television news shows. Anchors and reporters talk directly into the camera and address the audience directly; interviewees must look not at the audience but at the reporter, thus looking askance at the camera. In the same way, Stanton gave the privilege of direct transmission to no one but himself.

Given that extensive research and leading historians have not produced Civil War examples of inverted pyramid reports, the theories about the development of the form should be examined further: were there any journalists writing in this style before Stanton? If so, the history books should be revised to include Civil War examples. In any case, Stanton's writing of inverted pyramids at a time when chronological forms were still standard is interesting because of Stanton's special relationship with the press.

It would be hasty to suggest that Stanton developed the inverted pyramid; however, it does appear that he was writing inverted pyramids at a time when most news writing was still chronological and narrative. Stanton's role in the journalism history books needs to be revised; he was not a mere censor. He was harsh with the press, but he was also among the first to write in a style that would replace narrative with a hierarchical ordering of facts.

The two most widely held theories of the development of the inverted pyramid are (1) that the war and unreliable telegraphs pushed reporters to put their most important news in their first paragraphs; and (2) that wire services, notably the Associated Press, used the inverted pyramid because they had to be impartial. But there is no evidence that the telegraph or the wire services produced a basic shift in the way stories were written until *after* the Civil War. Telegraphs and press agencies may have influenced the

nalistic practice, which paralleled advances in other areas as well. First I will discuss the medical and journalistic response to the 1832 and 1849 cholera epidemics. Then I will outline, in the context of the journalistic response, the abundant changes in American society and culture as a whole. Finally I will return to cholera and show how medicine and journalism dealt with the epidemic of 1866. Together, these changes reflect a new way of thinking, a new scientific approach shared by the medical and journalistic communities. While the medical response to the cholera epidemics has been discussed at length in historical literature, notably in *The Cholera Years*, by Charles Rosenberg, the link between cholera and journalism has never been explored.

Antebellum Cholera, Antebellum Journalism

Cholera's first American appearance was on the dirty, pungent, impoverished streets of New York City. That was 1832. The first successful explosion of the penny press occurred on these same streets, about a year later. While many historical coincidences are contrived, the confluence of cholera and journalism, from the New York City birth through the 1860s, was no coincidence. The spread of cholera across the United States, by rail, wagon, and steamer, paralleled the spread of news by the same means. The disease, which is conveyed by drinking water polluted with human excreta, made the rounds from house to house and thrived in cramped cities. The penny papers also found a haven in the cities, where news too could be consumed and spread easily from door to door. By the 1860s the medical profession, using scientific method, data gathering, and technology, defeated cholera on the streets of New York City. Technology and science helped propel American journalism toward "objectivity" too.

Cholera first came to New York in July 1832. Before it had abated in late August, more than 2,200 deaths had been reported, which means that more than 1 percent of New York's inhabitants had been killed in less than two months. This figure is conservative, considering that in 1832 many of the deaths went unreported; bodies were often hastily buried, or half buried, the stench and the clouds of flies over St. Patrick's cemetery being a reminder of the city's inefficient response to the disease.[3]

The central belief of the medical profession, duly reported in the newspapers, was that the disease sprang from atmospheric conditions rather than from contagion. This was based on a "philosophical," not an empirical, view of the disease. According to Rosenberg, " 'empiric' was—as it had been for generations—a synonym for quack." One doctor, for example, upon seeing a cluster of cholera cases, felt that only contagion could explain the outbreak, but because he could not reject other causes, he felt that it was "unphilosophical" to accept the possibility of contagion.[4]

Dates of Principal Events Discussed in This Chapter

July 1832	**New York's first cholera epidemic begins**
1839	**Louis Daguerre invents photography**
May 1844	**Morse demonstrates his new invention, the magnetic telegraph**
July 1849	**New York's second major cholera epidemic begins**
1855	**Whitman publishes *Leaves of Grass***
1852–62	**Karl Marx is a correspondent for Greeley's *New York Tribune***
1859	**Darwin's *Origin of Species* is published**
1860	**Spencer publishes *First Principles***
1861–65	**American Civil War**
May 1866	**New York's third and final major cholera epidemic begins**
1870s	**The age of "realism" in art and literature begins in the United States** **Anesthesia, antiseptics, and aseptics are widely available**
1875	**The Tribune building rises above the New York skyline and dwarfs church spires**

The newspaper coverage of the 1832 outbreak reflected the view that "atmosphere" played the biggest role, but also reflected a disregard for scientific method and what we recognize as logic. James Watson Webb's *Courier and Enquirer* used up much of its ink in trying to calm readers' fears (often addressing merchants who might be scared to travel to New York) by discussing the "atmosphere." Before the extent of the cholera epidemic was apparent, the *Courier and Enquirer* announced that the city would be spared. "The purity of the atmosphere—the beauty of the weather for several days past was never surpassed," explained Webb in an editorial.[5] Less than three weeks later, however, the paper took solace in a seemingly contradictory sign: "A very severe thunder storm passed over the city yesterday morning, which will, we hope, have the effect of purifying the atmosphere."[6]

While the possibility of contagion was not accepted in the *Courier and Enquirer*, atmosphere was not the only cause discussed. After all, panicked New Yorkers wanted guidance in avoiding the disease. The pages of the *Courier and Enquirer* were filled with preventative advice. One doctor who had suffered from cholera himself, "Dr. De Kay," wrote to the paper to warn of "excess in diet, exposure to night air; fear, anxiety, &c."[7] Other reports warned against cold feet ("Keep on your flannels"), fruits, and vegetables.[8] Cucumbers were constantly cited as culprits ("take care of *cucumbers*"), leading one skeptical doctor to call cucumbers "the 'mad dog' of all our fruits . . . none is more abused, more slandered."[9]

Perhaps even more than the *Courier and Enquirer* realized, its ideas of cause and cure were wrapped up in its religious notions of morality and its view of the sizable destitute population of New York. "Drunkeness [*sic*], intemperance, dissipation and all their attendent [*sic*] evils," wrote the *Courier and Enquirer*, "are so many inducements for cholera attacks. . . . Be temperate."[10] The newspaper's point of reference seemed to be not science, but biblical notions of plague. A lead story sounds almost like a line from Exodus: "This pestilence, which walketh in darkness, continues its ravages among us, and is daily sacrificing hundreds of victims to its unmitigated fury."[11]

If God is at the bottom of the cholera epidemic, and God is just, the syllogism goes, his victims must be culpable. The authorities proposed a day of "fasting and humiliation," which the *Courier and Enquirer*'s editorials heartily endorsed, to purge the city of its sins. The victims, according to the medical records and newspaper accounts, were subject to a medical response characterized by violence. One doctor, the president of the New York State Medical Society, recommended an anal plug of beeswax or oilcloth to combat the diarrhea. Some used "tobacco smoke enemas," while others rubbed mercury into the gums of patients.[12] The *Courier and Enquirer* printed a series of cures, including one that advocated the immediate application "to the epigastric region [of] 20 or 40 leeches according to the severity of the case."[13] "The means used for my recovery," wrote

Charles Finney in remembering his own experience with cholera, "gave my system a terrible shock, from which it took me long to recover."[14]

The 1849 Epidemic

The city's next great cholera epidemic was in the summer of 1849, when the disease claimed more than four thousand New Yorkers. The 1849 epidemic stood between those of 1832 and 1866, both temporally and in terms of the relative sophistication of the response, as an investigation of the *New York Herald* during the epidemic reveals.[15]

From 1832 to 1849 many of the existing notions about the disease remained the same, including many of the ideas of cause and the level of invasiveness in the cures. Rosenberg found that the "atmosphere" was still the big culprit in 1849, and the *Herald* bears this out. "The return of electricity to the atmosphere," Bennett suggested in his paper, "has had on the whole, a favorable tendency."[16] Cases were still attributed to a plethora of preconditions, from drunkenness to national background, filth, fruits, exposure to the sun, and "offensive effluvia" from soap factories.[17] The biblical tone of 1832 was also present in 1849; Bennett thanked "Providence" for a relatively short mortality list.[18] Also remaining from 1832 were the contradictions found in the newspaper columns. One week after cautioning readers about the relationship between cholera and alcohol, the *Herald* praised a cure of "laudanum [an opium tincture] . . . camphor . . . cayenne pepper . . . ginger . . . peppermint . . . put into a quart of French brandy."[19] In 1849 medicine still shared with newspapers an inability to understand the cause, prevention, or cure of cholera; the newspapers were still operating without the facts they needed to make decisions and to help their readers make decisions.

Although it came too late to help the victims of the 1849 epidemic, the medical response to cholera was making gains in Europe. One London anesthetist, Dr. John Snow, had in fact discovered how the disease was spread and began publishing his findings in a British journal in 1849. Snow theorized correctly that cholera was spread through water contaminated by infected excreta. In 1849 Snow's theory was just one among many. What separated him from other theorists was that in 1854, when a cholera epidemic hit London, he was able to prove his theory. London in 1854 was served by two water companies, one that drew its water from the upper Thames River, and one that received its water from the lower Thames, south of where London dumped its sewage. Through massive data gathering and analysis, the type of "empirical" research so suspect in 1832, Snow was able to discover and prove that the customers from the latter water company were at a much greater risk than the customers of the former.[20]

The 1849 epidemic marked a paradoxical time in medical history. On the one hand, as Snow's research suggests and Rosenberg states, "statistics were becoming the reality of science." On the other hand, data gathering and scientific analysis were starting to be practiced in Europe while they were still woefully inadequate in the United States. In 1849 U.S. doctors and journalists still had no notion of how cholera was transmitted. And as in 1832, the New York doctors did little but harm; some of their more creative "cures" ranged from tobacco smoke enemas to electric shocks and immersion in ice water.[21]

While U.S. doctors and journalists were no closer in 1849 to understanding and accurately reporting the disease or finding a cure, an inchoate yet palpable respect for data and scientific inquiry is apparent in the pages of the *Herald*. It is no surprise that Bennett's *Herald* was highly critical of the medical profession (his modus operandi was unrelenting attack of everyone and anyone), but it is interesting that the focus of his criticism reflects a concern for empiricism and science. The *Herald* angrily presented evidence that not "a single . . . physician or student of medicine had made his appearance at any of the cholera hospitals for the purpose of observing and investigating the disease," and criticized the doctors' "dislike of anything like attentive study of the disease."[22] Columns of statistics, with lists of everything from mortality rates to national origin and age of victims to a comparison of the 1832 and 1849 epidemics, appeared regularly in the newspaper. There were even charts analyzing the correlation between the virulence of the disease and the average outdoor temperature, from which the *Herald* concluded that the statistics did not support a causal relationship.[23] This attempt to conduct scientific inquiry also reflected the paper's impatience with doctors for not finding a cure and for their indelicate experimentation: "The cholera is a most terrible infliction; but bad doctors and bad drugs are worse," announced one editorial.[24] The *Herald*, it seems, was ahead of the doctors in its concern for scientific method and data gathering.

A Changed World, 1849–66

The mortality rate had not changed significantly from the 1832 cholera epidemic to that of 1849. But in 1866 the medical response was able to cut the rate by 90 percent.[25] Paralleling this shift were fundamental changes in the way journalists practiced their craft. What happened in the seventeen years between 1849 and 1866? Everything. Mitchell Stephens looked at the antebellum era and cited the "haze" that covered the world. People simply did not know as much of the world and its workings as their children and grandchildren would, Stephens argued. In many areas—medicine, art, photography, fiction, social science, and journalistic communication, to name a few—fundamental shifts were occurring, allowing news producers and consumers a different, and often better, vision of the world. In some ways, of course, the haze had been lifting for centuries, ever since the Enlightenment overtook the Dark Ages. Before the printing press, for example, it was practically impossible to build on the innovations of others. With printing came widespread dissemination of books, pamphlets, journals, and newspapers, allowing scholars to review each other's work, replicate it, and build on it. The whole notion of the "public sphere," the space in society in which ideas and politics are debated, developed over time, before the period covered in this book. But after acknowlegding the debt the nineteenth century owed to centuries past, we must still understand the massive changes wrought in the thin sliver of time between 1849 and 1866. In those seventeen years, the haze had lifted considerably.[26]

The haze was certainly lifting for most New Yorkers during the middle of the nineteenth century. Simple innovations such as gaslight had profound consequences for people, extending days and allowing the consumption of ever more knowledge.[27] The expansion of New York City north of Fourteenth Street facilitated another innovation, public transportation. For the first time in human history ordinary citizens could ride to work in vehicles driven by someone else. Without having to keep their eyes on the road, they could read a newspaper or a book.[28] Meanwhile, during this time the *Herald*, *Times*, and *Tribune* went from four pages to eight, were published every day, and increasingly contained timely news from around the nation and Europe. Circulation boomed. Running concurrent to this rise in information consumption was a rise in literacy, which reached 94 percent in the free states by 1860, and in school enrollment, which went from less than 50 percent of children in 1850 to 72 percent in 1860.[29] And if people seemed more sober and clearheaded at the close of this period, it was probably because they were; liquor consumption fell markedly after 1830.[30]

People during this period could be increasingly confident about their doctors and the scientific and medical professions in general. The two greatest innovations of nineteenth-century surgery were born in this time—anesthesia and antiseptics. Before 1846, when ether was first used as an anesthetic in surgery, one leading hospital reported fewer than forty operations a year. After the Civil War more than seven hundred operations were performed there annually.[31] Antiseptics and aseptics greatly reduced the risk of infection; by the 1870s they were becoming widely available.[32] Finally, the Civil War itself, the first war for which data were carefully kept and the first war to use general anesthesia on a grand scale, produced many medical (particularly surgical) innovations and practitioners.[33] In the thirty years after 1849 the number of medical schools in the United States doubled.[34]

Medical patients of the postwar era were also more fortunate than antebellum patients in that many of the improvements of the 1860s were built on the excesses of the 1840s and 1850s. One of the leading gynecological surgeons of the nineteenth century, J. Marion Sims, gained his expertise by reckless experimentation on slaves in the South and on poor Irish women in the North; some unfortunate patients underwent as many as thirty operations. By the end of the war Sims had perfected a number of surgical techniques and had become a respected surgeon, heading the American Medical Association for a time and making a fortune from his many paying patients.[35]

Religion

Religion was a filter through which the cholera epidemics of 1832 and 1849 were seen, but this filter was being replaced in the minds of many. According to one writer, religion had dominated the professions until about the end of the eighteenth century. At this point the influence of religion was replaced by a growing reverence for law, and then for science, medicine, and empiricism.[36] The shift included a sense that the world was knowable and nameable ("naive empiricism"), if only we roll up our sleeves and investigate it. The penny newspapers saw themselves as a part of this shift. "Books have had their day," proclaimed Bennett's *Herald*, "the temple of religion has had its day. A newspaper can be made to take the lead of all these in the great movements of human thought."[37]

Newspapers played a role in the secularizing of America. Increasingly the Sabbath was defiled by newspaper extras (one of the earliest examples was the *Courier and Enquirer*'s special cholera edition of 1832)[38] until, by the Civil War, many major newspapers were printed seven days a week. And the Sunday reading was generally not religious in nature. The content of newspapers was becoming, as we shall see, more and more secular and "factual." All the penny papers read in this study asserted their own nonpartisanship, factuality, and accuracy, while few routinely asserted specific religious beliefs. Newspapers such as the *National Police Gazette* prospered and grew during the second half of the nineteenth century, in large measure because of their hard-nosed, factual approach to crime and other secular topics.[39]

A tangible reminder that the secular, in the form of the newspaper business, was replacing the religious came in the form of the great newspaper buildings that came to dominate New York in the years immediately following the Civil War. Before the war, New York's skyline was dominated by church spires. The white marble Herald building was completed in 1868 and was grander and more imposing than most churches. A huge Tribune building, the tallest in the city, reached 260 feet above City Hall in 1875.[40] The aspirations of newspaper business, aided by the secular science of modern architecture, were now towering above the spires of God.

Americans at midcentury were part of a society that was finding God increasingly less relevant to its thinking, and were purchasing "reality" at an ever increasing pace. The "dynamo," wrote Henry Adams at the turn of the century, had replaced the "Virgin" as the central metaphor for power.[41] The taste of Americans, from every level of society, was bending toward the real in areas as diverse as photography, art, literature, the social sciences, and philosophy.

Photography, Art, Literature, and Reality

The middle of the nineteenth century saw not only the decline of the religious paradigm, but also the birth of "realism" as an artistic form. In 1839 Louis Daguerre discovered a way for images to be stored on metal plates. By 1850 Americans were spending as much as $12 million a year on photographs; indeed, it was difficult to find a family of means who had not sat for photographic portraits.[42] The public by this time was increasingly interested in the "true" representation of life, and photographs were quickly replacing painted portraits as the preferred method of capturing reality. If photography helped to bring an appreciation of "reality" to the United States, this was never more true than the photographic exhibitions of the Civil War, which, according to the *New York Times*, virtually "brought bodies and laid them in our door yards and along streets."[43] Newspapers, laying claim to photographic realism, offered a "daily daguerreotype" and promised to be the "historical photographer of national acts."[44]

The art of the post–Civil War period also asserted its claim to be "real." "Art . . . is now seeking to get nearer [to] the reality," wrote one New York artist.[45] Many of the postwar artists, like their confreres in literature, felt less comfortable with sentimental topics in the wake of the staggering carnage of the Civil War. "Reality" began to replace sentimental themes. In the 1870s the trompe l'oeil or illusionist painters began to create art that might be mistaken for real (see figure 14). The most successful artist of this genre, William H. Harnett, painted many works that deceived the public (some wide-eyed viewers would touch the canvas just to make sure),[46] including paintings that depicted palpable and "real" objects such as pipes, matches, and . . . newspapers.

The term "realism" is often used to describe the era born during and after the Civil War. As often as not, "realism" is used specifically as a label of the literature of the age. David Shi, in his book *Facing Facts: Realism in American Thought and Culture*, traces much of the postwar realism to Walt Whitman, whose poems celebrated the everyday reality of American life.[47] Whitman's poetic celebration of the real began in his 1855 edition of *Leaves of Grass*, in which he basically invents what we now call free verse. Whitman's poetry is the opposite of the anti-empirical stance of the 1832 papers: Whitman's time is spent watching and interpreting what he sees. "You shall no longer take things at second or third hand," Whitman promises, but through your own eyes. And Whitman's eyes ranged across nineteenth-century America, never looking away from "opium eaters, prostitutes, presidents," or "patriarchs."[48] If his promiscuous purview resembled that of a snoopy reporter, it may be because Whitman had served as a reporter and editor of the *Brooklyn Eagle*. "The true poem is the daily paper," wrote Whitman.[49]

Whitman was not the only literary realist to start as a journalist; in fact, many realists did. William Dean Howells, perhaps the writer and editor

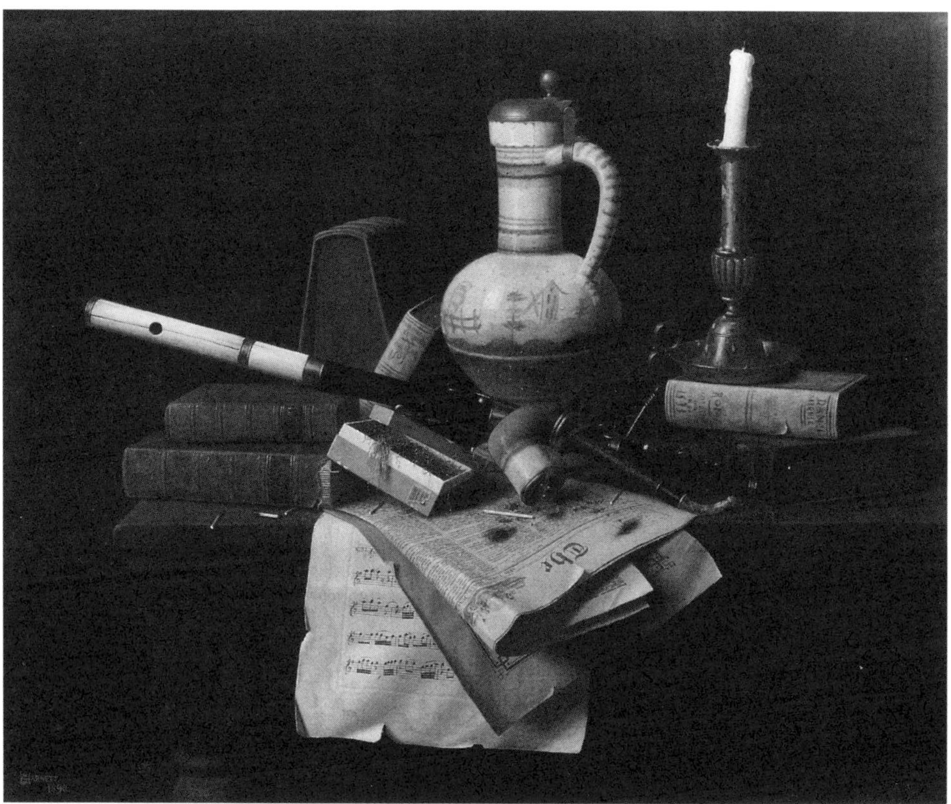

Figure 14. William M. Harnett, *Emblems of Peace*, 1890. Oil on canvas, 27½" high x 33¾" wide (Museum of Fine Arts, Springfield, Massachusetts. Gift of Charles T. and Emilie Shean). Reprinted by permission.

most associated with realism, started in a newsroom and called journalism "the school of reality." Mark Twain, Theodore Dreiser, and Stephen Crane also began as journalists.[50] Shi made the argument that the literature of realism can be traced in part to advertisers' claims that their products are real: "In a relentlessly commercial environment increasingly detached from spiritual priorities and the integrity of local markets," he wrote, "people craved the moorings of both product credibility and artistic veracity."[51] The claims of advertisers, as we have seen in chapters 1 and 2, were best supported by a seemingly "objective" news product, so here too we see a connection between the literature of "realism" and the journalism of "objectivity."

Darwin, Marx, and Spencer: The Social Sciences

During the middle of the nineteenth century a new secular, empirical, and scientific worldview was replacing religion and nonempirical philosophy in many areas of intellectual life. Darwin's *Origin of Species* was published during this time (1859), one of the most forceful arguments for a scientific worldview at the expense of religion to creep into popular consciousness. "When on board H. M. S. 'Beagle,' as naturalist," Darwin wrote in his introduction to *The Origin of Species*, "I was much struck with certain facts. . . . These facts . . . seemed to throw some light on the origin of species."[52] A reviewer in the *New York Times*, while skeptical, acknowledged that Darwin's "undeniable facts" would develop our understanding of the mutability of the species.[53]

Karl Marx was another key figure in the intellectual history of the mid-century. Although one journalism historian points out that Marx saw "objectivity" as serving the elite, Marx, through his writing, also helped the cause of empiricism and scientific analysis, both important to journalistic "objectivity." A champion of the secular for reasons more complicated than the famous line about religion being an opiate, Marx sought a philosophy grounded not on religion or abstractions, but on a careful, scientific analysis of social conditions. Marx argued that philosophy was successful only when used as a tool to solve real problems, and he himself applied a scientific approach to society. An examination of Marx's preface to *Capital* reveals his concern for "scientific" analysis and shows how he viewed himself as a scientist. Marx's scientific analysis of European society and politics reached American news consumers through the hundreds of articles and editorials he wrote during ten years (1852–62) that he was employed by Horace Greeley as a European correspondent for the *New York Tribune*.[54]

Herbert Spencer, whose theories of evolution complement (and in some cases predate) Darwin's, and who shared Marx's concern for social causes, wrote a mammoth ten-volume series, *Synthetic Philosophy* (1860–93), which tries to bring biology, psychology, philosophy, and sociology under a single umbrella. His first volume, *First Principles* (1860), which laid the groundwork for the nine volumes that followed, argued that much of the world *is* knowable and nameable, and that the various fields help us understand the world, at least the "laws of the highest certainty." His attempt to draw sociology into the sciences, *Principles of Sociology*, did much to shape that profession; U.S. journalists, too, took notice, and Spencer's work was discussed in newspapers and serialized in *Popular Science Monthly* (1874).[55]

Many fields of study, increasingly called the "social sciences," felt the pressure to be factual and scientific. One scientist, Simon Newcomb, was influenced by Darwin, Spencer, and John Stuart Mill, whose *System of Logic* (1843) was a call for philosophical empiricism. Newcomb preached the doctrine of "scientific method" to all who would listen, and the social sciences embraced scientific method, logical positivism, and "objectivity" in the years that followed.[56] Similarly Baconism, the belief that reality could be understood through the "collection, classification, and interpretation of facts," came to dominate the professions of sociology, political science, and economics; by the 1880s economics had become a "hard science," converted from antebellum notions of "political economy," with its "moral philosophy" and religious underpinnings.[57] By the 1880s "objectivity" was quickly becoming the "central norm" of the historical profession.[58] These changes in the social sciences paralleled the rise of "objective" notions in journalism: empiricism, data gathering, and scientific method.

The Telegraph and the Size of the World

Of all the scientific innovations of the nineteenth century, the telegraph was one of the most startling. The telegraph's impact on both science and journalism was profound. On May 1, 1844, a crowd gathered on a Washington, DC railroad platform to hear the latest news from nearby Baltimore, where the Whigs were meeting to nominate a presidential ticket. Long before the train arrived, Samuel F. B. Morse stepped onto the platform and announced to the incredulous crowd that a man at the Baltimore train station had "telegraphed" the Whigs' choice to him: "the ticket is Clay and Frelinghuysen," announced Morse.[59] "Who the devil is Frelinghuysen?" asked a spectator, who reasoned that if the news was confirmed, then the obscurity of the second name would prove that Morse's announcement wasn't a lucky guess. When the train finally arrived the news was confirmed, and so was the new invention, the Magnetic Telegraph.[60]

It is important to remember how much smaller the nation and the world became during the nineteenth century. The timeliness of news increased markedly. In 1817 John Calhoun, while contemplating the prospect of national "disunion," wrote, "Let us then bind the Republic together with a perfect system of roads and canals. . . . Let us conquer space."[61] At that time it took about a week for news from the capital to reach Boston. By the 1840s the roads, canals, and railroads greatly increased the speed of news to about two or three days.[62] But by 1846 the telegraph had cut the time to seconds. For the first time in human history, news could travel faster than its human carriers.[63] The notion of time itself was altered by the telegraph. Before the Civil War each city had its own "local time"; Boston and New York time, for example, differed by about twelve minutes. On the morning of November 18, 1883, called the "day of two noons," the nation adjusted to standard time, aided by time messages sent across telegraph lines. The rest of the world followed suit with the creation of time zones in the years ahead.[64]

The telegraph helped journalists and news consumers put a lasso around the believable world. Before the telegraph, outrageous stories and hoaxes were regular newspaper fare. In 1835, for example, the *New York Sun* ran its "moon hoax" about an astronomer whose giant telescope had explored the crevices of the moon. The story, which cited a fictitious scientific journal, the *Edinburgh Journal of Science*, reported on discoveries of mountains, forests, and—after days of building up to it—animals and "man-bats." The story was reprinted in the columns of the *Sun*'s rivals and was widely believed. A delegation from Yale was quickly dispatched to New York to investigate the reports.[65]

In 1835 a story about "man-bats" on the moon could still rouse a group of Ivy League scientists from their perch in New Haven; confirmation would take more than a month while ships carried letters to and from London.[66] But by 1866, with the birth of the transatlantic cable, the moon story's sources could have been checked, and in a matter of hours the astronomer's name and that of the journal would have proven to be false. The telegraph extended what one historian has called the "awareness of the impossible."[67] With the birth of the telegraph the world became smaller and the stories of monsters became increasingly less frequent. Nowadays "man-bats" and other monsters cannot be found in the "objective" news sources; to find monsters, one must turn to pages of certain supermarket tabloids.[68]

"What has become of space?" asked the *New York Herald* in 1844, the telegraph's first year. Providing its own answer, the paper announced that space had been "annihilated."[69] In 1844 the annihilation of space meant mainly a quicker reporting of events. In the years that followed, however, space was annihilated by what a number of critics refer to as the commodification of news by the telegraph and the press wire services. With the founding of the Associated Press in 1848, Wolff in 1855, and Reuter in 1858, a number of companies sought to market news as a salable commodity. James Carey wrote that telegraphic news demanded a " 'scientific' language," stripping news of "the local, the regional and colloquial."[70] Other studies confirm this, and while (as we have seen in the last chapter) the inverted pyramid form was not standard until the end of the century, researchers have discovered a decline of "bias" in news after 1872, especially in news sent over the wires.[71] In the middle part of the century, in order to sell to newspapers of different political positions—the elite Republican *New York Times*, the pro-South *Herald*, and the eccentric and socialistic *Tribune*, to name a few—the wire services had to repress partisan signals and seek to produce a commodity that would be palatable to all.[72]

By the late spring of 1866 (the time of the next major cholera epidemic in New York), the wire services and newspapers had stripped out of much of their partisan and local clothing, as Lawrence Gobright, the Washington agent for the Associated Press, explained:

> My business is merely to communicate facts. My instructions do not allow me to make any comments upon the facts which I communicate. My despatches are sent to papers of all manner of politics, and the editors say they are able to make their own comments upon the facts which are sent to them. . . . I do not act as politician belonging to any school, but try to be truthful and impartial. My despatches are merely dry matters of fact and detail.[73]

Gobright's "dry" and bland gruel, without the spice and piquancy of partisan criticism and local dialect, had helped to produce a unified journalistic voice, a scientific voice, and a faith that reporters could actually write to *everyone* and be understood by all. While science was triumphing over philosophy and religion, the newspapers and wire services were asserting a victory over partisanship and regionalism.

1866 and the Last Cholera Epidemic

In the weeks before the cholera epidemic of 1866, it was becoming apparent that New Yorkers would not place their faith in fasting, prayer, or vague notions of heavenly atmosphere; nor would they abide talk of speculative "cures" and "philosophical" and anti-empirical ideas of contagion.

Instead, the city mobilized an efficient bureaucratic machine with an aim to muscle out the disease with science and technology. The Metropolitan Board of Health organized its bureaucracy into distinct units: the Bureau of Vital Statistics, the Bureau of Complaints, with its Sanitary Superintendent and his Sanitary Inspectors, and a sophisticated hospital administration: each hospital district would be run by a Physician-in-Chief, who was required to make daily visits to his hospitals. There, Resident Physicians would keep an "accurate medical history," including "name, age, sex, nativity, occupation, residence, symptoms, and treatment."[74] "During the coming Summer," announced the *Times* in the late spring, "the City is, for all practical purposes, to be governed by the 'Board of Health.' "[75]

The rule of the Metropolitan Board of Health was an active one, and it reflected a faith in data gathering and a desire to take rapid and forceful measures based on pragmatic and empirical notions. The Code of Health Ordinances, passed in May 1866, required that all diseases be reported to the Board's Bureau of Records within twenty-four hours.[76] The Registrar of Vital Statistics would then put out statistics and corresponding charts, including the New York Mortality Table, breaking down all diseases by deaths per week and ward, comparisons with cholera epidemics in previous years and with epidemics in other countries, and the sex, nativity, and age of the victims. The table, "The Sanitary Police Report" (below), reveals both the extent of data gathering and the zeal of the "Sanitary Police" in their attempts to rid the city of sanitary "nuisances"[77]:

THE SANITARY POLICE REPORT.

Capt. Bowen G. Lord's report of the work of the Police Sanitary Company, for the week ending June 19, is as follows:

No. of complaints of nuisances received . . . : 536

No. of notices served for abatement . . . : 952

No. of sinks water-closets cleaned . . . : 437

Removed from City Limits

No. of Loads of night soil . . . : 1,796

Number of dead horses, cows, goats, hogs, dogs, and cats and calves seized . . . : 151

Number of barrels of offal—6,000.

Mentions of "atmosphere" could not be found in the reports of the Sanitary Police. They may well have been too busy carting away the dead horses and cleaning outhouses to worry about the weather.

If the organizing principle of the 1832 and 1849 newspapers' coverage of cholera was God and sin, that of 1866 was much less lofty. So much so, in fact, that it would not be too much to say that during that time, the newspapers' chief concern shifted from God to outhouses. Column after column in the three major New York dailies discussed, usually without the least mention of sin or God, the best ways to disinfect privies.[78] The *Times* reported that all doctors now agree that "the excreta, and especially the rice-water discharges of cholera patients are at least one means of propagating the cholera-poison and they urge . . . disinfection . . . of all privies, water-closets, and cess-pools connected with the sick."[79] A full majority of all news stories researched for this chapter had at least a mention of excreta. In a report on a woman's death, the *Herald* mentioned that she had just emptied all the water closets of her house and used the contents to fertilize her garden.[80] In the *Tribune* came a report of the worst centers of cholera in the city; the story described the "foul effluvia of . . . overflowing privies" and the fact that most outhouses in the district were not connected to sewers.[81] What more fitting way is there to enter the age of "realism" than with a replacement of God with the "foul effluvia of . . . overflowing privies"?

Rosenberg, in *The Cholera Years*, explained that "philosophical" arguments in medical journals gave way to ones based on "statistics and disciplined observation."[82] This can be said of the newspapers as well, which resembled medical journals in their scientific language. In an article in the *Tribune*, a writer describes the "pathognemonic [*sic*] characteristics of the disease": "Violent purging and vomiting, rice-water dejections, cold tongue, muscular cramps, and collapse,"[83] a description based on empirical evidence more than on religious notions. Similarly detailed and scientific were the descriptions of how to disinfect privies and clothing, with exact measurements of disinfecting agents provided for readers.

Given the level of detail about cause, contagion, and disinfecting procedures, it is surprising that there are few mentions of cures in the newspaper articles read for this study. One explanation of this may be that as doctors became truly members of a profession, and as hospitals became less charnel houses and more places for systematic care,[84] the business of curing became increasingly less a matter of public concern and consideration.

Gone in 1866 were the attacks on doctors seen in newspapers in past epidemics. In fact, the information that newspapers reported to the public came increasingly from doctors serving as designated sources of authority. While reporters did not have to operate under restrictions as severe as those imposed by Stanton, they did get much of their news from organized and tightly controlled sources. "The records in the office of the Registrar of

Vital Statistics show . . . ." began one report in the *Times*.[85] From this source, the Metropolitan Board of Health, the Bureau of Complaints, and the Physicians-in-Chief, the papers seemed to get most of their material. As it did during the Civil War, the telegraph played a major role in the dissemination of information in the summer of 1866. The Atlantic cable, completed at the height of the 1866 epidemic, brought cholera news from Europe, while in New York the cholera cases were reported to police precincts and then telegraphed to the Sanitary Superintendent, who in turn dispatched his Inspectors.[86] News reports of cholera were telegraphed from city to city and overseas as well.

Many of the shifts described in this chapter can be found in a single paragraph, a lead of a fine inverted pyramid article in the *New York Tribune*:

> The officers of the Board of Health, yesterday, took charge of the premises No. 14 Cherry St., thoroughly disinfected them and burned that portion of the clothing of the deceased, John Fitzgerald, which had been soiled by dejections during his illness.[87]

The article conveys the organization of the medical community, an understanding of how cholera is conveyed, and a concern not with religious issues, but with empirical investigation and concrete action to stop the spread of the disease.

Just as the transportation revolution coincided with the spread of journalism and cholera in New York in 1832, the epidemic of 1866 saw another confluence of forces: the first successful transatlantic cable and New York's last major cholera epidemic. The ascendancy of science and the growing understanding that empiricism was possible and profitable facilitated both developments. Once again, New York was frightened by the ships filled with cholera-stricken Europeans. But in 1866 doctors and journalists knew what to do, and the 90 percent decrease in mortality from 1849 to 1866 shows that the world had changed, in the journalism of the day, in the sciences, and in the culture in general. From 1832 to 1866 journalism and the wider culture had moved from a religious and philosophical paradigm to one of "naive empiricism" and scientific method. More and more people, including journalists, had moved their gaze from the heavens to the privies; and more and more had left the Virgin to view the dynamo.

The "objective" paradigm had advanced significantly.

5

Balance

A "Slanderous and Nasty-Minded Mulattress," Ida B. Wells, Confronts "Objectivity" in the 1890s

[Objective news] is the highest original moral concept ever developed in America and given to the world.

—Kent Cooper, AP General Manager

Objective journalism is a contradiction in terms.

—Hunter Thompson

Each chapter of this study covered an aspect of "objectivity": detachment, nonpartisanship, the inverted pyramid writing style, and a reverence for facts and empiricism all evolved over the course of the nineteenth century. By the 1890s, the period of this final chapter, all the elements covered so far came together; journalists and journalism were what the profession calls "objective." Through an examination of the mainstream newspapers' coverage of lynching[1] and a critique of this coverage by Ida B. Wells, an antilynching crusader, this chapter reveals a fascinating historical moment in which racism and "objectivity" meet and clash; in so doing, the chapter examines the concept of "objectivity," its construction, and how it can be compromised by racism and other factors. Even after the profession became "objective" it could not present a clear picture of lynching. In fact, "objectivity" helped to obscure an important piece of reality, the perceptions of Ida B. Wells and other African Americans.

"Objectivity" Comes of Age

In the 1890s "objectivity" became codified as the great law of journalism. Most historians of journalism agree that fin de siècle newspapers were less partisan, less "biased," more "independent," and more "objective" than their antebellum counterparts. By 1880 directories listed a fourth of all U.S. newspapers as politically "independent"; by 1890 a full third would be classified as such.[2] And nearly all the major newspapers of the major cities, especially those of the Northeast, regularly asserted their political independence. According to Willard G. Bleyer, an early twentieth-century press historian, antebellum "views-papers" were replaced by "news-papers."[3]

According to two researchers, Harlan Stensaas and Donald Shaw, "objectivity" rose while "bias" declined in the last quarter of the nineteenth century. In the decade after the Civil War only 40 percent of all surveyed stories were "objective," wrote Stensaas;[4] by the start of the new century "objective" stories comprised two-thirds of the total. With the rise of "objectivity," Stensaas argues, came a concomitant rise in the use of authoritative sources and the inverted pyramid form.[5] Shaw found a decline in "bias" after 1872 and suggested that the decline was due in part to the rise of the telegraph and news wire services.[6] My own research supports these claims. The personal, partisan, chronological, and religion-based articles of the early part of the century, as I have shown, were giving way to articles that contained the characteristics of "objectivity."

By the 1890s news and "editorial" had become two distinct forms of writing, and news writing was clearly dominant. Charles Dana, for example, used his editorials to smear President Grant in the 1870s, but instructed his news editors at the *Sun* to be strictly nonpartisan in their political coverage. The political voice of newspaper reporting was clearly on the wane, and by the late 1880s one editor who had begun his career with a strong political voice, Joseph Pulitzer, was even experimenting with doing away with editorials completely.[7]

The 1890s is a good place to end a history of "objectivity" because it is one of the first decades when "objectivity" was a recognized ethic in journalism, but also one of the last in which "objectivity" goes basically unquestioned. Michael Schudson addressed a number of factors, such as the First World War and the rise of public relations firms, that pushed journalists to question the idea of "objectivity" in the first half of the twentieth century.[8] In the 1890s consciousness and clearheadedness had not yet been complicated by Freud, observation had not yet been problematized by

Einstein, and perspective had not been challenged by Picasso, as they all would be in the first years of the twentieth century. The first journalism textbook to challenge "objectivity," with its pointed title, *Interpretative Reporting*, would not be written until 1938.[9] Although the "and that's the way it is" belief in "objectivity" still exists among many journalists, it may well have peaked as an ideal in the 1890s. The 1890s, therefore, can be described without much simplification as the first and last time that the ethic of "objectivity" existed in a laboratory-pure environment.

The Profession

The "objective" ethic that emerged in the last part of the nineteenth century paralleled a rising sense of journalism as a profession. Before the Civil War there were no professional societies, college programs, or textbooks for journalists in the United States.[10] This began to change after the Civil War, so much so that journalism quickly began to consider itself a profession. Recent scholarship suggests that American journalists thought of themselves as professionals as early as 1876, when the Missouri Press Association was formed, complete with its own code of ethics. The minutes of the meetings include numerous references to journalism as a profession, as well as comparisons of journalism with other professions such as medicine and law.[11]

Being a professional, of course, implies that others are "unprofessional." A number of journalists saw professionalization as an efficacious means to uplift journalists and keep out "unprofessionals." Whitelaw Reid, a leading journalist-turned-politician, declared in 1913, "we may hope for some of the sanctions of a profession. The age of Bohemia is gone."[12] Joseph Pulitzer waxed Darwinian in his plans to create his journalism school at Columbia: "I sincerely hope it will create a class distinction between the fit and the unfit," he wrote.[13]

Pulitzer's plans to create a school for journalists reflected his views about profession and class. Sounding almost Bennett-like in his optimism, he wrote, "I wish to begin a movement that will raise journalism to the rank of a learned profession"; he looked to journalism schools to create a "class feeling among journalists—one based not upon money, but upon morals, education, and character." As Pulitzer was calling for journalists to be less concerned with money, he may have been recalling the day in January 1896 when William Randolph Hearst hired away Pulitzer's entire Sunday staff, which included R. F. Outcault, the creator of the "Yellow Kid" cartoons from which "yellow journalism" got its name. At the end of a two-day wage battle, Hearst had bought the entire Sunday staff; only a secretary remained with Pulitzer. A little more "character" (read loyalty) and less concern for Hearst's astoundingly high wages might have saved some of Pulitzer's celebrated staff.[14]

Pulitzer's ideal of journalist-as-loyal-worker has a parallel in journalism education. Charles Ross, in a 1911 textbook, encouraged reporters to "keep yourself out of the story," and to observe this as the central "compact" with the publisher.[15] The act of taking oneself "out" of stories begs the question: what is left in? What remains? The answer is that "objectivity" remains, and the workers' voices are muted. According to James Carey, journalists during this period underwent a "conversion downwards" from "independent interpreters of events" to "brokers in symbols who mediated between audiences and institutions."[16]

Pulitzer's unprecedented multimillion-dollar endowment in 1903 to Columbia to found a journalism school was the best-known attempt to get academia to help professionalize journalism, but it was not the first.[17] In 1874 Cornell offered a "certificate of journalism," and in 1893 the University of Pennsylvania offered a full degree program.[18] During this time Edwin Shuman's *Steps into Journalism* (1894), probably the first comprehensive journalism textbook, was published as an "aid to students in certain collegiate courses and in schools of journalism."[19]

Shuman's 1894 textbook reflected many of the changes in journalism from the antebellum era. First, its concern with and support for formal education represented a departure from the old school of thought, exemplified by the belief of the *Herald* editor and newspaper historian Frederic Hudson that the newspaper office "is the true college for newspaper students. . . . Professor James Gordon Bennett or Professor Horace Greeley would turn out more real genuine journalists . . . than the Harvards, the Yales, and the Dartmouths could produce in a generation."[20] The book also shows how far newspaper establishments had come since the days of Bennett's one-man show in the basement of a run-down walk-up. The newspapers described in Shuman's book were great monuments to modern business. Shuman describes the various positions in the newspaper establishment: the copy editors, the book reviewers, the exchange editor, the sports editor. Journalists had become cogs in a great journalistic machine.

The greatest journalistic change reflected in Shuman's textbook is the ubiquitous style of writing called the inverted pyramid, which was employed by the wire services and by every major newspaper. Shuman mentions the inverted pyramid by name, probably the first textbook writer to do so. He explains, "the inverted pyramid . . . [is] the trick of serving the dessert first and the soup last." Shuman discussed the "five W" lead, a component of the inverted pyramid, as the "first and greatest commandment" of journalism.[21] The inverted pyramid style was already widely practiced in newsrooms across the country before Shuman's book was published. Editors told cub reporters that their leads should contain "Who or what? How? When? Where?"[22]

Dates of Principal Events Discussed in This Chapter

1877	**End of Reconstruction**
1883	**U.S. Supreme Court overturns the 1875 Civil Rights Act**
1889–94	**More than a thousand African Americans are lynched in the United States**
March 1892	**Moss and others are lynched in Memphis**
1893	**Chicago's Columbian Exposition**
1894	**Edwin Shuman's *Steps into Journalism***
	For the first time, Ida B. Wells is noticed by the *New York Times*
1896	**Supreme Court decision of *Plessy v. Ferguson* codifies "separate but equal"**

The Inverted Pyramid and the Coverage of Lynching

The inverted pyramid was not standard by the Civil War, but it was by the 1890s. This contention is supported by researchers and can be confirmed by a perusal of almost any major U.S. daily.[23] An 1898 story in the *Herald*, "Mob Murders a Negro Official," was a classic nineteenth-century inverted pyramid, which differed from the modern kind only because of its inclusion of specific details in the first paragraph. It began,

> Charleston, S.C., Tuesday. In Lake City, a town of five hundred inhabitants, sixty miles north of here, an angry mob of from three to five hundred men lynched Frazer B. Baker, the negro Postmaster, his three-year-old daughter Dora, early this morning, and wounded Baker's wife, two grown daughters and a ten-year-old son.[24]

Reading about lynching through articles written in an inverted pyramid, "objective" form is a queer and unpleasant experience: there was no outrage. The first reason there was no outrage is that the ethic of "objectivity," which tried to offend no one, discouraged writers from expressing "views." The second reason is that many whites, even in the North, even in newspaper offices, were not entirely antilynching, as these pages will show. In fact, when emotion was displayed in articles about lynching, it was generally outrage over the alleged crimes of the African Americans who were lynched.

Whites lynched African Americans by hanging them, shooting them, mutilating them, roasting them alive, and employing various other means of torture and death in each of the sixty-seven years between 1880 and 1947. During that time more than four thousand African American men, women, and children were lynched.[25] The practice peaked during the years of this chapter; more than a thousand African Americans were lynched from 1889 to 1894.[26] To gage the dimensions of lynching, consider the following: in the worst year, 1892, there were twice as many lynchings of blacks as there were legal executions of all races throughout the United States.[27] Many of the lynchings were covered by the leading white papers of the North, affording a rich opportunity for historians to examine the prisms through which newspapers saw "racial groups" and "race" violence. Through this examination, I will discuss the limitations of the ethic of "objectivity."

An 1892 article in the *New York Times*, "Negroes Lynched by a Mob," is a textbook inverted pyramid. It begins,

> Memphis, Tenn., March 9.—At dawn this morning the dead bodies of three negroes riddled with bullets and partly covered with brush were found in a lot about one and a half miles from the heart of the city. . . .
>
> The negroes, whose bodies were literally shot to pieces by this mob, were Calvin McDowell, William Stuart, and Theodore Moss.[28]

The Theodore Moss of the *Times*' story was actually Thomas Moss, a friend, as it turned out, of the newspaper editor Ida B. Wells; that fact put Wells in the position shared by anyone who has witnessed an event and read about it later: the position to see that the reporting of an event is often filtered by misperception and prejudice. Her position would allow Wells to change perceptions about lynching and to critique the mainstream press coverage of it. Her criticism of the white media will serve as a foundation for our discussion.

Wells, arguably one of the more heroic figures in American history, was born a slave in 1862. Orphaned in a yellow fever epidemic at fourteen, she had to begin work as a schoolteacher to support her five siblings. One day, at age twenty-two, Wells was riding the "ladies coach" of a train in Tennessee and was asked by a conductor to move to the smoking car, where the African Americans rode. She refused, and the conductor tried to remove her. Wells "fastened [her] teeth in the back of his hand" before she was dragged out by three trainmen. She independently sued the railroad and won a major (albeit temporary) blow against the growing list of Jim Crow laws. The case attracted much attention, and Wells found herself on the front page of papers across the South. The *Memphis Daily Appeal* announced, "A Darky Damsel Obtains a Verdict for Damages against the Chesapeake & Ohio Railroad."[29] Wells began to write articles, becoming a correspondent and then editor of the African American weekly the *Memphis Free Speech*. Wells's campaign to boost circulation of the *Free Speech* tripled its readership, and at age twenty-seven she became a part owner of the newspaper. Through Wells's efforts, the *Free Speech* became one of the leading African American newspapers in the South.[30]

The article in the *New York Times* about the lynching of Moss and his associates reflected racial stereotypes about whites and blacks, notably about bravery. The whites who lynched Moss, McDowell, and Stuart made a "quick and quiet march" to the county jail, where they searched for the "thoroughly alarmed" blacks. By both the *Times*' and Wells's account, Moss made a quick plea for blacks to leave the state, to go west. "If you are going to kill us turn our faces to the west," he was quoted as saying. But in the following sentence, the writer of the article reverted back to the stereotype of the weak black, describing how the whites had killed the "shivering negroes."[31] According to the *Times*' account, Moss and his associates were lynched because of their "ambushing and shooting down" of four "Deputy Sheriffs," who were "searching" for an outlaw.

The legality of the whites' position, among other things, was questioned by Wells in her next issue of *Free Speech*. Moss and his colleagues, wrote Wells, were simply businessmen who had opened a shop, the People's Grocery Company, that competed with a white-owned store in a predominantly black area. Whites began to harass the store, and planned to attack it on a Saturday night. When whites gathered in the back of the store and fired into it, the blacks in the store returned fire and wounded at least three men, the men the *Times* called "Deputy Sheriffs." More than a hundred African American men were arrested, and Moss, McDowell, and Stuart were taken from their jail cells and lynched. Following the lynching, the mob looted the People's Grocery Company and, according to Wells, "destroyed what they could not eat or steal."[32] The African American residents of Memphis were sufficiently horrified by the brutality of the lynching—Memphis had had relatively few lynchings for a Southern city—that hundreds of residents simply packed up and left town.[33]

Because Wells felt that the *New York Times* was wrong on so many points—Moss and his associates were not cowards, were not lawless, were not aggressors, were not outlaws, and were simply the victims of ruthless (not law-abiding) whites who feared economic competition—she suddenly came to realize that many aspects of lynching may have been misunderstood. For example, Wells herself had accepted as true that the "lawlessness" of blacks contributed to lynching, specifically that black men were lynched because they raped white women. In Wells's words,

> Thomas Moss, Calvin McDowell, and Lee Stewart had been lynched . . . with just as much brutality as other victims of the mob; and they had committed no crime against white women. This is what opened my eyes to what lynching really was. An excuse to get rid of Negroes who were acquiring wealth and property and thus keep the race terrorized and "keep the nigger down."[34]

After Moss's death Wells began to investigate lynchings across the South. She found a number of surprises. First, she discovered that despite the belief that most lynchings were a response to blacks raping whites, the fact was that rape was not even the stated cause in most cases. Second, she discovered that black victims were often charged with rape only *after* the lynchings became public. Third, through an investigation of specific cases, Wells learned that charges of "rape" were often cases involving a black man and a white woman caught in a consensual relationship. Wells wrote in an editorial, "Nobody in this section believes the old thread-bare lie that Negro men assault white women. If Southern white men are not careful they will over-reach themselves and a conclusion will be reached which will be very damaging to the moral reputation of their women."[35]

Wells had, to put it mildly, struck a nerve. We know this because of the

Figure 15. "Little Myrtle Vance Avenged," 1 February 1893. An African American accused of killing a child is lynched by slow burning in Paris, Texas, as hundreds look on (Library of Congress).

vehemence of the response to the editorial. The *Memphis Commercial Appeal*, thinking that the unsigned editorial was written by a man, suggested castration and lynching: "The black wretch who had written that foul lie should be tied to a stake . . . a pair of tailor's shears used on him and he should then be burned at a stake."[36] That week in Memphis, Wells joined history's long list of journalists attacked for their views. The *Free Speech* was quieted, its office and type destroyed, and its editors, including Wells, were chased out of town.

The "Threadbare Lie," Information, and Lynching

The "threadbare lie" as Wells called it, the belief that black men were lynched because they raped white women, was believed by practically everyone. The lynching of Moss and his associates was covered by most of the major newspapers in the North. It is very likely that Frederick Douglass, now in his last years of life, read about the case closely and was dismayed over the black "crimes." Douglass told Wells that until he read her evidence to the contrary, he too was troubled by "lasciviousness on the part of Negroes."[37] If Douglass, an untiring supporter of African American causes, could believe the "threadbare lie," then surely most everyone did as well. This impression, that blacks were culpable, was conveyed by the journalism of the elite newspapers.

By the 1890s the *New York Times* had embraced what Michael Schudson has called the "information" model of journalism, a reliance on "information" as opposed to the "story" model of Hearst's and Pulitzer's papers.[38] The coverage of lynching in the *Times* was generally written in a "balanced" way, with two opposing views presented. But how does one balance a story about lynching? The *Times* explained how in an 1894 editorial. On the one hand, the *Times* wrote, people who take the law into their own hands are savages. On the other hand, "the crime for which negroes have frequently been lynched [rape], and occasionally been put to death with frightful tortures, is a crime to which negroes are particularly prone." The solution, according to the *Times*, which could on one hand end lynching, and on the other satisfy the lynchers, would be "to make it again a capital offense, and to see that judicial processes are not so much slower and less exemplary than mob law as they are now." In other words, the solution would be for the government to hang blacks legally and nearly as quickly as the mobs did.[39] These views on lynching, recorded in the editorial pages of the *Times* in 1892, remained even beyond 1896, when Adolph Ochs bought the newspaper. Ochs, who in his inaugural editorial promised "no radical changes," evidently did not replace the writer who wrote that African Americans were "particularly prone to rape": this same phrase appeared again in an 1897 editorial.[40] Throughout the mid-1890s, even after Ochs took over, the *New York Times* remained strikingly consistent in its news and editorial policy toward lynching.

The above editorials reflected how the *Times* covered lynchings in the 1890s. On one typical day in 1892, the *Times* reported four cases of lynching. In each case, the guilt of the victims was assumed: "New-Orleans, La., July 6—Smith Tooley and John L. Adams . . . were hanged last night . . . in the Court House Yard. . . . Their crime was the murder of Mr. Benson Blake . . . last Thursday"; "Jasper, Ala., July 6—A negro was lynched here yesterday. He attempted to assault two white women"; "Weston, West Va., July 6— . . . Edgar Jones, the young negro who murdered Michael Tierney . . . was hanged by a mob"; "Richmond, Va., July 6—William

Anderson, colored, was taken from the jail . . . and lynched. He was awaiting trial for an attempt to assault Miss Shelburn, a white girl about fourteen years of age."[41] The four stories share at least three characteristics. First, each mentions that the victims were accused but not convicted of a crime. Second, the articles assume the guilt of the victims anyway: "Their crime was . . . ," and the other statements of guilt are regurgitations of the lynchers' claims, another practice that continued after Ochs bought the *Times*.[42] Today we would use terms like "alleged" or "accused," but the *Times* showed no such skepticism. Finally, the articles share an "objective" and "balanced" tone. A reporter conveys both the lynching and the charges against the accused.[43]

The ethic of "objectivity" demands that reporters take themselves out of the story, and nowhere in my research for this chapter did I find the reporter's view explicitly written ("I believe that x is guilty"). Occasionally a *Times* reporter would express outrage. But most stories were told matter-of-factly. On one hand, someone was accused of a crime; on the other hand, someone was lynched. But black guilt was assumed in nearly every story.[44] One reporter wrote, "A very young white girl was criminally assaulted by a negro . . . last week. The people rose en masse to lynch the brute." Later in the story we are told that a suspect was found, and despite the "girl's" statement that the suspect was not the right man, the angry mob of five hundred lynched him anyway. "Somebody has to die," a mob member shouted before they hanged him and mutilated his body. The *New York Times* reporter was horrified by the "angry, irrational, bloodthirsty" mob, but the horror was in response to killing the *wrong* person, not to the act of lynching in general.[45]

Wells's technique for responding to the mainstream coverage of lynching was to research the facts surrounding each lynching case. An Associated Press report on an 1892 lynching explains, "The big burly brute was lynched because he had raped the seven-year-old daughter of the sheriff." Wells visited the scene and discovered that facts were left out, including that the "girl" was a grown woman, that the lynched man was a worker on the sheriff's farm, and that the two were found in the black man's cabin.[46] Time after time Wells found that innocent blacks were lynched.

Operating under the belief that most lynching victims were criminals, the *New York Times* and other newspapers sought a common ground or balance between what they saw as the legitimate complaints about blacks and the need to quell mobs, as the following lead sentence in an editorial indicates: "The people of the South are doing themselves . . . a grievous

Figure 16. Ida B. Wells, 1880s (Library of Congress).

injury in so far as they give countenance to lynch law in dealing with negro criminals, however atrocious may be the crimes perpetrated by them."[47] Where the *New York Times* saw the lynching issue as a delicate balancing act, Wells saw murderous whites attacking innocent blacks.

We now know that Wells was right. History is, by its nature, a slippery business, but it is hard to imagine a "balanced" view on lynching based on what modern scholars now know. To deny this would be to slip into historical relativism. Modern scholarship supports all of Wells's major contentions.[48]

Historical Factors, Corroborating Scholarship

The lynchings during the 1889–94 period came at an especially difficult time for African Americans, particularly in the political arena. By 1889 the political and legal strides of 1864–70—the Thirteenth Amendment (ending slavery), the Fourteenth Amendment (granting blacks full citizenship), and the Fifteenth Amendment and Enforcement Act (granting and enforcing suffrage)—were under attack and in some cases overturned. In 1872 the Freedmen's Bureau, which despite some mismanagement had ameliorated the conditions of ex-slaves, was abandoned. In 1875 the Enforcement Act and the Fifteenth Amendment were virtually nullified by a series of Supreme Court decisions. In the 1876 presidential election, Democrats vowed to end Reconstruction altogether. When the election became deadlocked, Rutherford B. Hayes, the Republican presidential candidate, cut a deal to gain the presidency, a deal that included the removal of federal troops in 1877. The year 1877, therefore, is widely cited by historians as the end point of Reconstruction. After the Supreme Court in 1883 overturned the 1875 Civil Rights Act, most Southern states developed separate and unequal systems of schooling, transportation, and various other services. Although the 1896 Supreme Court decision of *Plessy v. Ferguson* is popularly seen as instituting the "separate but equal" doctrine, it merely codified existing practice.[49]

The year 1889 marked the start of what historian Joel Williamson called a "hot time" in the history of American race relations, during which white violence was just one of many tools to effect the total subjugation of blacks.[50] The five-year period beginning in 1889 was troubled perhaps most especially by an economic depression throughout the United States, which was most severe in the South.[51] This led to the emergence of an organized and increasingly radicalized labor force during this period. In 1886 the American Federation of Labor put out a call for a general strike to push for an eight-hour day, and 350,000 workers across the country boycotted their jobs; days later the violent Haymarket Riots in Chicago pitted workers against business interests; in 1888 Edward Bellamy wrote *Looking Backward*, a socialist book about inequality that sold more than a million copies; and Joseph Pulitzer could sell papers in 1883 with a message to workers on the front page that included a radical tax plan.[52]

In the South the Democratic Party saw erosion of its ranks due to the growing People's or Populist Party, which began to pick up many votes.[53] Labor became increasingly organized in the South, and white and black workers even marched together in a number of cases, horrifying white Southern conservatives.[54] At stake was nothing less than the Democratic hegemony of the South, and 1888 saw the election of a Republican president. While the economy was stricken in the South, two issues emerged that may well have contributed to white fears of economic competition from blacks. First, in 1889 the administration of Benjamin Harrison appointed more blacks to federal posts than any previous administration. Second, and perhaps most important, research has suggested that blacks worked harder and more productively than whites, for less pay.[55] It was only during this critical period of economic depression, growing labor strength, and a realization that blacks were a real and growing labor force that whites started to write about black rape.[56] Wells's suggestion that lynching had an economic component is supported by these facts.

Williamson wrote, "it is, indeed, one of the great ironies of American history that when the nation freed the slaves, it also freed racism." It also freed blacks to compete with whites on the open market; as Williamson notes, the rise of antiblack violence coincided with the time when the first young men born free, in 1865, were coming of age and entering into competition with whites.[57] Southern whites used countless methods of keeping blacks "down."[58] But the perception of black "lawlessness" was the excuse that undergirded the efforts. Perhaps the most potent vehicle for thwarting competition from blacks was the convict lease system by which prisons received free (mostly black) labor and made money by hiring out teams to mines, factories, and farms. From 1865 to the period of this study (the 1890s), the number of white prisoners in Southern jails did not change significantly and fell as a percentage of the white population as a whole; during that time the population of black prisoners rose about 900 percent.[59] In 1890 alone, more than 27,000 prisoners, nearly all African American, were taken out of the workforce and put to work for free in the South. The unpaid convicts, of course, were a boon for white capitalists, but may well have worsened conditions for other white and black laborers.[60]

Riots were another means by which whites intimidated blacks. Before this period, race riots had been two-sided affairs. Research shows, however, that by the 1890s they had changed: whites were now beating blacks at will, with little resistance.[61] In Springfield, Illinois, in 1908, just shy of the centennial of Abraham Lincoln's birth, whites rioted and lynched two blacks in a three-day spree. First a white woman claimed that she was raped by a black man. Then she recanted her story, admitting that she had been assaulted by a white whom she would not identify. Despite this information, a white mob destroyed African American homes and businesses, found an African American barber and lynched him next to his shop. The next day the mob lynched an eighty-four-year-old black man whose crime was to have been married to a white woman. The leaders of the lynching went unpunished.[62] The riot and lynchings illustrate a number of points argued by modern scholars. First, rape was more often charged than it was proven. Second, blacks were often lynched for economic reasons (as in the barber's case) or for consensual relationships (as in the case of the elderly man). Third, the legal system was not ready to punish lynchers. From 1919 to 1940 numerous antilynching bills were introduced in Congress. None passed.[63]

Williamson concluded that just as "the Negro as stereotypical child" during the antebellum period was the product of white slavers' imagination, the myth of the lawless African American was a creation of the 1890s white Southern racist. "The black beast rapist did not exist," wrote Williamson.[64] He was the product of the white Southern mind, conveyed to the general population in part by the conventions of "objective" journalism.

The Battle between Wells and the New York Times

After Wells printed her editorial about the "threadbare lie," a mob destroyed her printing type and chased her partners out of town. Wells herself barely missed lynching by the mob and fled to New York City. In New York, Wells worked for a leading African American newspaper, the *New York Age*, and published pamphlets about lynching, which sold well to a mainly black audience.[65] Wells's forced exile from Memphis was, ironically, a fortuitous event for the antilynching cause. Traveling between New York and London, the two newspaper capitals of the English-speaking world, Wells quickly began to gain access to an audience vastly wider than her four-thousand-copy *Free Speech* ever could.[66] Her trips to Britain awakened the activists of that country, much the same way that Frederick Douglass and other abolitionists had done two generations before. And Wells began to focus her attention on the white press, "since it was the medium through which I hoped to reach the white people of the country, who alone could mold public sentiment."[67] With British activists and clergymen speaking out and even sending antilynching delegations to the United States,[68] the *New York Times* and others began to take notice, and after Wells arrived back in New York, she was regularly featured in news stories.

The *Times* first noticed Wells in April 1894, when its London correspondent wrote that a "coffee-colored lady" was interviewed by the British *Chronicle*, "in which sensational charges, unhappily true in the main, are very skillfully mixed with stuff which I feel sure is not true." The correspondent called for "sober-minded, responsible Americans" to repudiate Wells's words.[69] If "sober-minded, responsible Americans" are needed to repudiate Wells, the syllogism goes, then Wells must be neither sober-minded nor responsible.

The *Times* here and elsewhere tried to place Wells outside the limits of Legitimate Controversy and cast her as a deviant.[70] Wells was seen as outside the *Times'* "rational" sphere of discussion, and she was associated with emotionality, dogmatism, and many of the traits that we might imagine when we think of people confined to the Sphere of Deviance. According to the *Times*' narrative, sober and responsible Americans, among whom the *New York Times* counted itself, discussed issues rationally, while Wells's views and appeal were based on emotion. "Wells . . . has deeply *excited* crowded gatherings by *tales* of lynching in the South [emphasis added]," wrote the *Times*, stressing Wells's emotionality.[71] The *Times* also suggested that Wells's motives for going to Britain were not pure, the purpose of the "enterprising missionary" being an "income rather than an outcome."[72] It may well have been that the *Times* considered that, as an African American and as a woman, Wells could not be "objective."[73] Never, in the articles read for this study, were her views balanced by those of whites; instead, the *Times* dealt with her charges directly in its editorial pages or balanced her views with those of blacks. Her views, depicted as emotional and dangerous, were not to be included in any debate with sober whites.

The *New York Times*, despite its criticism of Wells, was hardly without emotion itself, despite positioning itself in the sober and responsible camp. In addition to its habit of prejudging lynching victims and saving its greatest outrage for African American "brutes," the *Times* showed its true colors by embarking on a series of ad hominem attacks on Wells. When a British committee was formed to combat lynching, the *Times* fumed in an editorial that "it is especially to be deplored that it should take this action at the insistence of a slanderous and nasty-minded mulattress, who does not scruple to represent the victims of black brutes in the South as willing victims."[74] Another ad hominem attack came when Wells arrived back in New York. The *Times* announced that a "negro . . . wretch" had committed a "fiendish crime," an assault on a white woman in New York City. The crime, the *Times* wrote, "may serve to convince the mulatress missionary that the promulgation in New-York just now of her theory of negro outrages is, to say the least of it, inopportune."[75]

The *New York Times* had drawn a line between the emotionalism of Wells on the one hand and its own sober, responsible journalism on the other. In *Discovering the News*, Michael Schudson wrote about the dichotomy between "information" and "entertainment" journalism. The *Times* had set itself up as an example of the former and had set up Wells, intemperate and irresponsible, as an example of the latter. The act of casting out irresponsible journalists and spokespeople was a familiar exercise for the *New York Times* and other elite newspapers in the waning nineteenth century. For this we will briefly look at the Wells/*Times* battles in the context of newspaper wars of the 1890s.

The Newspaper Wars of the 1890s; Battle against the Upstart Journalists; "Civilization"

By the 1880s the upstart New York pennies—the *Sun*, *Herald*, *Times*, and *Tribune*—had long since vanquished the old antebellum press leaders, the now-dead partisan press. By the 1880s the former pennies *were* the establishment. In 1883 this group was shaken when Joseph Pulitzer bought the *New York World* and quickly injected it with his brand of sensationalism, popularizing huge headlines, pictures, women's pages, self-promotion, and immoderate writing. In 1895 William Randolph Hearst bought the *New York Journal* and "began where Pulitzer had the virtue to stop,"[76] producing even greater sensationalism and forcing Pulitzer to try to keep pace. The older papers recoiled in horror at the changes, for many journalistic and nonjournalistic reasons, including that they quickly saw their readership dwarfed by that of Pulitzer and Hearst.[77]

Much the same way Dan Rather asserted that he was "real" in the face of competition from below, the penny-cum-elite journalists asserted their "objectivity" and the immoderation of their rivals. The elite papers waged a "moral war" against the sensational and successful Pulitzer and Hearst, much like the one the old elite conducted against the sensational and successful Bennett a half century before. The former pennies and the yellows split roughly into two camps, the "information model" and the "story model."[78] This dichotomy is, of course, a construction; however, differences between, say, the *Times* and the *World* are apparent when one compares the two papers. After an explosion sank the U.S. battleship *Maine* in Havana Harbor in 1898, the *Times* printed a relatively dry account. In contrast, the *World* ran inflammatory pieces such as an imaginative illustration of a U.S. sailor at the instant of the explosion, startled in his hammock with outstretched arms clutching for his life. The picture ran in the days following the explosion when the idea of reparations from the Spanish (who, the *World* was convinced, were responsible) was raised; a caption below the picture reads, "CAN MONEY PAY FOR THIS?"[79]

In the 1890s the elite journalists defended themselves by attacking the yellows and nonobjective journalists; what they said was often more reflective of the critics than of the subjects. In this way "objective" journalists defined themselves by defining others. These definitions fell into three categories, each relating to Wells in some way. The elite newspapers depicted the yellows as deviant, feminine, and uncivilized.

The elites defined themselves first of all by casting the yellows as deviants, outsiders, and "freaks." Charles Dana, then the publisher of the *Sun*, embarked on a lively, often anti-Semitic campaign against Pulitzer, who was born Jewish but who had converted to Christianity. Dana asserted, "I have never published a falsehood." Pulitzer responded with the bravura of an earlier upstart, James Gordon Bennett, "that's another lie."[80] But Dana, known for his temper and angry that the *World* was overtaking his paper in circulation, became vituperative, regularly deriding his rival's ethnicity, calling him "Judas Pulitzer," and printing thrice-a-week editorials that typically contained the line "move on, Pulitzer, move on."[81]

The *New York Times*, meanwhile, drew a sharp distinction between itself and the yellows. In Adolph Ochs's inaugural editorial he wrote of his desire to publish an "impartial" and "high-standard newspaper, clean, dignified and trustworthy."[82] Six months later, when the *World* and *Journal* were publicly arguing over the veracity of a *Journal* illustration depicting a fair Cuban woman being strip-searched by sinister Spanish soldiers, the *Times* took notice of the "rivalry of our esteemed freak contemporaries."[83] Modern readers who have pondered the genesis and meaning of the *Times'* motto, "All the News That's Fit to Print," need only consider that the phrase was placed in the masthead by Ochs himself, at the height of the *unfit* yellows' war, when the *Times* had a circulation of 9,000 and the *World* 600,000.[84] The yellows, according to the elite papers, had little breeding or dignity, were "freaks" even, like the ones you would find in P. T. Barnum's museum.

The second way the elites defined themselves was by the suggestion that "objective" journalism, despite its relatively sedentary nature, was somehow a masculine endeavor. The "cult of the strenuous life" in the 1890s, exemplified by the hard-living Theodore Roosevelt, celebrated "rough sports" (including football and boxing) and "manly" strength as a means of reinforcing views of social Darwinism and even racial and cultural superiority. Emerging alongside this celebration of manliness was a "masculine" school of writers who celebrated these characteristics.[85] Journalists celebrated these characteristics too. Journalism requires "staying power," wrote Whitelaw Reid in 1913. "No man who cannot, like the pugilist, 'take punishment,' has any business in it."[86] In 1893 Charles Dana wrote that if a man reads political columns in the newspapers, he may become a good reporter, "but if, instead of that, he takes up a magazine and sits down to read a love story, you can not make a newspaper man out of him."[87] Dana's dig about love stories is a pretty good description of the newspaper of his nemesis, Pulitzer. The *World* included many columns that catered to women, including fashion, beauty, and etiquette articles and (quelle horreur!) love stories.[88]

The third way that the elite newspapers defined themselves by defining others was by calling non-"objective" journalists uncivilized and suggesting that elite journalists were closely tied to polite society and to the great Western civilization. As opposed to the colorful "yellow" journals, the *Times* claimed that its own paper "does not soil the breakfast cloth." The world of *Times* readers, the fiction went, was a place where white breakfast cloths existed—a place, suggested Schudson, that appealed to breakfast cloth–less readers who bought their *Times* (after Ochs lowered its price to a penny) as a mark of membership in high society.[89]

Thus "objectivity" was somehow connected to civilization. Charles Dana, for example, wanted his reporters to know Greek and Latin, to read Shakespeare, the Bible, and other "great" literary works.[90] For Dana, the paradigm for news gathering represented another Western tradition, the tradition of an industrialized and stratified society, one that gains its wealth from the service of others. The publisher saw a newspaper as having "its fingers reaching out toward every quarter of the globe . . . bring[ing] back the treasures of intellectual wealth that are stored up there."[91] With the newspapers' wire services, reporters, and editorial writers performing the "drudgery," editors are "emancipated" from hard labor and free to live an unburdened life of thought and devotion to civilized society.[92]

The three criticisms of the yellows by elite journalists—that the yellows were deviant, unmanly, and uncivilized—reflected prevailing views of race, gender, and civilization. All these views can be seen in Chicago's much-celebrated Columbian Exposition of 1893. The purpose of the exposition was to show the "progress of civilization in the New World." The exhibition was divided into two sections, the White City and the Midway. The section known as the White City was an intricate array of buildings celebrating the various achievements of white men; a smaller Woman's Building emphasized the domestic role of women. The Midway was a broad avenue devoted to "authentic" villages going from the more "civilized" European villages all the way to a tribe of androgynous Africans who wore grass skirts and danced to tom-toms. Exhibition-goers were encouraged to visit the White City first, then the Midway. "What an opportunity was here afforded to the scientific mind to descend the spiral of evolution," wrote the *Chicago Tribune*, "tracing humanity in its highest phases down almost to its animalistic origins." White men could define themselves as civilized and manly merely by comparing themselves to the skirted Africans.[93] Since their very existence belied the truth of both the White City and the dancing Africans, African Americans were not depicted at all, a fact that Wells and Frederick Douglass protested through the publication of a pamphlet, distributed from the tiny Haitian wing of the exhibit.[94]

The Columbian Exposition helps us understand both the elite journalists' views on lynching and their rejection of Wells as a reliable source. First, lynching was seen as a way for "civilized" whites to regulate the "savagery" of blacks. In the White City, blacks were portrayed as savages and contrasted with white "civilization"; similarly, lynched blacks were seen as savages so that white men could define themselves as noble and manly. Time after time, the elite media spoke of the unspeakable "crimes" of black men against white women. Research has shown that this had no basis in reality, but it did follow the belief system of the exposition and the society at large.[95] Wells was thwarted in her attempts to be heard because the idea that whites were more civilized than blacks was deeply ingrained in mainstream journalists' belief systems. Understanding lynching as white terrorism of blacks would undermine these beliefs. The second barrier against Wells was that she herself was considered less reliable because she belonged, according to the exposition narrative, in the three categories that the elites used to define non-"objectivity": she was an outsider, a woman, and a member of an "uncivilized race."

Not Ready to Take the Quotes off "Objectivity"

All the aspects of "objectivity" were in place in the 1890s, but the truth about lynching, or even a reasonable facsimile of the truth, was not conveyed by the mainstream media. Quite simply this is because reporters, despite their claims to be "objective," did not (and do not) operate in a vacuum. This is what makes the information/story dichotomy so untenable: information cannot be conveyed without an organizing narrative, and stories cannot be told without conveying information. In the case of lynching, the *Times* and other papers could not convey certain information without the intrusion of cultural biases and journalistic demands.

Cultural biases cannot be obliterated by "objectivity." The historian Robert Darnton, writing about his experiences as a young reporter for the *Newark Star Ledger* and *New York Times* in the late 1950s and early 1960s, recalled how he and other reporters often assembled facts around narratives that reinforced preset cultural frames. "We simply drew on the traditional repertory of genres. It was like making cookies from an antique cookie cutter," he wrote.[96] Writing for a newspaper that embraced all the elements of "objectivity," Darnton still had to conform to the expectations of his editors and readers.[97] Stories about Britain were a mixture of stock images: ascots, bowlers, cockneys, and royalty. Stories about blacks and whites also fit into a "cookie cutter," not unlike the one reporters used in the last century to cover stories of lynching.

The conventions of journalism, including timeliness and astonishment, what modern textbooks call "news values,"[98] also compete with "objectivity." Although journalists pride themselves on their ability to be detached, the quest to be *first* can often overwhelm this detachment. After his network beat the rest by a half hour on news of Bush's nomination of Quayle in 1988, Tom Brokaw reportedly cried tears of joy at the scoop.[99] One of the oldest and greatest journalistic commandments is that a news story should be interesting.[100] Articles that astonish the reader, sometimes called "man-bites-dog"[101] or "holy shit"[102] stories, reflect this commandment. Even "objective" newspapers are not immune; they too print stories that cater to the emotions and tastes of their readers.[103] The *Times* in 1896 may have called the yellows "freaks" for being obsessed with the Cuban woman who was searched by the Spanish, but when she arrived in New York harbor a few weeks later, the *Times* was there to get an interview.[104]

As readers, we are surprised when men bite dogs. We are surprised because of the reversal, what Roland Barthes called the "disturbed causality" of the situation. There is no human-interest news, Barthes wrote, without astonishment.[105] The astonishment of a story also tends to reinforce our prejudices about causality. If we read of a man biting a dog, we are subtly reminded that it is usually the dogs who do the biting. If we read about a rich, famous man who kills his wife and her lover, we are astonished because there is a relatively higher correlation between poverty and violence.[106] News should have "the structure of drama . . . including conflict," a television news producer instructed his staff.[107] Careful news consumers can often discern classic dramatic structure in, say, the O. J. Simpson trial or the funerals of the "People's Princess," Diana or the "Saint of Calcutta," Mother Theresa. "News is designed to resonate through to a society," wrote Mitchell Stephens,[108] and surprise happens where grounded cultural stereotypes are subverted.[109] It is difficult for a newspaper reporter to go against the grain of deeply embedded cultural beliefs. For an "objective" reporter, who has taken himself "out of the story" and given up his independent voice, it is doubly difficult.

Wells Tries to Break In

Wells tried to vault over these formidable barriers into the Sphere of Legitimate Controversy. Her limited success was achieved by two methods. First, she engaged "objectivity" on its own turf, fighting over facts and notions of "civilization." Second, she tried to do an end run around "objectivity," practicing what is now called "public journalism."

Wells had to enter the world of "objectivity" to combat it. She did this by engaging elite journalists in a discussion about two topics they held dear: "civilization" and facts. If the *New York Times* and others would claim "civilization," she reasoned, let them truly defend it. "Prove your man guilty, first,"[110] Wells told a London newspaper, "hang him, shoot him, pour coal oil over him and roast him, if you have concluded that *civilization* [emphasis added] demands this; but be sure the man has committed the crime first." This was a point raised time after time by Wells, a point that had some resonance in the elite newspapers. In one of the few times that Wells was quoted in the *Times*, she said, "we want at least to have [the guilt of a black man] established by a court competent to try him before he is executed, and we want the black man's home to be as sacred from invasion as that of any other man in the land."[111]

Wells also asserted her ability to be "factual." She carefully supported her argument with facts gleaned from white-owned papers; her statistics on lynching, for example, came from the columns of the *Chicago Tribune*.[112] In a pamphlet published by the African American newspaper the *New York Age*, Wells called her work a "contribution to truth, an array of facts." Echoing this sentiment, Frederick Douglass, in a foreword to that work, remarked that Wells "dealt with the facts with cool, painstaking fidelity and left those naked and uncontradicted facts to speak for themselves."[113] Here Douglass was casting Wells in the role that was guarded by the "objective" journalists: a "manly," information-centered investigator, unseduced by something more potent than any character in any love story, the "naked fact."

Lynching continued well into the twentieth century, long after the death of Wells in 1931. Given the narrow question of whether Wells was able to successfully break into the mainstream press, it appears that the story did not end happily for Wells (references to Wells in the *New York Times* index simply disappear after 1895). However, she was able to achieve some victories,[114] her antilynching work did earn her recognition among African Americans, and others built on her work and took up the fight.[115] She achieved all this not through the mainstream newspapers, but by practicing what journalists and media critics now call "public journalism."

The idea of public or "civic" journalism is one of the most hotly debated concepts in journalism today. Public journalism departs from the "objective" model in two basic ways. First, it seeks other sources beyond the standard authority spokespeople that "objective" journalists quote in their binary balancing act. Second, it helps to organize the public to act for themselves and it "crosses the line" from reporting to engaging citizens in seeking solutions. Although critics and proponents of public journalism often see these trends as "new," Wells was using these methods a century ago to achieve her aims.[116]

By the turn of the century, journalists had firmly embraced the idea that one can glean the truth by balancing quotes of figures of authority, a practice still in use today, as any astute news consumer would know. "No one looks for [news] anymore," wrote Julian Ralph, a correspondent for the *New York Sun*, in 1903. "That is an old-fashioned idea which outsiders will persist in retaining. News is now gathered systematically by men stationed at all the outlets of it, like guards at the gate of a walled city, by whom nothing can pass in or out unnoticed."[117] Ralph was supporting this practice, but Wells knew that balancing the views of any two people in the "walled city" of authority would be fruitless, because they were all white and nearly all of them shared certain basic beliefs about lynching.

Like the newspaper and AP reporters who filed stories about lynching, Wells packed her bags and traveled to the crime scenes. Unlike these reporters, however, Wells relied on African American eyewitnesses and her own observations. With one sentence, Wells was able to contradict the AP correspondent who reported that a lynched man had raped a seven-year-old: "I visited the place afterward and saw the girl, who was a grown woman more than seventeen years old."[118] The most important two words in the last sentence? They are "I" and "saw," two words that "objective" journalists almost never use together.[119]

The most important difference between the mainstream reporters and Wells was that Wells, after gathering her data, took action and counseled others to do the same. After investigating lynchings herself, Wells began to urge Northern blacks to establish a "bureau" to "procure authentic news," presumably as opposed to the stuff of the elite newspapers.[120] In response to lynchings, Wells often encouraged group action. Like public journalists, when confronted with apathy Wells would form groups herself, including the Negro Fellowship League, which became active in Chicago.[121] Her activist journalism may be best represented in the final section of her pamphlet *Southern Horrors*, titled "Self Help." In this section Wells calls for more proactive measures to end lynching—economic coercion, including migration away from the South and boycott of the rails, and self-defense. "A Winchester rifle should have a place of honor in every black home, and it should be used for that protection which the law refuses to give."[122] Wells had not taken herself "out" of the story; in fact, she tried to insert not only herself but all African Americans.

This chapter is about the failure of "objectivity" to recognize a truth, that African Americans were being terrorized across the nation. Ida B. Wells, through careful research and impassioned pleas, confronted "objectivity" and showed that mainstream journalists, while professing their "objectivity," were operating under flawed and culturally biased assumptions.

In the 1890s "objectivity" failed to understand lynching. This was true because each of the elements of "objectivity" discussed in this study contributed separately and together to obscure the truth. It was not useful to apply the detachment that emerged in the 1830s to the evil of lynching. The nonpartisanship that came about in the antebellum period could reveal only what the politicians were thinking about lynching, which did not illuminate actual conditions. The inverted pyramid structure of the 1860s and later only created a false balance where a genuine one did not exist. The rise of facticity and naive empiricism in the middle of the century did not help the understanding of lynching either, especially since journalists saw their ability to understand reality as mediated through authorities and not through "nasty-minded mulattresses" who showed emotion.

In the case of lynching, "objectivity" failed the truth. All the "objective" reporters and all the "objective" methods could not put together a reasonable understanding of lynching. That truth lay outside the rhetoric of "objectivity." Wells was not "objective," but perhaps some journalists ought not be.

Conclusion

Thoughts on a Post-"Objective" Profession

Aside from the stories they are paid to tell, professional journalists also invent myths about themselves. —John Pauly

One of the most powerful things about the declaration, "I'm objective," is the hidden corollary: "You're not." —Jay Rosen

Dan Rather's claim that his *CBS Evening News* program was "real" implied that his show was "objective" and others were not. This study has discussed similar protestations. Bennett and Webb battled over whose brand of journalism would prevail; both men claimed the "truth" and each smeared his opponent. Later, as we have seen in the final chapter, the *New York Times* and other papers conducted a "moral war" against what they called the "freak" journalists: Pulitzer, Hearst, and perhaps Wells. I will now take a parting look at the historical and present-day battles over "objectivity," and propose new journalistic standards for a post-"objective" world.

Whenever the hegemony of elite news brokers is threatened, intense debates over the nature of news occur. In the early 1830s Webb's *Morning Courier and New-York Enquirer* and other six-cent newspapers were the only source of newspaper news. Then came the upstart pennies, subverting the monopoly of the elite papers. The Webb-Bennett struggles took place against a backdrop of the *Courier and Enquirer*'s loss of circulation to the *Herald*. Webb tried to show that Bennett was no gentleman, and used his cane to demonstrate this. In return the rising Bennett called Webb's paper "dull," with the implication that the *Herald* would surpass the *Courier and Enquirer.*

A similar fight took place in the 1890s. This time it was the former pennies who played the part of the indignant elite. The upstarts, Pulitzer and Hearst, had reached a circulation hitherto unknown in the history of journalism, and the elite newspapers lashed out at them. The elite papers claimed it was the sensationalism of the *World* and *Journal* that angered them. But as we have seen in the last chapter, the elites were also irked by the success of the upstarts. The "freaks," as the yellows were called, were criticized because they agitated the New York masses, the "freaks" that read the colorful yellows.

The twentieth century has seen a series of media transfigurations that produced battles similar to the ones in the nineteenth century. The birth of commercial radio prompted the newspaper establishment to wage a war (not entirely unlike the "moral wars" of the last century) against the new medium.[1] When television news became increasingly popular in the 1950s, and eventually grew to surpass newspapers, again a struggle emerged between the monopoly (newspapers and radio) and the upstarts (television). Echoing past complaints about upstarts by elites, critics still claim that television is less serious than the older media.[2]

By the 1990s the news media landscape had shifted so significantly that Dan Rather, a representative of the formerly upstart television news, could publicly fret over encroachments from a new set of upstarts. New media, in many forms, and the assault on serious journalism from the entertainment world threatened television journalism even as television continued to threaten print. In the closing years of the twentieth century we are left with fewer and fewer daily newspapers, and network news divisions have had to cut their staffs substantially.[3] While these declines are occurring, an explosion in new media has again threatened the elite, "objective" journalists. With so many storytellers (each of the thousands of homepages, for example, is a separate news source), and with so many departing from the "information model" of "objective" news, journalists are called on once again to define themselves. It is no surprise that the nature of news and "objectivity" should reemerge as an issue so important to the profession.

Rather's assertion that the *CBS Evening News* was "real" came after a special report on "reality" television, the growing trend of basing made-for-TV [illegible]es on actual, sensational news events. Rather seemed to be [illegible]sure of "reality" television and arguing that it is not real. But [illegible]ther is real, other news sources are real too, a point not lost [illegible]xecutives. For example, Steven Brill, the founder of Court [illegible]e out his own slice of the "reality" market. Writing in an op-ed piece in the *New York Times*, Brill argued that his network, in providing a video camera inside the courtroom, was engaging in a "*real*-reality" brand of television.[4]

The competition Rather and associates feel from the other news outlets is intense. Rather's "This is real" comment was the first of many he made in the last few years regarding competition from non-"objective" media sources and the nature of his profession. One such comment came in a speech to the Radio and Television News Directors Association in 1993. In the speech Rather worried about the "glut of inanities now in 'access' time," urging news shows "to compete not with other news programs but with entertainment programs (including those posing as news programs) for dead bodies, mayhem and lurid tales." The "Hollywoodization of news," Rather warned, makes serious journalists into entertainers.[5] Since Rather's comments, a number of news outlets have been accused of adopting non-"objective" practices, notably NBC News and its recent emphasis on stories about health and other domestic issues. NBC's new format, called "You News" in the *Columbia Journalism Review*, was blasted by Rather in 1997 as "News Lite."[6]

Rather also challenged the competition in a letter to the *New York Times*, in which he responded to an op-ed piece by Bill O'Reilly, the anchor of *Inside Edition*, a sensational, syndicated television show. O'Reilly had written a piece discussing "checkbook journalism," a practice of paying subjects to interview them. King World, the parent company of *Inside Edition*, had paid Tonya Harding, the figure skater, an estimated $600,000 for an interview. O'Reilly's op-ed piece was not a defense of "checkbook journalism"; in fact, O'Reilly wrote, he would prefer not to participate in the practice. His argument was merely that competition from the broadcast networks, which could provide an interviewee with exposure and entertainment "deals," and from other syndicated shows, which could offer money, made paying for interviews necessary for *Inside Edition*'s survival.[7]

Rather's letter primarily sought to distinguish himself from O'Reilly. "I work in hard news," wrote Rather. "He is the anchor of 'Inside Edition,' a news-influenced entertainment show." But Rather's point has one crucial weakness: the difference between Rather and O'Reilly is not always clear. When arguing that CBS News avoids "checkbook journalism," Rather admitted that his organization had "on a very few occasions" been guilty of the practice.[8] Perhaps it is the lack of a clear distinction that compels Rather to write. For if O'Reilly's is a "news-influenced entertainment show," Rather's could be called an "entertainment-influenced news show."

Perhaps Rather's team did not pay Tonya Harding, but it did send Connie Chung to Norway for ten days to report on Harding during the Winter Olympics, an event covered exclusively by CBS Sports. Rather and Chung devoted more air time to the Winter Olympics than did NBC and ABC combined. During the ten days when Chung was in Norway, the crisis in Bosnia had escalated, a major spy, Aldrich Ames, had been caught by the United States, and a Jewish settler had massacred West Bank Muslims, all grist for "hard news" reporters, but not given the play of Harding's movements by the *CBS Evening News*.[9]

Without a monopoly on reality, and without a clear distinction between what he and O'Reilly do, Rather's next step could be to define "objectivity," to show that O'Reilly is not part of the club. What do Rather and the other "objective" journalists have that O'Reilly and others do not? This question is not easy to answer; it is made especially difficult by the rhetoric of "objectivity" itself. If you argue that you are like a window on the world, or a mirror held up against it, then what you do is passive and difficult to explain. That is why "objective" journalists define themselves primarily by defining others: it is much easier to define yourself by pointing out bias in others than by talking about what you do if you pretend you are in a passive role. Caught in this trap, Rather retreated. Instead of defining himself, he argued that the central difference between himself and O'Reilly was the perceptions of third parties: "we have our reputations," Rather wrote, "built over decades."[10] This was echoed in a longtime advertising slogan for the network's news division: "Experience. CBS News."[11]

As more and more information is printed, broadcast, faxed, phoned, and sent over the Internet, being a passive mirror is less and less relevant. With so much news and so many storytellers, there must be something more than passivity for responsible journalists to offer. Reputation may be part of the answer, but reputation is something you earn, not something you do. And experience at doing something passive is little comfort either. Nor is it a fair representation of what journalists do. Rather himself has built his reputation on his nonpassive relationship with public figures, including his tough on-air questioning of George Bush about the Iran-contra affair in 1988.[12]

I believe that Rather's best chance to keep our attention in the years ahead is not by touting his reality and "objectivity," or even by defining others. It is, I believe, through the honest admission that he actually does something. Reality is a big thing. We cannot have it all. We should not expect Rather and company to give us the world, whether he has twenty-two minutes or even much longer. What Rather actually does offer is not reality but mediation between out there and in here. What we must ask Rather and company is that their filters be *better* than those of O'Reilly and company. What we need Rather to do is explain his filters, to tell us how he interprets reality and why we should buy his interpretation. To do so would mean abandoning the myth of "objectivity."

If we accept that true objectivity is unattainable, with what are we left? If, as this study suggests, "objectivity" must be clothed in quotes to have any validity as a concept, what standards do we still have to apply? If there is no "objectivity," what is there for journalists to strive for? Winston Churchill once said that democracy is the worst form of government, except for all the other forms.[13] Might the same be said about "objective" journalism? Perhaps. But if journalists want to keep the professional ethic they call "objectivity," at least they should clearly understand it and be able to argue its merits without claiming "reality" as a defense. This work is an attempt to elevate the discussion by putting "objectivity" into a historical frame.

This study has attempted to break down "objectivity" into a number of characteristics: detachment, nonpartisanship, inverted pyramid writing, reverence for facts, and balance. Implicit in this work is the call to look beyond "objectivity" to these characteristics. If we understand "objectivity's" components, we will be better able to develop a new set of ethics. If we understand the structure, possibilities, and limits of detachment and nonpartisanship, the major topics of the first two chapters, we will be able to discuss them as distinct values from "objectivity." This can lead to a more specific language about what a reporter is doing. Perhaps nonpartisanship as a value, which studies have shown is possible, could be kept. But what kind of nonpartisanship? Chapter 2 discusses three examples of nonpartisan journalists: the centrist Bennett, the antipartisan Garrison, and the activist Douglass, each unaffiliated with party, but significantly different from each other. Chapter 2 offers the modern journalist the option to choose between three distinct nonpartisan models.

The inverted pyramid is another aspect of "objectivity" that could be kept, although chapter 3 offers a cautionary tale about how the form can be entwined with issues of government press manipulation. Understanding that the history of the inverted pyramid is tied to some of the worst aspects of the government's control of the press can remind journalists of the dangers of seeking truth in the balance of authorities' truth claims.

Chapters 4 and 5 describe the rise of facticity and the difficulty of trying to understand the world free of cultural filters. After reading chapter 4, one might still want to reject superstition and revere science (this did help nineteenth-century journalists combat cholera). But chapter 5 tells us that journalists should not assume that "objectivity" equals a correct picture of reality; journalists must always remember that their vision is colored by their culture.

This is not to embrace relativism. I am not suggesting that the search for truth is futile. There is an out there out there. To suggest that the *Times'* account of lynching was just as valid as that of Ida B. Wells is to deny a preponderance of evidence that shows that blacks were unfairly victimized by whites. Perhaps the best a reporter can do is to strive to tell the truth, as the reporter sees it, negotiated with his or her editors and readers.

This study has examined the evolution of "objectivity" across the cultural landscape of the nineteenth century. It has also sought to replace one word, "objectivity," with many others (detachment, nonpartisanship, the inverted pyramid, facticity, balance). Unfortunately, as we get more specific about "objectivity," we must use more words, which is exactly the opposite of what journalists seek to do as they try to make difficult concepts understandable for news consumers. But given the rising din of people hawking reality, we need to step back and honestly figure out what we do, what we make, what we see, in a world of filters, in a world without "objectivity."

Notes

NOTES TO THE INTRODUCTION

1. Quoted in W. B. Blankenburg and R. Walden, "Objectivity, Interpretation, and Economy in Reporting," 591–92.

2. Jon Katz, "No News Is Good News."

3. Until 1996 "objectivity" was the central ethic of the Society of Professional Journalists' Code of Ethics. Jay Black, "Codes."

4. For an account of the struggles between print and radio, see Gwenyth L. Jackaway, "The Press-Radio War, 1924–1937: A Battle to Defend the Professional, Institutional and Political Power of the Press."

5. Erik Barnouw, *Tube of Plenty: The Evolution of American Television*, 100–104. By 1974 television had replaced newspapers as the main source of news. Michael Schudson, *Discovering the News: A Social History of American Newspapers*, 182. Walter Goodman, "What's Bad for Politics Is Great for Television," 36.

6. *CBS Evening News with Dan Rather,* 11 February 1993.

7. Vladimir Nabokov, *Lolita*, 330.

8. Once, after discovering that the quotation marks can make for difficult reading, I removed them from the word wherever it appeared in the manuscript. After all, I told myself, "objectivity" does have a tangible presence in the lives of many reporters and editors. But "objectivity" looked unclothed without quotes, and this book asks journalists to move beyond the term, to find better words. I put back the quotation marks.

9. In *The Press and America: An Interpretive History of the Mass Media*, 8th ed., Michael Emery and Edwin Emery write that the number of cities with competing dailies has steadily declined in the second half of the twentieth century, from 181 in 1940 to 61 in 1961 to 33 in 1994 (545); Robert Goldberg and Gerald Jay Goldberg, *Anchors: Brokaw, Jennings, Rather and the Evening News*, 106, 229, 320–23; Andie J. Tucher, "You News," 27.

10. S. Elizabeth Bird, *For Enquiring Minds: A Cultural Study of Supermarket Tabloids*, 178.

11. Tom Baxter, "New Allegations against Clinton: Web Gossip Purveyor Hits Pay Dirt Again"; Francis X. Clines, "Gossip Guru Stars in 2 Roles at Courthouse"; Alicia Shepard, "A Scandal Unfolds," 24.

12. Ken Auletta, "Demolition Man."

13. Nan Robertson, *The Girls in the Balcony: Women, Men and the New York Times*, 144.

14. Jill Nelson, *Volunteer Slavery: My Authentic Negro Experience,* 86.

15. James B. Reston, "The Job of the Reporter," 101; Jay Walljasper, "What Is the Alternative Press?" 7.

16. Christiane Amanpour, "Television's Role in Foreign Policy."

17. *New York Herald*, 6 May 1835, 3.

18. Schudson, *Discovering the News*, 7.

19. Black, "Codes."

20. The claim is made a few times an hour by WINS Radio in New York City.

21. Gaye Tuchman, *Making News: A Study in the Construction of Reality*, 1.

22. "Docudrama Strikes Again."

23. David Bartlett, "Viewers Like It."

24. Even standard mirrors distort, as the following exercise will reveal. Stand at a mirror at arm's length and trace the outline of your head. You may be surprised to learn that the image of your head is about the size of an orange. It is our human filter that makes sense of the image.

25. Mark Crispin Miller, *Boxed In: The Culture of TV*, 102.

26. Tuchman, *Making News*, 21.

27. Phone interview with Tom Hannon, Cable News Network (CNN) political director, 27 April 1992.

28. Salant is quoted in Edward J. Epstein, *News from Nowhere: Television and the News*, epigraph, ix.

29. Tuchman, *Making News*, 21.

30. Oswald Garrison Villard, "Press Tendencies and Dangers," 23.

31. Cable News Network (CNN) advertisement, 1993. For a wider discussion of the idea of "objective" journalism as a seesaw, see Gaye Tuchman, "Objectivity as Strategic Ritual: An Examination of Newsmen's Notions of Objectivity," 665–67.

32. *Time* Magazine advertisement, *New York Times*, 20 December 1993, A20.

33. Miller was awarded the Pulitzer Prize in 1976. John Hohenberg, *The Pulitzer Prize Story II: Award-Winning News Stories, Columns, Editorials, Cartoons, and News Pictures, 1959–1980*, 353.

34. Jay Rosen, "Journalism and the Production of the Present," 110. The distinction between making and faking was made by Michael Schudson in Dan Berkowitz's book, *Social Meanings of News: A Text-Reader*, 7. See page 206 in the same book for the claim that news does not reflect.

35. Fred Fedler, *Reporting for the Print Media*. Melvin Mencher, *News Reporting and Writing*. Mitchell Stephens, *Broadcast News*. Mitchell Stephens and Gerald Lanson, *Writing and Reporting the News*. The Missouri Group (George Kennedy, Daryl

R. Moen, and Don Ranly), *Beyond the Inverted Pyramid: Effective Writing for Newspapers, Magazines, and Specialized Publications.*

36. Stephens and Lanson, *Writing and Reporting the News*, 57–58. For "detachment" also see Fedler, *Reporting for the Print Media*, 22; Mencher, *News Reporting and Writing*, 23; Stephens, *Broadcast News*, 44.

37. Mencher, *News Reporting and Writing*, 23. Also see Stephens and Lanson, *Writing and Reporting the News*, 57; Fedler, *Reporting for the Print Media*, 119–34; Stephens, *Broadcast News*, 308; and Missouri Group, *Beyond the Inverted Pyramid*, 193–94.

38. Mencher, *News Reporting and Writing*, 97–108; Stephens and Lanson, *Writing and Reporting the News*, 57, 78; Fedler, *Reporting for the Print Media*, 73–76; and Missouri Group, *Beyond the Inverted Pyramid*, 102–8.

39. Mencher, *News Reporting and Writing*, 23; Stephens and Lanson, *Writing and Reporting the News*, 57; Fedler, *Reporting for the Print Media*, 22; and Stephens, *Broadcast News*, 44.

40. Stephens, *Broadcast News*, 44; Mencher, *News Reporting and Writing*, 35; Stephens and Lanson, *Writing and Reporting the News*, 57, 78; Fedler, *Reporting for the Print Media*, 119–34; and Missouri Group, *Beyond the Inverted Pyramid*, 102–8.

41. Missouri Group, *Beyond the Inverted Pyramid*, 192–97.

42. See especially Mike Hoyt, "Chuck-Gate: When Can Journalists Act Like Citizens?"; Alicia Shepard, "The Revolving Door," 19; and Amanpour, "Television's Role in Foreign Policy."

43. Hoyt, "Chuck-Gate."

44. Katz, "No News Is Good News."

45. Jon Katz, "Um, Hello?"; "Woe Is Hillary"; "Um, Hello?"; "Talk amongst Ourselves."

46. *New York Times*, 9 August 1974, 1. The *Times*, in the days that followed, also included editorial clips from leading newspapers around the country.

47. Alison Mitchell, "Standoff Deepens as G.O.P. Calls Off Talks."

48. Tuchman, "Objectivity as Strategic Ritual," 665–67.

49. Schudson, *Discovering the News*, 161.

50. Schudson, *Discovering the News*, 4.

51. Hazel Dicken-Garcia, *Journalistic Standards in Nineteenth-Century America*, 98. The term "objectivity" was used widely in the nineteenth century, including numerous times by Herbert Spencer, who wrote, "objective facts are ever impressing themselves upon us." Quoted in David Shi, *Facing Facts: Realism in American Thought and Culture, 1850–1920*, 69.

52. Thomas Paine, *Common Sense*, 32.

53. *Publick Occurrences*, 25 September 1690, 1.

54. Mitchell Stephens, *A History of News: From the Drum to the Satellite*, 268.

55. In 1835 the nation's leading newspaper was the *Morning Courier and New-York Enquirer*. James L. Crouthamel, *James Watson Webb: A Biography*, 68–69. In

1865 the *New York Herald, Times,* and *Tribune* were the only three eight-page dailies in the country, and had the largest staffs and budgets. Louis M. Starr, *Bohemian Brigade: Civil War Newsmen in Action,* 11. By the 1890s Hearst and Pulitzer were battling for supremacy of the New York City newspaper market, the nation's largest, with unprecedented budgets, manpower, and enthusiasm. See W. A. Swanberg's two books, *Pulitzer* and *Citizen Hearst.*

56. Oliver Gramling, *AP: The Story of News,* 19.

57. *Liberator,* 1 January 1831, 1.

58. In *Making News,* Gaye Tuchman writes about the "web of facticity" that ties journalists and figures of authority. This web allows reporters access but connects them to their sources and their legitimacy. This idea is discussed throughout chapters 5 and 6 of her book. See also Robert A. Hackett, "Decline of a Paradigm? Bias and Objectivity in News Media Studies."

59. *New York Sun,* 25 January 1868, 3.

60. *New York Times,* 2 August 1894, 7.

61. *New York Times,* 2 August 1894, 7.

NOTES TO CHAPTER 1

1. Mitchell Stephens, *A History of News: From the Drum to the Satellite,* 207–8.

2. *New York Herald,* 21 April 1836, 1; 4 May 1836, 3; 18 April 1836, 3; 10 May 1836, 1.

3. James L. Crouthamel, *James Watson Webb: A Biography,* 31, 68.

4. *New York Herald,* 21 April 1836, 2; 30 April 1836, 2; 7 May 1836, 2; 20 April 1836, 2.

5. James L. Crouthamel, *Bennett's New York* Herald *and the Rise of the Popular Press,* 26.

6. In the context of the Jacksonian era, "nonpartisanship" means that for the first time since the ratification of the Constitution in 1789, U.S. newspapers would increasingly separate themselves from direct affiliation with political parties.

7. Michael Schudson, *Discovering the News: A Social History of American Newspapers,* 15.

8. John C. Nerone et al., "The Mythology of the Penny Press," 387. Nerone argues an opposite point, that the pennies' circulation may have been high, but their readership may have not been significantly higher than that of the shared elite newspapers. Nerone and his critics offer an interesting discussion of this period.

9. Carl Prince, in *The Federalists and the Origins of the U.S. Civil Service,* discusses the inns of the Federalist era as places to read and be read to. The inns, post offices, printers, and newspapers were often connected through political affiliation, and during the years before Jefferson's presidency in 1801, were generally Federalist (224–25). Circulation did not depend on the number of subscribers. However, the pennies did vastly increase personal ownership of newspapers.

10. Schudson, *Discovering the News*, 13; Daniel Schiller, *Objectivity and the News: The Public and the Rise of Commercial Journalism*, 12.

11. Crouthamel, *Webb*, 31; *New York Herald*, 21 April 1836, 3. The rise in circulation was facilitated by advances in printing technology, although Schudson argues in *Discovering the News* (33–34) that the advances generally followed the need established by the increases in circulation. The growing urbanization of the Northeast, coupled with a rise in literacy, is also frequently cited by historians as important in the rise of the penny press. Frank Luther Mott, *American Journalism: A History: 1690–1960*, 304–5; Schudson, *Discovering the News*, 35–39.

12. There is a rich literature on the pre-penny press and the political aspects of printing. For the Federalist period press, see Prince, *The Federalists*, esp. 183–225; and Carl Prince, "The Federalist Party and the Creation of a Court Press, 1789–1801." Also see Donald Stewart, *The Opposition Press of the Federalist Period*; Eugene Perry Link, *Democratic-Republican Societies, 1790–1800*; the introduction to Nobel Cunningham, Jr., *Circular Letters of Congressmen to Their Constituents, 1789–1829*; and Gerald Baldasty, "The Press and Politics in the Age of Jackson," 7–21. Baldasty's monograph is informative and thorough, but focuses on the partisan press at the expense of the pennies.

13. In Gerald J. Baldasty, *The Commercialization of the News in the Nineteenth Century*, 124, the author presents evidence that political news declined and crime and other news rose after the advent of the pennies; the *New York Transcript* is quoted in Willard G. Bleyer, *Main Currents in the History of American Journalism*, 167.

14. Frank L. Mott, author of *American Journalism*, titled a chapter on the pre-penny era the "Dark Ages of Partisan Journalism," a phrase countered by the author's laudatory title for the penny period: "Sunrise"! Michael Emery and Edwin Emery, in their popular book *The Press and America*, called the changes "revolutionary," and announced that the pennies supplied "news" not "views." The Emerys also cited the "democratic ferment" and "emergence of common people" during the Jacksonian age. Mitchell Stephens, in *A History of News*, connected the pennies' rise with the "spread of Jacksonian democracy." Mott, *American Journalism*, 215; Michael Emery and Edwin Emery, *The Press and America: An Interpretive History of the Mass Media*, 8th ed., 90–104. The Emerys do not explain how one might express oneself without a "view"; Stephens, *A History of News*, 205.

15. Schudson, *Discovering the News*, 44, 56, 16.

16. Schudson, *Discovering the News*, 3, 4. First, as Mitchell Stephens points out in *A History of News* (and a quick perusal of pre-Jacksonian papers will support this), journalists had been claiming fairness, balance, and truthfulness, crucial elements of "objectivity," since well before the American Revolution. See especially Stephens, *A History of News*, 57, 256–70. And the very presence of the newspapers proves that "news" existed before the 1830s. In fact Schudson himself, when he discusses the era before " 'news' itself was invented," writes, "newspapers had in-

creasingly tried to be up-to-date, especially in reporting the arrival of ships and in printing the *news* they brought with them" (26; italics mine). Mitchell Stephens and Michael Schudson debated this claim in "Schudson and Stephens Debate: The 'Invention' of News, Other Sundry Matters," 7. For the literature on the pre-penny news, see note 12, above.

17. Schudson, *Discovering the News*, 12.

18. Schudson, *Discovering the News*, 43–44.

19. Schlesinger's *Age of Jackson* is widely seen by historians as the culmination of the "progressive" school, which viewed the period, and American history as a whole, as a conflict between "the people" and special interests. Jackson and his associates, according to this view, represent "the people." Much of what came after Schlesinger responded to this interpretation. Bray Hammond, *Banks and Politics in America: From the Revolution to the Civil War* departed from Schlesinger's view that the elite controlled the Bank of the United States (B.U.S.) and Jackson and "the people" opposed it. The Democrats, Hammond argued, were impelled to fight the B.U.S. less for idealistic reasons than for a desire for speculation unrestrained by a strong bank. Richard Hofstadter, in *The American Political Tradition and the Men Who Made It*, cautioned against comparing the genuine achievements of the New Deal with Jacksonian democracy, which was, in many ways, a vehicle for "small capitalists" (70–71). By the time Edward Pessen's *Jacksonian America: Society, Personality, and Politics* was published, a new critique of Jacksonian "democracy" was emerging, based not on economics or politics as much as on social aspects of the era. Lee Benson, in *The Concept of Jacksonian Democracy: New York as a Test Case*, suggested that class may not have been as important as ethnic, religious, or national background in molding party identity. Others, such as Leon F. Litwack in *North of Slavery: The Negro in the Free States, 1790–1860*, looked at specific communities and concluded that the age of Jackson was anything but democratic. The plight of women, African Americans, and Native Americans in *The Age of Jackson* is, as Schlesinger himself admits in hindsight, "shamefully out of mind." Gerald N. Grob and George A. Billias, *Interpretations of American History: Pattern and Perspectives*, vol. 1, 281. Pessen used the new "social historians" in his critique of the "progressive" school. Since Pessen's book, much has been written about the age of Jackson, and the notes that follow will provide a representative group from the revisionist "social historians." There are a number of historiographies of the Jacksonian age. Grob and Billias, *Interpretations of American History*, vol. 1, 254–69 is a good introduction to the topic; also see Pessen, *Jacksonian America*, 329–67; Sean Wilentz, "On Class and Politics in Jacksonian America"; and Daniel Feller, "Politics and Society: Towards a Jacksonian Synthesis," 135.

20. Pessen, *Jacksonian America*, 100, 327. Here, as elsewhere, I quote from the second edition (1978). While the edition comes after Schudson's, the first (1969) edition, which precedes it, contains nearly identical quotes and is no less emphatic in its revision of the "progressive" school.

21. Schiller, *Objectivity and the News*, 10, 17.

22. As I shall discuss in the following pages, Webb had switched parties after receiving "loans" from the head of the Bank of the United States, Nicholas Biddle. For Webb's support of the Whigs in the 1832 election, see the *Courier and Enquirer*, 8 November 1832, 3.

23. *New York Herald*, 19 January 1836, 2. For part of the early pennies' history, the first page of the newspaper was for advertisements. On this day the "disclosures" were published on page 2, column 1; *New York Herald*, 20 January 1836, 2; 21 January 1836, 2.

24. *New York Herald*, 21 January 1836, 2.

25. *New York Herald*, 23 January 1836, 2. Circulation figures are unreliable, as Nerone ("The Mythology of the Penny Press," 386) pointed out, but certainly the *New York Sun* and probably the *New York Herald* were overtaking Webb's paper by this point.

26. Schiller, *Objectivity and the News*, 33–40.

27. Isaac Clark Pray, *Memoirs of James Gordon Bennett and His Times: By a Journalist*, 199.

28. Crouthamel, *Webb*, 40–43. Crouthamel argues that the House committee was biased and used Webb for partisan reasons, to show that the bank should not be rechartered. Webb himself denied that he knew the source of the "loans." But the evidence against Webb is compelling. First, Webb's support of the bank grew stronger as each loan was received (Crouthamel, *Webb*, 9). Second, within a year of the third "loan" he abandoned the Democratic Party altogether, professing "impartiality" but supporting the Whigs, Biddle's party (Crouthamel, *Webb*, 39–40). And finally, Biddle himself, writing during the year of the questionable "loans," justified paying editors for their support: "If a grocer wishes to apprize the public that he had a fresh supply of figs, the printer whom he employed, for that purpose, never thinks of giving his labor for nothing, but charges him for his trouble in inserting the advertisement. If the Bank, in like manner, wishes a printer to insert information about its concerns, why should it not pay him for his trouble?" Baldasty, "The Press and Politics," 18–19.

29. *Working Man's Advocate*, 8 November 1834, quoted in Phillip S. Foner, *American Labor Songs of the Nineteenth Century*, 35.

30. See Schudson, *Discovering the News*, 51–55 on Bennett and the *Courier and Enquirer*. In a section titled "A Penny Press for the Common People," Emery and Emery in *The Press and America*, 8th ed. (101–2) accept Schudson's theory about Bennett and the other pennies coming from "the growth of mass democracy." Stephens, *A History of News*, 200–208. Schiller, *Objectivity and the News*, 35–37 (Webb) and 47–65 (Bennett).

31. Pessen, *Jacksonian America*, 81. According to Charles Sellers, "the rise from rags to riches was statistically mythical." *The Market Revolution: Jacksonian America, 1815–1846*, 239.

32. Jack Larkin, *The Reshaping of Everyday Life: 1790–1840*, 60–61.

33. This view is put forth by Schiller in *Objectivity and the News*, 59.

34. There is convincing evidence that Robinson was indeed the murderer—a fact that may have been known by all, including Bennett—and that Bennett may have run an extortion operation out of his editorial office, taking money from the rich customers in return for a promise to not publish their names and for his support of Robinson. For this compelling theory, see Andrea J. Tucher, " 'Froth and Scum': Truth, Beauty, Goodness, and the Axe-Murder in the First Years of the New York Penny Press," 95–98. See also *The Life and Writings of James Gordon Bennett, Editor of the New-York Herald.*

35. Patricia Cline Cohen, "Unregulated Youth: Masculinity and Murder in the 1830s City," 44.

36. Many elite mobs felt that the abolitionists were responsible for everything they feared about the roiling age. Leonard Richards, *"Gentlemen of Property and Standing": Anti-Abolition Mobs in Jacksonian America*, 3–19.

37. The Tappan family of New York City, the chief patrons of abolition, were often the victims of vandalism. Sellers, in *The Market Revolution*, points out that the Tappans were antilabor. Thus the Tappan family, while great supporters of slaves and free blacks, the most downtrodden segments of antebellum society, were reviled by many whites (388).

38. George Dangerfield, *The Awakening of American Nationalism, 1815–1828*, 1–8; Sean Wilentz, *Chants Democratic: New York City and the Rise of the American Working Class, 1788–1850*, 23–24.

39. Washington Irving, *The Sketch Book*, 48.

40. Crouthamel, *Webb*, 70. Bennett noted the difference often, as he does in the following editorial:

> We do not, as the Wall-street lazy editors do, come down to our office about ten or twelve o'clock—pull out a Spanish segar—take up a scissors—puff and cut—cut and puff for a couple of hours—and then adjourn to Delmonico's to eat, drink, gormandize and blow up our cotemporaries. We rise in the morning at five o'clock—write our leading editorials, squibs, sketches &c., before breakfast. From nine till one we read all our papers, and the original communications, the latter being more numerous than those of any other office in New York. . . . We also give audience to visitors—gentlemen on business—and some of the loveliest ladies in New York, who call to subscribe—God bless them. At one, we sally out among the gentlemen and loafers of Wall-street. . . . We dine moderately and temperately—thank God for his mercies—read our proofs—take in cash and advertisements, which are increasing like smoke—and close the day by going to bed always at ten o'clock. . . . That's the way to conduct a paper with spirit and success.

New York Herald, 16 August 1836, quoted in Bleyer, *Main Currents*, 189–90. Later, as the *New York Herald* became increasingly successful, Bennett traveled more and took longer vacations.

41. Alexis de Tocqueville, *Democracy in America*, 221.

42. *Morning Courier and New-York Enquirer*, 5 May 1836, 2 (hereafter cited as *Courier and Enquirer*).

43. *New York Herald*, 6 May 1836, 1.

44. *New York Herald*, 12 May 1836, 4.

45. *New York Herald*, 29 April 1836, 1; *Courier and Enquirer*, 29 April 1836, 3.

46. Pessen, *Jacksonian America*, 103.

47. See Washington Irving, "Rip Van Winkle" and "The Legend of Sleepy Hollow"; James F. Cooper's "Leatherstocking" series, especially *Deerslayer, or The First Warpath*; Nathaniel Hawthorne, *Scarlett Letter*, "Young Goodman Brown"; and "My Kinsman, Major Molineaux"; and Melville's sea narratives, which include *Typee, A Peep at Polynesian Life*; *Redburn: His First Voyage*; and, of course, *Moby Dick*.

48. See Pessen, *Jacksonian America* for a general account. For the plight of free blacks, see Litwack, *North of Slavery*. For women's views on themselves as slaves, see Nancy F. Cott, *The Bonds of Womanhood: "Woman's Sphere" in New England*; the "bonds" in the title are those of friendship and of slavery.

49. Ronald G. Walters, *American Reformers: 1815–1860*, 8.

50. Pessen, *Jacksonian America*, 172.

51. Pessen, *Jacksonian America*, 69; Keith J. Hardman, *Charles Grandison Finney*, 151–52. The idea that God is present in humans was not developed, but popularized by the revivalists. Quakers, for example, believed this long before the Jacksonian era.

52. William S. McFeely, *Frederick Douglass*, 123; Pessen, *Jacksonian America*, 68–70.

53. Hardman, *Finney*, 262–67. Finney was an influential and fascinating figure of the Jacksonian era. In addition to his preaching, he went on to become one of the early presidents of the progressive Oberlin College. For Tappan, see the *Liberator*, 12 July 1832, 2.

54. *New York Herald*, 1 September 1845, 3.

55. *New York Herald*, 21 April 1836, 1.

56. *New York Herald*, 10 May 1836, 1; for the reference to Moses, see Stephens, *A History of News*, 242.

57. Richards, *"Gentlemen of Property and Standing,"* 3–19.

58. Richards, *"Gentlemen of Property and Standing,"* 29.

59. Crouthamel, *Webb*, 72–76. Webb led bloody riots in the 1832 elections as well. See his paper for the week of 2–8 November 1832.

60. Larkin, *The Reshaping of Everyday Life*, 286. In *The Market Revolution*, Sellers shows that liquor consumption peaked in the 1830s (260).

61. Carl Prince, "The Great 'Riot Year': Jacksonian Democracy and Patterns of Violence in 1834," 18–19.

62. Pessen, *Jacksonian America*, 321.

63. Dangerfield, *The Awakening of American Nationalism*, 46–50; Jackson killed "any and all Indians wherever he could," writes Sellers in *The Market Revolution*, 98.

64. Pessen, *Jacksonian America*, 172; Robert V. Remini, *Andrew Jackson and the Course of American Democracy, 1833–1845*, vol. 3, 51.

65. For more on the nullification crisis, see Richard Ellis, *The Union at Risk: Jackson Democracy, States' Rights, and the Nullification Crisis*, esp. 78, 37.

66. *New York Evening Post*, 4 February 1835, 3.

67. Remini, *Andrew Jackson*, 227, 434, 69.

68. Prince, "The Great 'Riot Year,' " 1–2.

69. Litwack, *North of Slavery*, 123–31.

70. Richard Hofstadter and Michael Wallace, *American Violence: A Documentary History*, 477; Prince, "The Great 'Riot Year,' " 18, 7.

71. Kenneth S. Greenberg, *Masters and Statesmen: The Political Culture of American Slavery*, 23–24.

72. Greenberg, *Masters and Statesmen*, 144–46.

73. Schiller, *Objectivity and the News*, 39–40.

74. Ben H. Bagdikian, *The Media Monopoly*, 44–48.

75. The above was gleaned from the *New York Herald* of 26 and 27 February 1838; Crouthamel, *Webb*, 72–73; and Greenberg, *Masters and Statesmen*, 28–39.

76. *New York Herald*, 28 February 1838, 2–4.

77. *New York Transcript* and *New York Sun*, 27 Februrary 1838, quoted in *New York Herald*, 28 February 1838, 4.

78. *New York Herald*, 3 March 1838, 2.

79. Schiller, *Objectivity and the News*, 46.

80. Richards, *"Gentlemen of Property and Standing,"* 157.

81. The *Courier and Enquirer* declined after the birth of the pennies; the pennies and former pennies, by the early 1850s, including the *Sun*, *Herald*, *Tribune*, and *Times*, were the leading New York papers, far outpacing the commercial and mercantile press. Crouthamel, *Webb*, 149–50.

NOTES TO CHAPTER 2

The epigraphs in this chapter are quoted in Jay Rosen, "Beyond Objectivity," 50; and Herbert Gans, *Deciding What's News*, 207.

1. For Bennett's endorsements, see James L. Crouthamel, *Bennett's New York* Herald *and the Rise of the Popular Press*, 73–74. Since I offer Bennett as an example of an early nonpartisan editor, I should clarify this statement. Other newspapers, including the mercantile press of the 1820s, often had interests apart from politics

altogether. So Bennett's claim to the history of nonpartisanship may be that he was one of the first practitioners of nonpartisanship who was interested in politics.

2. See Donald L. Shaw, "News Bias and the Telegraph: A Study of Historical Change," 5–11. Shaw finds that political partisanship declined after the 1870s. There were a few stragglers: "A newspaper is naturally an organ of a party," said Charles A. Dana, the editor of the *New York Sun*, in 1895. Charles A. Dana, *The Art of Newspaper Making*, 86.

3. For the Vietnam study, see Daniel Hallin, *The Uncensored War: The Media and Vietnam*, 107, 231 n. 14; Robert A. Hackett, "Decline of a Paradigm? Bias and Objectivity in News Media Studies," 245.

4. Anna Quindlen, "Talking about the Media Circus," 54.

5. See the epigraph by Donaldson at the start of the chapter. In "Beyond Objectivity" (50), Jay Rosen noted, however, the intellectual danger of rejecting criticism because it comes from both the right and the left. It can create a way of discounting all critics and "a way of living without criticism." Walter Cronkite, *A Reporter's Life*, 258, 27.

6. Herbert Gans, *Deciding What's News*, 198.

7. Hackett, "Decline of a Paradigm?" 245.

8. Cable News Network (CNN) advertisement, 1993.

9. For the studies of nonpartisanship, an "electorally oriented notion of bias," and the FCC ruling, see Hackett, "Decline of a Paradigm?" 245.

10. Trying to reduce fifty years of historical scholarship about politics to a few paragraphs is a violent act. Still, we must try in order to explain the need for this study. While more detailed historiographies of the era can be found easily (see chapter 1, n. 19), the following discussion, centering around five books, will have to suffice.

11. Writing through the filter of New Deal politics, Schlesinger saw a connection between the Democrat Jackson and the later Democrat Franklin D. Roosevelt, whom he named a number of times in his book. Arthur M. Schlesinger, Jr., *The Age of Jackson*, esp. foreword and 401–26, 520.

12. Bray Hammond, *Banks and Politics in America: From the Revolution to the Civil War*, esp. 326–46, where Hammond lists a number of prominent anti-bank Democrats and discusses their wealth, desire to speculate, and interest in laissez-faire economic policy. See Lee Benson, *The Concept of Jacksonian Democracy: New York as a Test Case*; and Edward Pessen, *Jacksonian America: Society, Personality, and Politics*, esp. 233–60.

13. Charles Sellers, *The Market Revolution: Jacksonian America, 1815–1846*, 348–59. For his analysis of party and faction, Sellers relied on a number of other studies, including Richard McCormick, *The Presidential Game: The Origins of American Presidential Politics*.

14. Arthur M. Schlesinger, Jr., "The Ages of Jackson."

15. Schlesinger, *Age of Jackson*, 445.

42. Thomas and Hyman, *Stanton*, 90–91. In 1859, his last year of private practice, Stanton cleared $40,000, a huge sum.

43. Thomas and Hyman, *Stanton*, 111–13.

44. Thomas and Hyman, *Stanton*, 63–65, 124.

45. Stanton, however, was unfairly accused in this century of plotting Lincoln's death. For a discussion of the accusation, and a forceful repudiation of it, see Oates, *Abraham Lincoln: The Man behind the Myths*, 170–77.

46. F. B. Marbut, *News from the Capital: The Story of Washington Reporting*, 124.

47. David H. Bates, *Lincoln in the Telegraph Office*, 389.

48. Oates, *Abraham Lincoln: The Man behind the Myths*, 173.

49. I thank Will McCormack for his suggestions here.

50. Henry Villard, *The Memoirs of Henry Villard, Journalist and Financier, 1835–1900, in Two Volumes*, vol. 1, 339.

51. Geoffrey C. Ward, Ric Burns, and Ken Burns, *The Civil War: An Illustrated History*, 90.

52. Dana, *Recollections*, 5; Stanton Papers.

53. Thomas and Hyman, *Stanton*, 152.

54. J. Cutler Andrews, *The North Reports the Civil War*, 56–58; Stanton Papers; *New York Tribune*, 11 February 1862, 8.

55. James Ford Rhodes, *History of the Civil War, 1861–1865*, 350; Bishop, *The Day Lincoln Was Shot*, 16.

56. Dana, *Recollections*, 237.

57. Before Stanton took over, the Treasury and then the State Department were in charge of censorship. According to an 1862 congressional report (U.S. House of Representatives, Judiciary Committee, "Telegraphic Censorship," 1–14), the administration transferred the responsibility for censorship from the State to the War Department on Februrary 25, 1862. Stanton's censors, according to the report, were more consistent than Secretary of State Seward's, although Stanton, as we shall see, could be severe with those who disobeyed his orders; Starr, *Bohemian Brigade*, 95.

58. Thomas and Hyman, *Stanton*, 301–2.

59. Starr, *Bohemian Brigade*, 318–19.

60. U. S. Grant, *Memoirs and Selected Letters*, 460–61.

61. Welles, *Diary*, vol. 1, 83, 127–29.

62. William T. Sherman, *Memoirs of General W. T. Sherman*, 850–54.

63. Sherman, *Memoirs*, 866; Dana, *Recollections*, 289–90.

64. Grant, *Memoirs*, 769.

65. Salmon P. Chase, *The Diary and Correspondence of Salmon P. Chase*, 87.

66. Bates, *Lincoln*, 282.

67. Bishop, *The Day Lincoln Was Shot*, 15.

68. Bishop, *The Day Lincoln Was Shot*, 44.

69. Oates, *With Malice toward None*, 417.

70. Bates, *Lincoln*, 138–43. Much of Lincoln's important business was conducted

in the telegraph office; he wrote the first draft of the Emancipation Proclamation there, and on another occasion, Welles reported finding Lincoln lying on Stanton's couch, reading dispatches (vol. 1, 371). On the night of his reelection, Lincoln was at the War Department reading returns.

71. Welles, *Diary*, vol. 1, 319–21.

72. Oates, *With Malice toward None*, 409; Rhodes, *History*, 196.

73. Oates, *With Malice toward None*, 427–28.

74. Oates, *Abraham Lincoln: The Man behind the Myths*, 174.

75. Thomas and Hyman, *Stanton*, 300.

76. *New York Tribune*, 7 May 1864, 1.

77. National Archives; also Department of War, *The War of the Rebellion*, series 1, chap. 48, 471.

78. Marbut, *News from the Capital*, 127.

79. Ward, Burns, and Burns, *The Civil War*, 273.

80. Schudson, *Discovering the News*, 65.

81. Daniel Hallin, *The Uncensored War: The Media and Vietnam*, 8.

82. Mark Hertsgaard, *On Bended Knee: The Press and the Reagan Presidency*, 141–43.

83. I thank Peter Filardo for this observation; Shaw, "At the Crossroads," 49. One hundred and twenty years after Stanton's "War Diary," the Reagan administration took the concept to its logical conclusion with a daily "Line of the Day." Although derided by journalists as a "known quantity," the "Line" was still duly reported. Hertsgaard, *On Bended Knee*, 34–35.

84. *New York Herald*, 1 October 1864, 5.

85. Dana, *Recollections*, 152.

86. Starr, *Bohemian Brigade*, 16. Civil War reporters occasionally held telegraph lines by sending portions of the Bible until their story was composed. See Julian Ralph, *The Making of a Journalist*, 193.

87. Ward, Burns, and Burns, *The Civil War*, 281.

88. Dana, *Recollections*, 83.

89. Gaye Tuchman, "Objectivity as Strategic Ritual: An Examination of Newsmen's Notions of Objectivity."

90. James Randall, "The Newspaper Problem in Its Bearing upon Military Secrecy during the Civil War," 310–12.

91. *New York Times*, 19 January 1865, 1.

92. Department of War, *The War of the Rebellion*, series 1, vol. 46, pt. 2, 155–56.

93. *New York Herald*, *Tribune*, and *Times*, 4 September 1864, 1; *New York Tribune*, 5 September 1864, 1.

94. National Archives.

95. *New York Times* and *Herald*, 4 April 1865, 1.

96. *New York Tribune*, 4 April 1865, 1.

97. Stensaas found a relationship between the inverted pyramid form and the use of governmental sources. "The Objective News Report," 67.

NOTES TO CHAPTER 4

1. David Shi, *Facing Facts: Realism in American Thought and Culture, 1850–1920*, 69.

2. Melvin Mencher, *News Reporting and Writing*, 23; Mitchell Stephens and Gerald Lanson, *Writing and Reporting the News*, 57; Fred Fedler, *Reporting for the Print Media*, 22; and Mitchell Stephens, *Broadcast News*, 44.

3. *Morning Courier and New-York Enquirer*, 30 August 1832, 3 (hereafter cited as *Courier and Enquirer*). Charles Rosenberg, *The Cholera Years: The United States in 1832, 1849, and 1866*, 90. In his *Memoirs of Rev. Charles G. Finney, Written by Himself*, Finney, the evangelist, writes of seeing five hearses pull up at once, to five different doors on his street (320).

4. Rosenberg, *The Cholera Years*, 79.

5. *Courier and Enquirer*, 7 July 1832, 2.

6. *Courier and Enquirer*, 26 July 1832, 2.

7. *Courier and Enquirer*, 18 June 1832, 2.

8. *Courier and Enquirer*, 16 June 1832, 2.

9. *Courier and Enquirer*, 27 June 1832, 2.

10. *Courier and Enquirer*, 26 June 1832, 2.

11. *Courier and Enquirer*, 25 July 1832, 2.

12. *Courier and Enquirer*, 3 August 1832, 2; Rosenberg, *The Cholera Years*, 60–67.

13. *Courier and Enquirer*, 21 June 1832, 2.

14. Finney, *Memoirs*, 320.

15. I read each issue of the *New York Herald* from the summer of 1849 and compared that newspaper's coverage with that of the earlier and later epidemics.

16. *New York Herald*, 23 July 1849, 2.

17. *New York Herald*, 5 July 1849, 1; 10 July 1849, 1, 2; 15 July 1849, 3; 17 July 1849, 3.

18. After this report, however, the number of cholera deaths rose exponentially. *New York Herald*, 1 July 1849, 3.

19. *New York Herald*, 15 July 1849, 2.

20. John Snow, *Snow on Cholera, Being a Reprint of Two Papers by John Snow, M.D.*, 63–75; Rosenberg, *The Cholera Years*, 193–94.

21. Rosenberg, *The Cholera Years*, 152–53. The homeopathic doctors were an exception to this, for while their cures did little good, they were not nearly as dangerous as the standard medical cures (161).

22. *New York Herald*, 27 July 1849, 2; 8 August 1849, 2.

23. *New York Herald*, 21 August 1849, 3.

24. *New York Herald*, 12 August 1849, 2.

two articles, "New Journalism, Metaphor and Culture," and "On Journalistic Authority: The Janet Cooke Scandal."

9. Curtis MacDougall, *Interpretative Reporting.*

10. Joseph A. Mirando, "Journalism by the Book: An Interpretive Analysis of News Writing and Reporting Textbooks, 1867–1987," 1–30.

11. Stephen A. Banning, "Discovering a Mid-Nineteenth Century Drive for Journalistic Professionalization," 2–18. Banning's research places professionalism earlier than does the leading work on the subject, Hazel Dicken-Garcia, *Journalistic Standards in Nineteenth-Century America.*

12. Whitelaw Reid, *American and English Studies,* vol. 2, *Biography, History, and Journalism,* 219.

13. Joseph Pulitzer, "The College of Journalism," 649.

14. Pulitzer, "The College of Journalism," 657; W. A. Swanberg, *Pulitzer,* 206.

15. Charles G. Ross, *The Writing of News: A Handbook with Chapters on Newspaper Correspondence and Copy Reading,* 18. Ross's book may be the first to contain a reference to journalistic "objectivity." Ross quotes a newspaper article that begins, "The three notes of modern reporting are clarity, terseness, and objectivity" (17).

16. James W. Carey, "The Communications Revolution and the Professional Communicator," 32.

17. For details of the endowment, see Swanberg, *Pulitzer,* 303–6, 413–14.

18. Mirando, "Journalism by the Book," 1.

19. Edwin L. Shuman, *Steps into Journalism: Helps and Hints for Young Writers,* viii. The two most complete discussions of early journalism textbooks are Mirando, "Journalism by the Book" and Joseph A. Mirando, "Journalism's First Textbook: Creating a News Reporting Body of Knowledge."

20. Frederic Hudson, *Journalism in the United States, from 1690 to 1872,* 713.

21. Shuman, *Steps into Journalism,* 60–62.

22. Theodore Dreiser, *Newspaper Days,* 67.

23. Harlan S. Stensaas, in "The Objective News Report: A Content Analysis of Selected U.S. Daily Newspapers for 1865 to 1954," finds that the inverted pyramid form was common by the 1880s and standard by the turn of the century (57). I discussed this issue at greater length in chapter 3.

24. *New York Herald,* 23 February 1898, 1.

25. Joel Williamson, *The Crucible of Race: Black-White Relations in the American South since Emancipation,* 118. See also John Hope Franklin and Alfred A. Moss, Jr. *From Slavery to Freedom: A History of African Americans,* 312.

26. Arthur F. Raper, *The Tragedy of Lynching,* 480. According to Walter White, *Rope and Faggot: A Biography of Judge Lynch,* more than a thousand blacks were lynched from 1889 to 1894 (231).

27. Williamson, *The Crucible of Race,* 185. I use "race" in its cultural context here, as I do words such as "black" and "white," which are problematic scientifically. Without going into the centuries-old debate on naming, I use terms such as

"black" and "African American" because they are shorter than a more accurate and descriptive title would be.

28. *New York Times*, 10 March 1892, 1.

29. Ida B. Wells Barnett, *Crusade for Justice: The Autobiography of Ida B. Wells*, 7–19. (In subsequent notes and in the bibliography I refer to her by her maiden name, Wells—the name she used during the period covered in this chapter.) The state supreme court later overturned Wells's award and forced her to pay court costs.

30. Wells, *Crusade for Justice*, 19–41; Julius E. Thompson, *The Black Press in Mississippi, 1865–1985*, 8.

31. *New York Times*, 10 March 1892, 1. Wells, *Crusade for Justice*, 50–51.

32. Wells, *Crusade for Justice*, 49–51.

33. Wells, *Crusade for Justice*, 50–55.

34. Wells, *Crusade for Justice*, 64.

35. Wells, *Crusade for Justice*, 65–66.

36. Wells, *Crusade for Justice*, 66.

37. Wells, *Crusade for Justice*, 72.

38. Schudson, *Discovering the News*, 88–120.

39. *New York Times*, 2 August 1894, 4.

40. Ochs's first editorial was on 19 August 1896, 4. The editorial about lynching appeared on 9 June 1897, 4.

41. *New York Times*, 7 July 1892, 8.

42. See, for example, *New York Times*, 26 June 1897, 1; and 11 December 1897, 2–3.

43. It is possible to have the facts but not the context; see Richard E. Neustadt and Ernest R. May, *Thinking in Time: The Uses of History for Decision Maker.* Neustadt and May suggest that decision makers ask "journalists' questions," including the "five w's and an h" (107), but also should work to see "time as a stream," to understand the greater context behind the facts (246).

44. See Thomas N. Page, "The Lynching of Negroes—Its Cause and Its Prevention," an article written in a detached and "objective" style. Page asserts that innocent blacks are never lynched, and calls for the death penalty for blacks convicted of rape.

45. *New York Times*, 27 April 1893, 11.

46. Wells, *Crusade for Justice*, 65.

47. *New York Times*, 22 September 1893, 4.

48. The first major work on the Reconstruction period was William A. Dunning, *Reconstruction, Political, and Economic, 1865–1877*. Reconstruction, according to Dunning, was a terrible era, most especially because of free blacks. The Dunning school, as the early twentieth-century Reconstruction historians came to be called, depicted blacks as stupid, drunken, murderous beasts, "little above the intellectual level of the mules they drove." Quoted in Gerald N. Grob and George A. Billias, *Interpretations of American History: Pattern and Perspectives*, vol. 2, 119. The Dunning

school's findings were popularized by *Birth of a Nation*, the 1915 film celebrating the victory of the Ku Klux Klan over powerful and lusty blacks. Since the 1920s, historians have been correcting the myths perpetuated by the Dunning school. John Hope Franklin, *Reconstruction: After the Civil War*; Franklin and Moss, *From Slavery to Freedom*; and Eric Foner, *Reconstruction: America's Unfinished Revolution, 1863–1877* are three later works that deal with the period and point out the Dunning school's many misrepresentations. For two detailed historiographical essays, see Franklin and Moss, *From Slavery to Freedom*, 593–96, and Grob and Billias, *Interpretations of American History*, vol. 2, 116–42.

49. Franklin and Moss, *From Slavery to Freedom*, 253–65. In *The Crucible of Race*, 344, Williamson called the *Plessy* decision a "progressive" one since separate systems already existed and the Court added the criterion of equality. The use of 1877 as the final year of Reconstruction is discussed in Foner, *Reconstruction*, xxvii.

50. Williamson, *The Crucible of Race*, 513.

51. Edward L. Ayers, *Vengeance and Justice: Crime and Punishment in the Nineteenth-Century American South*, 250.

52. For a discussion of the labor movement in the 1880s, see Howard Zinn, *A People's History of the United States, 1492–Present*, 247–89; Pulitzer's progressive manifesto was largely adopted in later years. It reads, "1. Tax Luxuries. 2. Tax Inheritances. 3. Tax Large Incomes. 4. Tax Monopolies. 5. Tax the Privileged Corporation. 6. A Tariff for Revenue. 7. Reform the Civil Service. 8. Punish Corrupt Officers. 9. Punish Vote Buying. 10. Punish Employers who Coerce their Employees in Elections. This is a popular platform of ten lines. We recommend it to the politicians in place of long-winded resolutions." Swanberg, *Pulitzer*, 76.

53. Williamson, *The Crucible of Race*, 114.

54. Ayers, *Vengeance and Justice*, 216.

55. Williamson, *The Crucible of Race*, 114.

56. Williamson, *The Crucible of Race*, 117.

57. Williamson, *The Crucible of Race*, 109–11.

58. Franklin and Moss write, "The law, the courts, the schools, and almost every institution in the South favored whites. This was white supremacy." *From Slavery to Freedom*, 263.

59. Ayers, *Vengeance and Justice*, 180–81.

60. Ayers, *Vengeance and Justice*, 193–220.

61. Williamson, *The Crucible of Race*, 189.

62. Franklin and Moss, *From Slavery to Freedom*, 316–17; Wells, *Crusade for Justice*, 299, 309.

63. Franklin and Moss, *From Slavery to Freedom*, 355. A few bills passed in the House of Representatives, only to be defeated in the Senate, where Southerners had greater leverage to block bills.

64. Williamson, *The Crucible of Race*, 309–10.

65. Wells, *Crusade for Justice*, 60–65, 72.

66. The suppression of *Free Speech* provides a lesson for would-be press censors: Wells was forced out of her small community and gained an international forum. In 1894 the *Brooklyn Eagle*, unsympathetic to Wells's views, offered to pay Wells's transportation back to Memphis and her salary to keep her relatively quiet as the editor of her "one horse" paper, *Free Speech*. Quoted in Wells, *Crusade for Justice*, 221.

67. Gail Bederman, " 'Civilization,' the Decline of Middle-Class Manliness, and Ida B. Wells's Antilynching Campaign (1892–94)," 13.

68. *New York Times*, 11 September 1894, 2.

69. *New York Times*, 29 April 1894, 1.

70. Here, as in chapter 2, I use Hallin's construction of objective journalism (see chapter 2, figure 5).

71. *New York Times*, 20 May 1894, 1.

72. *New York Times*, 2 August 1894, 4.

73. The historian Nathan I. Huggins argues that until recently this had been the prevailing view in the historical profession; black historians were always seen as having an "ax to grind." In Grob and Billias, *Interpretations of American History*, vol. 2, 160.

74. *New York Times*, 2 August 1894, 4.

75. *New York Times*, 27 June 1894, 4. The *Times*' response to Wells was much milder than that of the Southern papers. The *Memphis Commercial* printed an attack against Wells so "coarse" that no British paper would quote it, according to an article in the *Liverpool Post*. Wells, *Crusade for Justice*, 183–85.

76. Swanberg, *Pulitzer*, 67; the criticism of Hearst is in S. Elizabeth Bird, *For Enquiring Minds: A Cultural Study of Supermarket Tabloids*, 18.

77. In 1883 the *Sun* was New York's circulation leader, followed by the *New York Herald*, the *Tribune*, the *Times*, and the *World*. By 1895 the *World*'s morning and evening circulation was greater than that of all these papers combined. Steele, *The Sun Shines for All*, 142–43.

78. These are Schudson's distinctions. Schudson, *Discovering the News*, 88–120.

79. *New York Times*, 16 February 1898, 1; *New York World*, 25 February 1898, 1. There are, of course, stories in information-based newspapers and information in entertaining papers. One press historian, John Pauly, has called the information-entertainment distinction "intellectually feeble"; but Pauly did acknowledge that the distinction is a way for journalists to "defend a particular style of professional practice." John J. Pauly, "Rupert Murdoch and the Demonology of Professional Journalism," 252.

80. Mitchell Stephens, *A History of News: From the Drum to the Satellite*, 121.

81. Steele, *The Sun Shines for All*, 143–44; Swanberg, *Pulitzer*, 146.

82. *New York Times*, 19 August 1896, 4.

83. *New York Times*, 16 February 1897, 4. The battles between the *World* and

Journal continued throughout the Spanish-American War. The *Journal* got its revenge on the *World* when the latter paper cribbed news from the former that a Colonel Reflipe W. Thenuz had died. The *Journal* gleefully announced that the news was a hoax to trap the *World*. The letters in "Reflipe W. Thenuz," the *Journal* revealed, can be rearranged to read, "We pilfer the nuz." Swanberg, *Pulitzer*, 251–52.

84. Schudson, *Discovering the News*, 111.

85. David Shi, *Facing Facts: Realism in American Thought and Culture, 1850–1920*, 216–20.

86. Reid, *American and English Studies*, 343.

87. Charles A. Dana, *The Art of Newspaper Making*, 41.

88. For a rich discussion of the *World* and women, see George Juergens, *Joseph Pulitzer and the New York World*, 132–74, esp. 133–59.

89. Schudson, *Discovering the News*, 112.

90. Dana, *The Art of Newspaper Making*, 32, 48.

91. Dana, *The Art of Newspaper Making*, 5.

92. Dana, *The Art of Newspaper Making*, 64.

93. This analysis of the exhibit relies on Bederman, " 'Civilization,' the Decline of Middle-Class Manliness, and Ida B. Wells's Antilynching Campaign," 9–11.

94. Bederman, " 'Civilization,' the Decline of Middle-Class Manliness, and Ida B. Wells's Antilynching Campaign," 11–12.

95. In addition to articles already cited, see Page, "The Lynching of Negroes—Its Cause and Its Prevention."

96. Robert Darnton, "Writing News and Telling Stories," 189.

97. The expectations of readers were also the focus of Robert Entman, *Democracy without Citizens*.

98. Mitchell Stephens and Gerald Lanson, in *Writing and Reporting the News*, list a number of characteristics that together make up "news judgement." They include "impact," "weight," "controversy," "emotion," "uniqueness," "prominence," "proximity," "timeliness," and "currency," all values that compete with the information or "objective" model of journalism (67–70).

99. Dan Berkowitz, *Social Meanings of News: A Text-Reader*, 303.

100. A news article should "possess interest for the reader," wrote Jesse Haney in *Haney's Guide to Authorship, Intended as an Aid to All Who Desire to Engage in Literary Pursuits for Pleasure or Profit*, 88.

101. Stephens, *A History of News*, 136.

102. Carlin Romano, "What? The Grisly Truth about Bare Facts," 44. As an example of a "holy shit" story, Romano lists a headline in the *Philadelphia Inquirer*: "Guest Drowns at Party for 100 Lifeguards."

103. Pauly, "Rupert Murdoch and the Demonology of Professional Journalism," 254. David M. White, in "The 'Gate Keeper': A Case Study in the Selection

of News," 386, studied the selection process of a telegraph editor over the course of a week. White found that the editor's biggest reason for rejecting stories was that they were not "interesting." The tabloid tastes and those of the "objective" journalists often collide; the coverage of the trial of O. J. Simpson offers a case in point. In 1986, when I was working for CNN, a number of news stories were covered the same way by CNN and the *Weekly World News*, one of the most sensationalistic supermarket tabloids.

104. Schudson, *Discovering the News*, 113–14.

105. Roland Barthes, "Structure of the *Fait-Divers*." Walter Lippmann, in *Public Opinion*, wrote extensively about how journalists use stereotypes (53–100, esp. 63).

106. This "reversal of the situation" is central to the dramatic form of tragedy as well. Aristotle, *Poetics*, 72.

107. Berkowitz, *Social Meanings of News*, 133.

108. Stephens, *A History of News*, 139.

109. As any etymological dictionary will reveal, "stereotype" and "cliché" are printing terms, dating from the eighteenth and nineteenth centuries, respectively. The development of the stereotype press is discussed in Charles Sellers, *The Market Revolution: Jacksonian America, 1815–1846*, 369–70.

110. Bederman, " 'Civilization,' the Decline of Middle-Class Manliness, and Ida B. Wells's Antilynching Campaign," 17.

111. *New York Times*, 30 July 1894, 8.

112. Wells, *Crusade for Justice*, xxii.

113. Ida B. Wells, *Southern Horrors: Lynch Law in All Its Phases*, 1–3.

114. Wells, *Crusade for Justice*, 253, 312–17.

115. Antilynching articles can be found in the NAACP journal *Crisis* and elsewhere; White's *Rope and Faggot* was a scathing denunciation of lynching.

116. Articles that outline the basic ideas of public journalism include Davis Merritt and Jay Rosen, "Imagining Public Journalism: An Editor and Scholar Reflect on the Birth of an Idea"; Mike Hoyt, "Are You Now, or Will You Ever Be, a Civic Journalist?"; and Jay Rosen, "Making Things More Public: On the Political Responsibility of the Media Intellectual." Also see Davis Merritt, *Public Journalism and Public Life: Why Telling the News Is Not Enough.*

117. Julian Ralph, *The Making of a Journalist*, 10–11.

118. Wells, *Crusade for Justice*, 65.

119. In "Who? Sources Make the News," in Manoff and Schudson's *Reading the News*, Leon V. Sigal writes, "News is not what happens, but what someone says has happened. . . . even when reporters are in a position to cover an event directly, they feel bound by [the conventions of objectivity] to record what sources say has occurred rather than to venture, at least explicitly, their own version of the event" (15).

120. *New York Times*, 30 July 1894, 8.

121. In 1909 Wells encouraged young men in Chicago to found the Negro

Fellowship League to respond to the Springfield riots. Wells, *Crusade for Justice*, 299–300.

122. Wells, *Southern Horrors*, 22–23.

NOTES TO THE CONCLUSION

The epigraphs are found in John J. Pauly, "Rupert Murdoch and the Demonology of Professional Journalism," 246; and in William Glaberson, "Fairness, Bias and Judgment."

1. For an account of the struggles between print and radio, see Gwenyth L. Jackaway, "The Press-Radio War, 1924–1937: A Battle to Defend the Professional, Institutional and Political Power of the Press."

2. Erik Barnouw, *Tube of Plenty: The Evolution of American Television*, 100–104. By 1974 television had replaced newspapers as the main source of news. Michael Schudson, *Discovering the News: A Social History of American Newspapers*, 182; Walter Goodman, "What's Bad for Politics Is Great for Television," 36.

3. Michael Emery and Edwin Emery, *The Press and America: An Interpretive History of the Mass Media*, 8th ed., 545. Robert Goldberg and Gerald Jay Goldberg, *Anchors: Brokaw, Jennings, Rather and the Evening News*, 106, 229, 320–23.

4. Steven Brill, "The Eye That Educates."

5. Dan Rather, "Call It Courage."

6. Andie J. Tucher, "You News," 26–28.

7. Bill O'Reilly, "We Pay for News. We Have To."

8. Dan Rather, "When News and Entertainment Look Alike."

9. Vanderbilt Television News Archive, *Television News Index and Abstracts*, 165–315.

10. Rather, "When News and Entertainment Look Alike."

11. CBS News, Advertisement, 11 February 1993.

12. I thank Jay Rosen for helping me develop this point; Goldberg and Goldberg, *Anchors*, 238–40.

13. Robert R. James, *Winston S. Churchill: His Complete Speeches, 1897–1963*, vol. 7, *1943–1949*, 7566.

Bibliographic Essay

Journalists call journalism the "first draft of history," and this is true, both in terms of its importance as a historical record and in its unfinished, often sketchy quality. Much of my time researching this book was spent in front of microfilm machines viewing nineteenth century newspapers, or in the New York Historical Society and other libraries, thumbing through the actual copies. Over the years I looked at most of the press run of the *New York Herald* from 1835 to 1865.

Michael Schudson's *Discovering the News* still provides the primary conceptual frame in journalism history. If I have argued a great deal with this book it is only because of its importance. Three other press histories were especially helpful: Mitchell Stephens, *A History of News*; Frank L. Mott, *American Journalism*; and the first draft of journalism histories, Frederic Hudson, *Journalism in the United States, from 1690 to 1872*. Stephens's book, Hazel Dicken-Garcia, *Journalistic Standards in Nineteenth-Century America*, and articles by James Carey are important models of the kind of intellectual history of journalism that this book seeks to emulate.

CHAPTER I

Bennett's *New York Herald* and Webb's *Morning Courier and New-York Enquirer* are undervalued but rich resources for historians of the Jacksonian period. For the history of the Jacksonian period, the best synthesis is still Edward Pessen, *Jacksonian America: Society, Personality, and Politics*, a thorough rebuttal to Schlesinger and the "progressive" historians. Another valuable (and more recent) synthesis is Charles Sellers, *The Market Revolution: Jacksonian America, 1815–1846*. Other books helped to clarify the inequalities and violence of the era, notably Leon F. Litwack, *North of Slavery: The Negro in the Free States, 1790–1860*; Kenneth S. Greenberg, *Masters and Statesmen: The Political Culture of American Slavery*; Richard Ellis, *The Union at Risk: Jackson Democracy, States' Rights, and the Nullification Crisis*; Paul A. Gilje, *The Road to Mobocracy: Popular Disorder in New York City, 1783–1834*; and Leonard L. Richards, *"Gentlemen of Property and Standing": Anti-Abolition Mobs in Jacksonian America.*

Dan Schiller, *Objectivity and the News: The Public and the Rise of Commercial Journalism* offers a good rebuttal to some of Schudson's views on the Jacksonian promise.

James L. Crouthamel, *Bennett's New York* Herald *and the Rise of the Popular Press* and

James Watson Webb: A Biography are the best biographies of the two editors, even though Crouthamel himself points out that most of what we know of Bennett comes from the editor's own columns.

CHAPTER 2

James Gordon Bennett's *New York Herald*, William Lloyd Garrison's *Liberator*, and Frederick Douglass's *North Star* and *Frederick Douglass' Paper* provide the best examples of their conflicting views about party and their common mistrust of partisanship. For background on the three journalists, James L. Crouthamel, *Bennett's New York* Herald *and the Rise of the Popular Press*; Walter McIntosh Merrill, *Against Wind and Tide: A Biography of William Lloyd Garrison*; and William S. McFeely, *Frederick Douglass* were invaluable. For the abolition movement and a response to it, Ronald G. Walters, *The Antislavery Appeal: American Abolitionism after 1830*; and Leonard Richards, *"Gentlemen of Property and Standing": Anti-Abolition Mobs in Jacksonian America* were helpful in filling in missing pieces. For the African American press one work was extremely helpful: Carter Bryan, "Negro Journalism in America before Emancipation." An excellent analysis of presidential politics can be found in Richard McCormick, *The Presidential Game: The Origins of American Presidential Politics*. Two books that address nineteenth-century journalism are Alexander Saxton, *The Rise and Fall of the White Republic*; and Gerald J. Baldasty, *The Commercialization of the News in the Nineteenth Century*.

CHAPTER 3

The chief sources for this chapter are a one-hundred-volume compilation of the dispatches of the Civil War commanders, including all Stanton's dispatches to Dix, *The War of the Rebellion: A Compilation of the Official Records of the Union and Confederate Armies*; the *New York Herald* and other dailies during the Civil War period; Stanton's papers, held in the Library of Congress; and the War Department's handwritten dispatches in the National Archives.

Diaries and autobiographies from military figures provided important primary sources, notably U. S. Grant, *Memoirs and Selected Letters*; the *Memoirs of General W. T. Sherman*; Charles A. Dana, *Recollections of the Civil War: With the Leaders at Washington and in the Field in the Sixties*; and the voluminous *Diary of Gideon Welles: Secretary of the Navy under Lincoln and Johnson*. An exceptional little book by a telegraph clerk in Stanton's office, David H. Bates, *Lincoln in the Telegraph Office*, revealed much about Lincoln, Stanton, and the flavor of the war office.

For Stanton, Benjamin S. Thomas and Harold M. Hyman, *Stanton: The Life and Times of Lincoln's Secretary of War* was thorough and authoritative.

CHAPTER 4

Charles Rosenberg, *The Cholera Years* was the inspiration for this chapter. It is one of the most thorough and accessible medical histories that I have read. My research, which mainly focused on the newspaper coverage of the epidemics, follows Rosenberg's book closely. As the notes to chapter 4 reveal, I mainly used the *Morning Courier and New-York Enquirer* for the 1832 epidemic, the *New York Herald* for 1849, and the *New York Times* for 1866. David Shi's book, *Facing Facts: Realism in American Thought and Culture, 1850–1920*, helped to place medicine and journalism in the wider social context of nineteenth-century realism. Ira Rutkow, *Surgery: An Illustrated History* is a well documented (albeit whiggish) chronicle of the sweeping changes in nineteenth-century medicine.

CHAPTER 5

Ida B. Wells's autobiography, *Crusade for Justice*, and her pamphlet *Southern Horrors* are still the best records of her life and thought. These two works, alongside the mainstream newspaper coverage of lynching, were the main sources for this chapter. Gail Bederman, " 'Civilization,' the Decline of Middle-Class Manliness, and Ida B. Wells's Antilynching Campaign (1892–94)" is an excellent analysis of Wells's critique of mainstream notions of "civilization." The racism and violence of the 1890s are analyzed at length in three broad histories: Joel Williamson, *The Crucible of Race: Black-White Relations in the American South since Emancipation*; Edward L. Ayers, *Vengeance and Justice: Crime and Punishment in the Nineteenth-Century American South*; and John Hope Franklin and Alfred A. Moss, *From Slavery to Freedom: A History of African Americans*, which contains a valuable bibliographical essay about race relations and violence (601–2).

Works Cited

PAPERS, COLLECTIONS, AND ARCHIVAL RECORDS

Douglass, Frederick. *The Frederick Douglass Papers.* Series 1, vol. 2, 1847–1854. Ed. John Blessingame. New Haven: Yale University Press, 1982.

Johnson, Andrew. *The Papers of Andrew Johnson.* Vol. 7: 1864–1865. Ed. Leroy P. Graf. Knoxville: University of Tennessee Press, 1986.

Lamont, Daniel S., Secretary of War, et al. *The War of the Rebellion: A Compilation of the Official Records of the Union and Confederate Armies.* Washington, DC: Government Printing Office, 1895. Series 1, vol. 47, pt. 3; vol. 38 pts. 1, 5; vol. 46, pts. 2, 3; vol. 36, pt. 3; vol. 51, pt. 1.

Stanton, Edwin M. Papers. Library of Congress.

U.S. House of Representatives, Judiciary Committee. "Telegraphic Censorship." 37th Cong., 2d sess., Report 64. 20 March 1862.

U.S. War Department Dispatches. National Archives.

NEWSPAPERS

Frederick Douglass' Paper, selected dates.

Freedom's Journal, selected dates.

Harper's Weekly, 1861–65, most dates.

Liberator, 1831–40, most dates.

Morning Courier and New-York Enquirer, 1832–38, most dates.

New York Evening Post, 1830s, selected dates.

New York Herald, 1835–65, most dates; 1865–95, selected dates.

New York Journal, selected dates.

New York Sun, 1832–94, selected dates.

New York Times, 1851–94, selected dates.

New York Transcript, selected dates.

New York Tribune, selected dates.

New York World, selected dates.

North Star, selected dates.

Publick Occurrences, 25 September 1690.

———. "Technology and Ideology: The Case of the Telegraph." *Prospects* 8 (1982): 302–25.

Carlson, Oliver. *The Man Who Made News: James Gordon Bennett*. New York: Duell, Sloan and Pearce, 1942.

Chase, Salmon P. *The Diary and Correspondence of Salmon P. Chase*. New York: De Capo, 1971.

Clines, Francis X. "Gossip Guru Stars in 2 Roles at Courthouse." *New York Times*, 12 March 1998, A25.

Cohen, Patricia Cline. "Unregulated Youth: Masculinity and Murder in the 1830s City." *Radical History Review* 52 (winter 1992): 33–52.

Cooper, James F. *Deerslayer, or The First Warpath*. New York: New American Library, 1980.

Cott, Nancy F. *The Bonds of Womanhood: "Woman's Sphere" in New England*. New Haven: Yale University Press, 1977.

Cranberg, Lawrence. "Plea for Recognition of Scientific Character of Journalism: Responsible Journalists Are Practicing Scientists (Commentary)." *Journalism Educator* 44 (winter 1989): 46–49.

Cronkite, Walter. *A Reporter's Life*. New York: Knopf, 1996.

Crouthamel, James L. *Bennett's New York* Herald *and the Rise of the Popular Press*. Syracuse: Syracuse University Press, 1989.

———. *James Watson Webb: A Biography*. Middletown, CT: Wesleyan University Press, 1969.

Cunningham, Nobel, Jr., ed. *Circular Letters of Congressmen to Their Constituents, 1789–1829*. Vol. 1, 1789–1807. Chapel Hill: University of North Carolina Press, 1978.

Dana, Charles A. *The Art of Newspaper Making*. New York: D. Appleton, 1895.

———. *Recollections of the Civil War: With the Leaders at Washington and in the Field in the Sixties*. New York: D. Appleton, 1898.

Dangerfield, George. *The Awakening of American Nationalism, 1815–1828*. New York: Harper and Row, 1965.

Darnton, Robert. "Writing News and Telling Stories." *Daedalus* 104, no. 2 (spring 1975): 175–94.

de Tocqueville, Alexis. *Democracy in America*. New York: New American Library, 1956.

Dicken-Garcia, Hazel. *Journalistic Standards in Nineteenth-Century America*. Madison: University of Wisconsin Press, 1989.

"Docudrama Strikes Again." Editorial. *New York Times*, 10 February 1985, 26.

Donahue, Hugh C. "Censorship of Battlefield News during the Civil War: The Beginnings of Bureacratization." Paper presented at the Symposium on Ante-Bellum and Civil War Press, University of Tennessee, Chattanooga, November 1994.

Douglass, Frederick. *Autobiographies: Narrative of the Life of Frederick Douglass, an*

American Slave, My Bondage and My Freedom, Life and Times of Frederick Douglass. Washington, DC: Library of America, 1994.

———. *My Bondage and My Freedom.* Urbana: University of Illinois Press, 1987.

Dreiser, Theodore. *Newspaper Days.* Philadelphia: University of Pennsylvania Press, 1991.

Dunning, William A. *Reconstruction, Political, and Economic, 1865–1877.* New York: Harper and Brothers, 1907.

Eason, David L. "New Journalism, Metaphor and Culture." *Journal of Popular Culture* 15, no. 4 (1982): 142–48.

———. "On Journalistic Authority: The Janet Cooke Scandal." *Critical Studies in Mass Communication* 3 (December 1986): 429–47.

Ellis, Richard. *The Union at Risk: Jackson Democracy, States' Rights, and the Nullification Crisis.* New York: Oxford University Press, 1987.

Emery, Michael, and Edwin Emery. *The Press and America: An Interpretive History of the Mass Media.* 8th ed. Englewood Cliffs, NJ: Prentice Hall, 1996.

Entman, Robert. *Democracy without Citizens.* New York: Oxford University Press, 1989.

Epstein, Edward J. *News from Nowhere: Television and the News.* New York: Vintage, 1973.

Fedler, Fred. *Reporting for the Print Media.* 2d ed. New York: Harcourt Brace Jovanovich, 1979.

Feller, Daniel. "Politics and Society: Towards a Jacksonian Synthesis." *Journal of the Early Republic* 10, no. 2 (1990): 135–61.

Finney, Charles G. *Memoirs of Rev. Charles G. Finney, Written by Himself.* New York: A. S. Barnes, 1876.

Folkerts, Jean, and Dwight L. Teeter, Jr. *Voices of a Nation: A History of Media in the United States.* New York: Macmillan, 1989.

Foner, Eric. *Reconstruction: America's Unfinished Revolution, 1863–1877.* New York: Perennial Library, 1988.

Foner, Phillip S. *American Labor Songs of the Nineteenth Century.* Urbana: University of Illinois Press, 1975.

Frankenstein, Alfred. *The Reality of Appearance: The Trompe L'oeil Tradition in American Painting.* New York: New York Graphic Society, 1970.

Franklin, John Hope. *Reconstruction: After the Civil War.* Chicago: University of Chicago Press, 1961.

Franklin, John Hope, and Alfred A. Moss, Jr. *From Slavery to Freedom: A History of African Americans.* 7th ed. New York: McGraw-Hill, 1994.

Furner, Mary O. *Advocacy and Objectivity: A Crisis in the Professionalization of American Social Science, 1865–1905.* Lexington: University Press of Kentucky, 1975.

Gans, Herbert. *Deciding What's News.* New York: Pantheon, 1979.

Gilje, Paul A. *The Road to Mobocracy: Popular Disorder in New York City, 1783–1834.* Chapel Hill: University of North Carolina Press, 1987.

Glaberson, William. "Fairness, Bias and Judgment: Grappling with the Knotty Issue of Objectivity in Journalism." *New York Times*, 12 December 1994, D7.

Gobright, Lawrence. *Recollections of Men and Things at Washington during the Third of a Century*. Philadelphia: Claxton, Remson and Haffelfinger, 1869.

Goldberg, Robert, and Gerald Jay Goldberg. *Anchors: Brokaw, Jennings, Rather and the Evening News*. New York: Birch Lane Press, 1990.

Goodman, Walter. "What's Bad for Politics Is Great for Television." *New York Times*, 27 November 1994, 33 (Arts and Leisure section).

Gramling, Oliver. *AP: The Story of News*. New York: Farrar and Rinehart, 1940.

Grant, U. S. *Memoirs and Selected Letters*. Ed. Mary Drake McFeely et al. Washington, DC: Library of Congress, 1990.

Greeley, Horace. *Recollections of a Busy Life*. New York: Ford, 1873.

Greenberg, Kenneth S. *Masters and Statesmen: The Political Culture of American Slavery*. Baltimore: Johns Hopkins University Press, 1985.

Grob, Gerald N., and George A. Billias. *Interpretations of American History: Pattern and Perspectives*. 2 vols. New York: Free Press, 1992.

Habermas, Jürgen. *The Structural Transformation of the Public Sphere: An Inquiry into a Category of Bourgeois Society*. Trans. Thomas Burger. Cambridge: MIT Press, 1995.

Hackett, Robert A. "Decline of a Paradigm? Bias and Objectivity in News Media Studies." *Critical Studies in Mass Communication* 1, no. 3 (September 1984): 229–59.

Hallin, Daniel. *The Uncensored War: The Media and Vietnam*. New York: Oxford University Press, 1986.

Halttunen, Karen. *Confidence Men and Painted Women: A Study of Middle-Class Culture in America*. New Haven: Yale University Press, 1982.

Hammond, Bray. *Banks and Politics in America: From the Revolution to the Civil War*. Princeton: Princeton University Press, 1957.

Haney, Jesse. *Haney's Guide to Authorship, Intended as an Aid to All Who Desire to Engage in Literary Pursuits for Pleasure or Profit*. New York: Haney and Co., 1867.

Hardman, Keith J. *Charles Grandison Finney*. Syracuse: Syracuse University Press, 1987.

Hausman, Carl. *Crisis of Conscience: Perspectives on Journalism Ethics*. New York: HarperCollins, 1992.

Hawthorne, Nathaniel. "My Kinsman, Major Molineux," "Young Goodman Brown," and *The Scarlett Letter*. In *The Complete Novels and Selected Tales of Nathaniel Hawthorne*, ed. Norman H. Pearson. New York: Modern Library, 1965.

Hertsgaard, Mark. *On Bended Knee: The Press and the Reagan Presidency*. New York: Schocken Books, 1989.

Hoffert, Sylvia. "New York City's Penny Press and the Issue of Women's Rights, 1848–1860." *Journalism Quarterly* 70 (autumn 1993): 656–65.

Hofstadter, Richard. *The American Political Tradition and the Men Who Made It.* New York: Vintage, 1974.

Hofstadter, Richard, and Michael Wallace. *American Violence: A Documentary History.* New York: Knopf, 1970.

Hohenberg, John. *The Pulitzer Prize Story II: Award-Winning News Stories, Columns, Editorials, Cartoons, and News Pictures, 1959–1980.* New York: Columbia University Press, 1980.

Homer. *The Iliad of Homer.* Trans. Richard Lattimore. Chicago: University of Chicago Press, 1951.

Howe, Daniel Walker. *The Political Culture of the American Whigs.* Chicago: University of Chicago Press, 1979.

Hoyt, Mike. "Are You Now, or Will You Ever Be, a Civic Journalist?" *Columbia Journalism Review* (September–October 1995): 27–33.

———. "Chuck-Gate: When Can Journalists Act Like Citizens?" *Columbia Journalism Review* (May–June 1996): 57–60.

Hudson, Frederic. *Journalism in the United States, from 1690 to 1872.* New York: Harper and Brothers, 1873.

Hyde, Grant M. *Newspaper Reporting and Correspondence: A Manual for Reporters, Correspondents, and Students of Newspaper Writing.* New York: D. Appleton, 1912.

Irving, Washington. "Rip Van Winkle" and "The Legend of Sleepy Hollow." In *The Sketch Book.* New York: New American Library, 1961.

Jackaway, Gwenyth L. "The Press-Radio War, 1924–1937: A Battle to Defend the Professional, Institutional and Political Power of the Press." Ph.D. diss., University of Pennsylvania, 1992.

James, Robert R. *Winston S. Churchill: His Complete Speeches, 1897–1963.* Vol. 7, *1943–1949.* 9 vols. New York: Chelsea House, 1974.

Jones, Charlotte. "The Penny Press and Origins of Journalistic Objectivity: The Problem of Authority in Liberal America." Ph.D. diss., University of Iowa, 1985.

Jones, Robert W. *Journalism in the United States.* New York: Dutton, 1947.

Juergens, George. *Joseph Pulitzer and the New York World.* Princeton: Princeton University Press, 1966.

Kamm, Samuel R. "The Civil War Career of Thomas A. Scott." Ph.D. diss., University of Pennsylvania, 1940.

Katz, Jon. "No News Is Good News." *HotWired.* http://www.hotwired.com/ (9 October 1996).

———. "Talk amongst Ourselves." *HotWired.* http://www.hotwired.com/ (20 January 1997).

———. "Um, Hello?" *HotWired.* http://www.hotwired.com/ (17 November 1996).

———. "Woe Is Hillary." *HotWired.* http://www.hotwired.com/ (27 October 1996).

Kimball, Bruce. *The "True" Professional Ideal in America: A History*. Cambridge, MA: Blackwell, 1992.

Kluger, Richard. *The Paper: The Life and Death of the New York* Herald Tribune. New York: Vintage Books, 1989.

Larkin, Jack. *The Reshaping of Everyday Life: 1790–1840*. New York: Perennial Library, 1988.

The Life and Writings of James Gordon Bennett, Editor of the New-York Herald. New York: n.p., 1844.

Link, Eugene Perry. *Democratic-Republican Societies, 1790–1800*. New York: Columbia University Press, 1942.

Lippmann, Walter. *Public Opinion*. New York: Free Press, 1949.

Litwack, Leon F. *North of Slavery: The Negro in the Free States, 1790–1860*. Chicago: University of Chicago Press, 1961.

MacDougall, Curtis. *Interpretive Reporting*, 8th ed. New York: Macmillan, 1982.

Manoff, Robert K., and Michael Schudson, eds. *Reading the News: A Pantheon Guide to Popular Culture*. New York: Pantheon, 1986.

Marbut, F. B. *News from the Capital: The Story of Washington Reporting*. London: Southern Illinois University Press, 1971.

Marszalek, John F. *Sherman's Other War: The General and the Civil War Press*. Memphis: Memphis State University Press, 1981.

McCormick, Richard. *The Presidential Game: The Origins of American Presidential Politics*. New York: Oxford University Press, 1982.

McFeely, William S. *Frederick Douglass*. New York: Touchstone, 1991.

McPherson, James M. *Ordeal by Fire: The Civil War and Reconstruction*. New York: Knopf, 1982.

———. *What They Fought For: 1861–1865*. Baton Rouge: Louisiana State University Press, 1994.

Melville, Herman. *Collected Poems of Herman Melville*. Ed. Howard P. Vincent. Chicago: Packard, 1947.

———. *Moby Dick*. Indianapolis: Bobbs-Merrill, 1964.

———. *Redburn: His First Voyage*. Evanston: Northwestern University Press, 1969.

———. *Typee, A Peep at Polynesian Life*. Evanston: Northwestern University Press, 1968.

Mencher, Melvin. *News Reporting and Writing*. 6th ed. Madison: Brown and Benchmark, 1994.

Merriam, George S. *The Life and Times of Samuel Bowles, in Two Volumes*. New York: Century, 1885.

Merrill, Walter McIntosh. *Against Wind and Tide: A Biography of William Lloyd Garrison*. Cambridge: Harvard University Press, 1963.

Merritt, Davis. *Public Journalism and Public Life: Why Telling the News Is Not Enough*. New York: Lawrence Erlbaum, 1995.

Merritt, Davis, and Jay Rosen. "Imagining Public Journalism: An Editor and

Scholar Reflect on the Birth of an Idea." *Roy W. Howard Public Lectures in Journalism and Mass Communication Research* 5 (April 1995).

Miller, Mark Crispin. *Boxed In: The Culture of TV.* Evanston: Northwestern University Press, 1989.

Mindich, David T. Z. "Edwin M. Stanton, the Inverted Pyramid, and Information Control." *Journalism Monographs* 140 (1993): 1–31.

———. "That's the Way It Was." *Media Studies Journal* 11 (spring 1997): 165–76.

Mirando, Joseph A. "Journalism by the Book: An Interpretive Analysis of News Writing and Reporting Textbooks, 1867–1987." Ph.D. diss., University of Southern Mississippi, 1992.

———. "Journalism's First Textbook: Creating a News Reporting Body of Knowledge." Paper presented at the annual meeting of the Association for Education in Journalism and Mass Communication, Kansas City, August 1993.

Missouri Group (George Kennedy, Daryl R. Moen, and Don Ranly). *Beyond the Inverted Pyramid: Effective Writing for Newspapers, Magazines, and Specialized Publications.* New York: St. Martin's, 1993.

Mitchell, Alison. "Standoff Deepens as G.O.P. Calls Off Talks." *New York Times,* 18 January 1996, A1.

Mott, Frank Luther. *American Journalism: A History: 1690–1960.* 3d ed. New York: Macmillan, 1962.

———. *American Journalism: A History of Newspapers in the United States through 260 Years: 1690 to 1950.* 1st ed. New York: Macmillan, 1950.

———. *The News in America.* Cambridge: Harvard University Press, 1952.

Moyer, Albert E. *A Scientist's Voice in American Culture: Simon Newcomb and Rhetoric of Scientific Method.* Berkeley: University of California Press, 1992.

Nabokov, Vladimir. *Lolita.* New York: Knopf, 1992.

Nelson, Jill. *Volunteer Slavery: My Authentic Negro Experience.* New York: Penguin, 1993.

Nerone, John C. "The Mythology of the Penny Press." With criticism by Michael Schudson, Dan Schiller, Donald L. Shaw, and John J. Pauly. *Critical Studies in Mass Communication* 4 (December 1987): 376–422.

Neustadt, Richard E., and Ernest R. May. *Thinking in Time: The Uses of History for Decision Makers.* New York: Free Press, 1986.

Nord, David P. "William Lloyd Garrison." In *Dictionary of Literary Biography.* Vol. 43. Detroit: Gale, 1985.

Novick, Peter. *That Noble Dream: The "Objectivity Question" and the American Historical Profession.* Cambridge: Cambridge University Press, 1988.

Oates, Stephen B. *Abraham Lincoln: The Man behind the Myths.* New York: Harper, 1984.

———. *With Malice toward None: The Life of Abraham Lincoln.* New York: Harper and Row, 1977.

O'Malley, Michael. *Keeping Watch: A History of American Time*. New York: Viking Penguin, 1990.

O'Reilly, Bill. "We Pay for News. We Have To." *New York Times*, 26 February 1994, A23.

Page, Thomas N. "The Lynching of Negroes—Its Cause and Its Prevention." *North American Review* 178 (January 1904): 33–48.

Paine, Thomas. *Common Sense*. In *Basic Writings of Thomas Paine*. New York: Willey, 1942.

Pauly, John J. "Rupert Murdoch and the Demonology of Professional Journalism." In *Media, Myths, and Narratives: Television and the Press*, ed. James W. Carey. Newbury Park, CA: Sage, 1988.

Pessen, Edward. *Jacksonian America: Society, Personality, and Politics*. Homewood, Ill.: Dorsey, 1969. Rev. ed., Urbana: University of Illinois Press, 1985.

Plum, William Rattle. *The Military Telegraph during the Civil War in the United States*. 2 vols. New York: Arno, 1974.

Pratt, Fletcher. *Stanton: Lincoln's Secretary of War*. Westport, CT: Greenwood, 1953.

Pray, Isaac Clark. *Memoirs of James Gordon Bennett and His Times. By a Journalist*. New York: Stinger and Townsend, 1855.

Prince, Carl. "The Federalist Party and the Creation of a Court Press, 1789–1801." *Journalism Quarterly* 53 (1976): 238–41.

———. *The Federalists and the Origins of the U.S. Civil Service*. New York: New York University Press, 1977.

———. "The Great 'Riot Year': Jacksonian Democracy and Patterns of Violence in 1834." *Journal of the Early Republic* 5 (spring 1985): 1–19.

Pulitzer, Joseph. "The College of Journalism." *North American Review*, May 1904.

Quindlen, Anna. "Talking about the Media Circus." *New York Times Magazine*, 26 June 1994, 28–62.

Ralph, Julian. *The Making of a Journalist*. New York: Harper and Brothers, 1903.

Randall, James. "The Newspaper Problem in Its Bearing upon Military Secrecy during the Civil War." *American History* 23, no. 2 (January 1918): 303–23.

Raper, Arthur F. *The Tragedy of Lynching*. New York: Dover, 1933.

Rather, Dan. "Call It Courage." Speech to the Radio and Television News Directors Association. *Communicator* (November 1993): 10–16.

———. "When News and Entertainment Look Alike." Letter. *New York Times*, 8 March 1994, A20.

Reid, Whitelaw. *American and English Studies*. Vol. 2, *Biography, History, and Journalism*. Freeport, NY: Books for Libraries Press, 1968.

Remini, Robert V. *Andrew Jackson and the Course of American Democracy, 1833–1845*. Vol. 3. New York: Harper and Row, 1984.

Reston, James B. "The Job of the Reporter." New York Times Staff, *The Newspaper: Its Making and Meaning*. New York: Scribner's, 1945.

Rhodes, James Ford. *History of the Civil War, 1861–1865*. Ed. E. B. Long. New York: Frederick Ungar, 1961.

Rhodes, Jane. "Breaking the Editorial Ice: Mary Ann Shadd Cary and the Provincial Freeman." Ph.D. diss., University of North Carolina at Chapel Hill, 1992.

Richards, Leonard L. *"Gentlemen of Property and Standing": Anti-Abolition Mobs in Jacksonian America*. London: Oxford University Press, 1971.

Robertson, Nan. *The Girls in the Balcony: Women, Men and the New York* Times. New York: Fawcett Columbine, 1992.

Romano, Carlin. "What? The Grisly Truth about Bare Facts." In *Reading the News: A Pantheon Guide to Popular Culture*, ed. Robert K. Manoff and Michael Schudson. New York: Pantheon, 1986.

Rosen, Jay. "Beyond Objectivity." *Nieman Reports* (winter 1993): 48–53.

———. "Journalism and the Production of the Present." *Tikkun*, September–October 1994, 13–14, 109–13.

———. "Making Things More Public: On the Political Responsibility of the Media Intellectual." *Critical Studies in Mass Communication* 11 (December 1994): 362–88.

Rosenberg, Charles. *The Cholera Years: The United States in 1832, 1849, and 1866*. Chicago: University of Chicago Press, 1987.

Ross, Charles G. *The Writing of News: A Handbook with Chapters on Newspaper Correspondence and Copy Reading*. New York: Henry Holt, 1911.

Rutkow, Ira. *Surgery: An Illustrated History*. St. Louis: Mosby-Year Book, 1993.

Ryan, Michael, and James W. Tankard. *Basic News Reporting*. Palo Alto: Mayfield, 1977.

Saxton, Alexander. *The Rise and Fall of the White Republic: Class, Politics, and Mass Culture in Nineteenth-Century America*. London: Verso, 1990.

Schiller, Daniel. *Objectivity and the News: The Public and the Rise of Commercial Journalism*. Philadelphia: University of Pennsylvania Press, 1981.

Schlesinger, Arthur M., Jr. *The Age of Jackson*. New York: Book Find Club, 1945.

———. "The Ages of Jackson." *New York Review of Books*, 7 December 1989, 48–51.

Schudson, Michael. *Discovering the News: A Social History of American Newspapers*. New York: Basic Books, 1978.

Schudson, Michael, and Mitchell Stephens. "Schudson and Stephens Debate: The 'Invention' of News, Other Sundry Matters." *Clio among the Media* 29, no. 3 (spring 1997): 7.

Sellers, Charles. *The Market Revolution: Jacksonian America, 1815–1846*. New York: Oxford University Press, 1991.

Shaw, Donald L. "At the Crossroads: Change and Continuity in American Press News, 1820–1860." *Journalism History* 8, no. 2 (summer 1981): 38–50.

———. "News Bias and the Telegraph: A Study of Historical Change." *Journalism Quarterly* 44 (spring 1967): 3–31.

Shepard, Alicia. "The Revolving Door." *American Journalism Review* 19 (July–August 1997): 18–25.

———. "A Scandal Unfolds." *American Journalism Review* 20 (March 1998): 20–28.

Sherman, William Tecumseh. *Memoirs of General W. T. Sherman.* Washington, DC: Library of Congress, 1990.

Shi, David. *Facing Facts: Realism in American Thought and Culture, 1850–1920.* New York: Oxford University Press, 1995.

Shilen, Ronald. "The Concept of Objectivity in Journalism in the United States." Ph.D. diss., New York University, 1955.

Shuman, Edwin L. *Steps into Journalism: Helps and Hints for Young Writers.* Evanston, IL: Correspondence School of Journalism, 1894.

Sigal, Leon V. "Who? Sources Make the News." In *Reading the News: A Pantheon Guide to Popular Culture,* ed. Robert K. Manoff and Michael Schudson. New York: Pantheon, 1986.

Snow, John. *Snow on Cholera, Being a Reprint of Two Papers by John Snow, M.D. Together with a Biographical Memoir by B. W. Richardson, M.D. and an Introduction by Wade Hampton Frost, M.D., Professor of Epidemiology, the Johns Hopkins School of Hygiene and Public Health.* New York: Commonwealth Fund, 1936.

Starck, Kenneth, and John Soloski. "Effect of Reporter Predisposition in Covering Controversial Story." *Journalism Quarterly* 54 (spring 1977): 120–25.

Starr, Louis M. *Bohemian Brigade: Civil War Newsmen in Action.* New York: Knopf, 1954.

Steele, Janet E. *The Sun Shines for All: Journalism and Ideology in the Life of Charles A. Dana.* Syracuse, NY: Syracuse University Press, 1993.

Stensaas, Harlan S. "Development of the Objectivity Ethic in U.S. Daily Newspapers." *Journal of Mass Media Ethics* 2, no. 1 (fall–winter 1986–87): 50–60.

———. "The Objective News Report: A Content Analysis of Selected U.S. Daily Newspapers for 1865 to 1954." Ph.D. diss., University of Southern Mississippi, 1987.

Stephens, Mitchell. *Broadcast News.* 2d ed. New York: Holt, Rinehart and Winston, 1986.

———. *A History of News: From the Drum to the Satellite.* New York: Viking, 1988.

Stephens, Mitchell, and Gerald Lanson. *Writing and Reporting the News.* Fort Worth: Holt, Rinehart and Winston, 1986.

Stewart, Donald. *The Opposition Press of the Federalist Period.* Albany: State University of New York Press, 1969.

Storey, Moorfield. "Dickens, Stanton, Sumner, and Storey." *Atlantic Monthly* 145 (April 1930): 463–65.

Swanberg, W. A. *Citizen Hearst.* New York: Collier, 1961.

———. *Pulitzer.* New York: Scribner, 1967.

Thomas, Benjamin S., and Harold M. Hyman. *Stanton: The Life and Times of Lincoln's Secretary of War.* New York: Knopf, 1962.

Thomas, John L. *The Liberator, William Lloyd Garrison: A Biography*. Boston: Little, Brown, 1963.

Thomas, Leonard. *The Power of the Press: The Birth of American Political Reporting*. New York: Oxford University Press, 1986.

Thompson, Julius E. *The Black Press in Mississippi, 1865–1985*. Gainesville: University Press of Florida, 1993.

Thoreau, Henry D. *Walden*. In *The Portable Thoreau*, ed. Carl Bode. New York: Penguin, 1975.

Tucher, Andie J. "You News." *Columbia Journalism Review* (May–June 1997): 26–31.

Tucher, Andrea J. " 'Froth and Scum': Truth, Beauty, Goodness, and the Axe-Murder in the First Years of the New York Penny Press." Ph.D. diss., New York University, 1990.

Tuchman, Gaye. *Making News: A Study in the Construction of Reality*. New York: Free Press, 1978.

———. "Objectivity as Strategic Ritual: An Examination of Newsmen's Notions of Objectivity." *American Journal of Sociology* 77, no. 4 (January 1972): 660–79.

Tucker, Robert C., ed. *The Marx-Engels Reader*. 2d ed. New York: Norton, 1978.

Vanderbilt Television News Archive. *Television News Index and Abstracts*. Ed. John Lynch. Nashville: Vanderbilt University Press, 1994.

Villard, Henry. *The Memoirs of Henry Villard, Journalist and Financier, 1835–1900, in Two Volumes*. Boston: Houghton, Mifflin, 1904.

Villard, Oswald Garrison. "Press Tendencies and Dangers." In *The Profession of Journalism: A Collection of Articles on Newspaper Editing and Publishing, Taken from the Atlantic Monthly*, ed. Willard G. Bleyer. Boston: Atlantic Monthly Press, 1918.

Walljasper, Jay. "What Is the Alternative Press?" Meredeth Lecture, Drake University, April 1994.

Walters, Ronald G. *American Reformers: 1815–1860*. New York: Hill and Wang, 1978.

———. *The Antislavery Appeal: American Abolitionism after 1830*. New York: Norton, 1984.

Ward, Geoffrey C. et al. *The Civil War* (video). 1990.

———. *The Civil War: An Illustrated History*. New York: Knopf, 1990.

Welles, Gideon. *The Diary of Gideon Welles: Secretary of the Navy under Lincoln and Johnson*. 3 vols. Boston: Houghton Mifflin, 1911.

Wells, Ida B. *Crusade for Justice: The Autobiography of Ida B. Wells*. Chicago: University of Chicago Press, 1970.

———. *Southern Horrors: Lynch Law in All Its Phases*. Pamphlet. New York: *New York Age* Print, 1892.

Welter, Barbara. "The Cult of True Womanhood: 1820–1860." *American Quarterly* 18 (summer 1966): 151–74.

White, David M. "The 'Gate Keeper': A Case Study in the Selection of News." *Journalism Quarterly* 27 (1951): 383–90.

White, Walter. *Rope and Faggot: A Biography of Judge Lynch.* New York: Knopf, 1929.

Whitman, Walt. *Leaves of Grass.* New York: Penguin, 1986.

Wilentz, Sean. *Chants Democratic: New York City and the Rise of the American Working Class, 1788–1850.* New York: Oxford University Press, 1984.

———. "On Class and Politics in Jacksonian America." *Reviews in American History* 10 (December 1982): 45–64.

Williamson, Joel. *The Crucible of Race: Black-White Relations in the American South since Emancipation.* New York: Oxford University Press, 1984.

Wyatt-Brown, Bertram. *Yankee Saints and Southern Sinners.* Baton Rouge: Louisiana State University Press, 1985.

Zinn, Howard. *A People's History of the United States, 1492–Present.* New York: Harper Perennial, 1995.

INTERVIEW

Hannon, Tom (Cable News Network [CNN] political director). 27 April 1992.

Index

About the Author

David T. Z. Mindich is an assistant professor of journalism at Saint Michael's College, Vermont, where he teaches writing, mass communication, journalism history, and new media. A former assignment editor for CNN, Mindich is also a longtime freelance print journalist; his articles have appeared in *Media Studies Journal, New York Magazine, Quill, Christian Science Monitor, New York Newsday, Burlington Free Press, Journalism and Mass Communication Quarterly, American Journalism,* and *Journalism and Mass Communication Monographs.*

Mindich earned a Ph.D. in American Studies from New York University in 1996, where he was awarded a Dean's Dissertation Fellowship. Mindich is also the head of the History Division of the Association for Education in Journalism and Mass Communication and the founder of Jhistory, an Internet group for journalism historians. He lives in Burlington, Vermont, with his wife, Barbara Richmond, a former field producer for CNN, and their two children.